GW00367564

The Manx Norton

Mick Walker

Published in 2001 by Redline Books
2 Carlton Terrace, Low Fell, Tyne & Wear, NE9 6DE

Copyright Mick Walker 2001

All rights reserved. Apart from any fair dealing for the purpose of private study, research, criticism
or review, as permitted under the Copyright, Designs and Patents Act, 1988, no part of this
publication may be reproduced, stored in a retrieval system, or transmitted in any form or by any
means, electronic, electrical, chemical, mechanical, optical, photocopying, recording, or otherwise,
without prior written permission. All enquiries should be addressed to the publisher.

British Library Cataloguing in Publication Data

A catalogue record for this book is available
from the British Library

ISBN: 0 9531311 4 9

Designed and published by Redline Books

This book is dedicated to all racers and fans, both past and present,
and to the special memory of Gary Walker and Peter Goodwin.

Contents

Forward by Ken Kavanagh

First Australian to win the TT - 1956. British Champion 350 and 500 - 1952. First Australian to win a World Championship Grand Prix - 1952. Works rider for Norton, Moto Guzzi, MV and Ducati.

Ken Kavanagh at the 1951, 350cc Italian Grand Prix.

'FUNCTIONAL HARMONISATION'

JOE CRAIG invented this term to describe his beloved Camshaft Engines in an article for the book by G.S. Davidson *The TT Races Behind the Scenes*. Manx Nortons were not toys! They were machines built by professionals, and even if the power of one of the early 100mm stroke models read 38bhp, that is Bracebridge hp, few riders were able to race the machine at its absolute limit, and whoever did so was at once noted by Norton, Velocette, AJS, Moto Guzzi, Gilera, BMW and other factories.

I was fortunate to have owned six new Manxes and had the use of a seventh from Norton Motors to learn the Isle of Man circuit in 1951. My first Manx was a 1948 single camshaft 499cc (79.6 x 100mm); it was the third imported to Australia after the war, bought with my savings as a motorcycle engineer and prize money from scrambles. I paid full list price. The machine won its first race, the richest run up to that time in Australia, beating, among many others, the great Harry Hinton. In its second outing, at Adelaide in October 1948, it broke the connecting rod, and forever afterwards I worried about Norton con-rods, earning the nickname in Australia of 'Kenny Conrod'. My second Manx was a 1950 500cc twin-cam, perhaps the prettiest racing Norton ever built. By now the front forks had real damping and finally extensive use of light alloy.

By 1951, I was at the works in Bracebridge Street as one of the official Australian team to take part in the TT. The Managing Director of 'our company', Gilbert Smith, kindly loaned me for one month the experimental shop's 1950 350cc Manx to learn the Isle of Man circuit. This was the machine that had done the 1950 season in the hands of Australia's George Morrison.

For the races, I was assigned two of the new 'Featherbeds', only a few of which were ready in time for the TT. Again, both of these machines broke connecting rods in the races, the 500 whilst in fifth place at the Guthrie Memorial on the last lap of the Senior TT. Desperation. But it really didn't matter, for by now I had been noticed and was on Joe Craig's short list together with Rod Coleman and Ray Amm.

I was to stay at Bracebridge Street, Aston, Birmingham, with Joe Craig and Gilbert Smith for three years, and by nature being very curious, became rather competent in many questions regarding Norton Motors and Norton Motorcycles. I was one of those who felt betrayed when 'our company', as Frank Cope called it, was put under the 'protection' of our natural enemies, 'Associated Motorcycle Wreckers' of London, which for workers' morale had the same effect as if the Seaforth Highlanders had been sold to that western oriental gentleman of Tripoli.

Then in 1959, going private once more, I bought two new Short Strokers. Never was there built a worse or slower Manx Norton, any difference was in the way it was ridden.

Maintenance was almost nil; check the tappet clearance, adjust the chains, blow up the tyres. A whole European season could be done with three sets of valve springs, two spare valves, some spare rings and one big-end - maybe no more than fifty quid - and it could be overhauled in anybody's backyard with a few spanners. Some riders didn't even bother to change the gear ratios, for on going over to the Continent they fitted the 'Europa gears'. This was the true spirit of racing machines for the perennially poor private rider, not the expensive junk that the makers foist off on today's boys, obliging them to fall under the grasp of sponsors. A Manx was genuine 'do it yourself'.

The first post-war machines could break the frame near the rear suspension. The long-strokers could break con-rods using regulation rpm - 350cc, 7,000; 500cc, 6,250. The problem was the material in the forgings (the works rods were machined from solid bar). The 'Featherbeds' could be 'twittery' in the front end if the springs were too hard. But all in all they were very forgiving bicycles.

I was also to race Guzzi, MV and Ducati; Geoff Duke was to ride Gilera, Benelli and BMW, but when any of we old racing gentry get together, including the great Guzzi designer Ing. Carcano, conversation always filters back to those amazing racing Nortons and their more amazing technician, 'Professor Joe Craig'. According to Carcano a Manx Norton should not work, on the other hand, in 1959 Ing. Taglioni of Ducati was only too pleased to copy the squish head from one of my machines in Bologna.

Ken Kavanagh testing at MIRA (Motor Industry Research Association) near Nuneaton, Warwickshire, February 1953. The bike is "Old Faithful" – the 350 works Norton used by Geoff Duke until his crash at Schotten in July 1952.

Although many years have gone by, when I'm here alone or laying in bed, relaxing, I pretend I'm with Joe Craig again and redesigning the 'Manx' to compete with the four-cylinder, two-stroke monsters of today.

We are applying the few simple formulae from Phil Irving's *Tuning for Speed,* 1963 edition, and *Collins' Engineers Diary,* 1953, courtesy of Castrol, and using as a starting point one of the most famous replies by Joe Craig to a question before the Institute of Mechanical Engineers, when he presented his white paper in 1947 or thereabouts:

Question: 'How did you get so much power with such a long stroke?'

Answer: 'I was not proud of the piston speed.'

The 'not proud' piston speed in question was, I remember, 4,500rpm.

So we, that is Joe Craig and I, have settled on a stroke of 32mm and a bore of 141mm at 21,500rpm, that is a 'not proud' piston speed of 4,500rpm. It will develop 140bhp, and with its lighter weight and simplicity, will once more make the single-cylinder Norton a force to be reckoned with.

I realise that Vic Willoughby will worry about the 'harmonic variation' and the 'acceleration rate of the piston', but, as Joe Craig said, 'If we ignore the problem, it will give us no trouble'. Impossible, it could not work. But the most improbable situation of all is that that impossible bicycle, the Manx Norton, and its impossible inventor make it possible for you and me to recall the once glorious British motorcycle industry.

So readers, when you look at any Norton, please spare a thought for the three most unapproachable characters in British motorcycle history for whom, really, this book has been written:

The impossible Manx Norton, the impossible Gilbert Smith, and the even more impossible Joe Craig, who all had one thing in common: For them, nothing was 'impossible'.

Kenny 'Conrod' Kavanagh

Bergamo, Italy, 1989

Introduction

Superbly restored 1960, 348cc 40M Manx; late 1980s.

With a history stretching back almost to the very dawn of motorcycling itself, the Norton single is without doubt the greatest of all the over-the-counter production racers. Not only that, but in works guise these cammy Nortons dominated road racing at Grand Prix level until they were finally eclipsed by the Italian multis during the early 1950s. Even then, both factory and privately entered Manx models put up some tremendous performances, often against fantastic odds, to win countless races until well into the 1960s.

After Godfrey Nash's final Norton Grand Prix win in Yugoslavia during 1969, the Bracebridge singles languished in lockups and garden sheds gathering dust, as so many racing machines have done before and since, once they are no longer competitive on the track. Then, with the birth of the Classic movement in the early 1980s, these very same bikes were reborn.

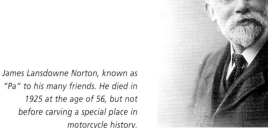

James Lansdowne Norton, known as "Pa" to his many friends. He died in 1925 at the age of 56, but not before carving a special place in motorcycle history.

This book sets out to record the full story of the Manx legend. Not just the bikes, with their track performances and technical background, but the myriad of people who, over the years, played such a vital part in the creation of this legend. In doing this I have uncovered many little-known facts.

The Manx Norton story is diverse, covering not just two but three and four wheels as well. Furthermore, how many other engines can claim to have won major titles on two, three and four wheels? Not many, I would speculate. But Manx Norton-powered motorcycles, sidecar combinations and cars have all been championship winners in their own particular racing field.

In parts the plot is almost akin to a novel, but in this case fact really is quite often stranger than fiction.

What I enjoy best about compiling a new title is the number of both old and new friends one meets in the process, and The Manx Norton was no exception.

I must therefore record my sincere thanks to all those who have contributed both their time and expertise in the preparation of this book. Included is a wide range of enthusiasts from all forms of motor sport, among them former works riders Ken Kavanagh and John Surtees.

Four times Formula 3 car champion Jim Russell not only spent much time reliving his experiences, but kindly put his extensive archives at my disposal. Other four-wheel help was provided by Peter Wright.

I was also extremely fortunate to count the leading tuner, the late Francis Beart, as a personal friend and was able to interview him before his death.

Thanks also to the following who provided both photographs and useful information; Dan Shorey, Steve Lancefield, Fred Walmsley, Derek Minter, Phil Kettle, David May, Percy May, Tina May, Eric Kirk, Kim and Andy Molnar, Stewart Rogers, Andy Farrer, Dan Nash, Linda Hadwin, Alan Preston, Mr. and Mrs. R.B. Sharpe, Bernie Allan, the Summerfield brothers, Denis Parkinson, Allen Dudley-Ward, Francis Beart, Richard Thirkell, Michael Steel, John Douds, Colin Seeley, Brenda Scivyer, Suzette Bradnam, Lawrence and Sylvia Stanhope plus fellow journalists Rob Carrick and Philip Tooth.

Many of the photographs that illustrate the book came from private collectors and enthusiasts; but several vital ones were from The Classic Motorcycle archives. A special thank you to Christopher Marshall for allowing us to use his fine drawing on the title page. If I have missed anyone, I can only apologise, it was not my intention.

I have dedicated this book to all those countless Norton riders and drivers around the world who, down the years, have provided race-goers with such superb sport on two, three and four wheels.

Finally I hope you have as much enjoyment reading The Manx Norton saga as I have had writing it.

Mick Walker,
Wisbech,
Cambridgeshire,
January 2001.

Evocative picture of a 1915 type single-speed belt-drive Norton with a 1930's de Havilland DH-82 Tiger Moth.

The Wisbech & District Motor Cycle Club float at the Annual Rose Fair, July 1970. Machine number 74 is a 499cc Manx raced by the author's brother-in-law, Tony Plumridge. Mick Walker is seated on his 250 Ducati ridden to 7th in that year's Thruxton 500 miler.

1 The Birmingham Connection

James L. Norton (centre with beard) and the Norton racing team, Douglas, Isle of Man, June 1920.

James Lansdowne Norton was born in 1869, the son of a Birmingham cabinet-maker. He was destined to play a vital role in the creation of an entirely new industry, where his name was to mean sporting success and mechanical excellence.

It can be stated with confidence that the contributions he made to the design and development of the motorcycle during the first quarter of the twentieth century, were probably of more signficance than those from any other single source; when he died in 1925, at the age of 56, his passing was mourned wherever motorcycles were ridden, many observers simply referring to him as 'The Father of the Industry'.

Even as a boy he had clearly displayed a talent for making things. For example, by the age of ten he had constructed his own model steam engine. The sight of it running in the front-room window was enough to earn a visit from a member of the local constabulary, who instructed James's mother 'to get that thing moved'. Not, I hasten to add, because of anything untoward, but merely because its presence was causing a congestion of

Dennis Mansell (centre) receives the Palmer Challenge Trophy after becoming British Sidecar Trials Champion, 20th November, 1929.

bodies outside the said front window, with people crowding to view its operation, and so obstructing the road!

After leaving school the young James was apprenticed to a local jeweller; but his interest in engineering was always close to his heart, and it was not long before he entered a new career more akin to this inclination, in the bicycle and cycle chain business.

In 1898 saw James L. Norton, now aged 29, branched out on his own, as The Norton Manufacturing Company. The basis of this new enterprise was the idea of a mechanically propelled bicycle. Shortly after this, some experimental work directed towards this goal was to play a vital role in his later designs, but most important of all to the fledgling concern was his tie-up with the Frenchman Charles Garrard. In the first years of the new century, Garrard was importing the small-capacity Clement internal combustion engine from his native country under the title of the Clement-Garrard. In many ways the forerunner of the present-day moped, the little Clement 63cc engine unit was attached to the front downtube of a conventional pedal cycle, and was reputed to produce 1.30bhp. Its more interesting technical features included an external flywheel, which allowed the use of a conveniently small crankcase, and a push-rod-operated overhead exhaust valve alongside the usual (for the era) automatic inlet valve. In place of the rawhide belt drive direct to the rear wheel, James Norton offered a countershaft two-speed gear, mounted below the engine, and all-chain drive. The latter features were obviously influenced by Norton's earlier experiences in the cycle business.

In addition, the Norton enterprise was also manufacturing components for the large number of new firms coming into the two-wheel industry in 1902-3 - and in some cases, even complete machines. One of those built at the tiny works at 320 Bradford Street, Birmingham, was sold in 1903 to Sydney Turner of Derby, for his wife to ride. This machine sported an open frame, making it one of the very first models expressly intended for ladies. It was during this time that the other young engineers connected with the infant motorcycle industry would often call on James Norton, generally after the cessation of the day's business, to exchange ideas and so further progress. Norton's office subsequently becoming known as 'the club'.

By 1905 Norton had progressed to the title of motorcycle manufacturer, although his company was still using other people's engines. One such machine was a lightweight, sold under the Norton Energette label. This was powered by the Swiss-designed Moto Reve engine, a tiny v-twin that was obtained from Basil Feeny, who was building the Moto Reve in Acton, North West London.

First to lap the TT Mountain circuit at 60 and 70mph, Jimmy Simpson broke the 80mph barrier during the 1931 Senior – seen here that year raising the front wheel at Ballig Bridge.

Alec Bennett after winning the Senior TT of 1927.

The larger Norton machines used French Peugeot engines, either singles or v-twins, with automatic inlet valves. Significantly, it was one of the latter with which the Norton marque was to gain its first sporting success, when private owner Rem Fowler took his bike to victory in the twin-cylinder class and won the Hele Show Trophy in the very first Tourist Trophy race on the Isle of Man during 1907.

Fowler's victorious ride was also instrumental in founding a tradition that the Norton racers were built to a standard specification, and were the 'same as you could buy', even down to the now famous silver and black tank.

Norton motorcycles had by this time, except for the retention of pedalling gear, moved away from their pedalcycle ancestry. The power unit was now mounted low and far forward with an extra long frame and tank, known by the term 'Ferrets' until the majority of other producers adopted similar designs, to give the motorcycle an appearance it was to generally retain until the end of the Vintage era.

Back at his workshop in Birmingham, James Norton had been giving his full attention to the design of his own engine, which was introduced in 1908 and known as the Big Four because of its 4hp rating. It was a long-stroke side-valve 633cc single with a bore of 82mm and a massive stroke of no less than 120mm! This was soon followed by a 490cc (79 x 100mm) model called the 3½. These models were to form the basis of the standard production line for many years and to survive two world wars, until finally deleted as late as 1954.

By the end of the first decade of the 20th century, the Norton Manufacturing Company had moved to a new home at Deritend Bridge, Floodgate Street, Birmingham.

In 1909 James Norton decided to run in the Isle of Man, the first time he had done so, even though he had previously gained a string of short-distance successes, including occasional visits to show the London based manufacturers how to do it by winning the important Streatham Club's hill climb. Norton also competed in the Isle of Man in 1910 and 1911. Unfortunately, his Isle of Man visits were not destined to meet with success, for he retired on each occasion.

CS1

confidence was to prove well-founded, with Bennett riding a CS1-engined machine winning the Senior TT by over eight minutes. What an incredible debut and one of the best ever in motorcycle racing history. Alec Bennett's winning speed (a new record) was 68.41mph.

The CS1 employed the traditional long-stroke Norton dimensions of 79 x 100mm. In fact Moore utilised the technology of several existing ohv engine components, including the crankcases, crank flywheels, connecting rod and piston from the Model 18. But the big difference was the set of bevel gears and shafts which ran up the offside of the cylinder and crankshaft.

Again Moore pinched the oil pump design from a type first used on the 1925 works TT bikes; this being enclosed in the bottom bevel housing. The magneto, situated at the rear of the barrel, was driven by a chain.

The honour of being the first ever overhead camshaft Norton single-cylinder engine goes to the CS1 (Cam Shaft One). The design was the work of Walter Moore who had joined the company in 1924 to take over from the ailing James Norton.

Conceived during 1926, the engine, which replaced the overhead valve Model 18 at the top of Norton's range, was first used at the Isle of Man TT series in 1927. As the story goes the engine had never actually been properly tested, and Walter Moore himself took the first two completed engine assemblies to the Island, hiring a small boat to get himself there overnight. He personally persuaded the team riders, including Alec Bennett to use them. This

But ultimately the CS1 was to be a relatively shortlived model due to a combination of events. First Moore tried, unsuccessfully, to extract extra performance from 1928 - which affected both reliability and race success. Then in 1929 Moore left Norton to work for NSU in Germany and his first design for his new employers was virtually an unlicenced CS1! This was the final straw as far as the Norton management was concerned, the result being a new 'cammy' engine designed by Arthur Carroll, which was to be the real father to the Manx itself.

1932 NSU 501SS Super Sport designed by former Norton chief engineer, Walter Moore and clearly based on the Norton CS1.

Norton's chief designer Walter Moore quit the Bracebridge Street firm after seeing his plan to join the board of directors come to nought. The year was 1929 and Moore saw a bigger future for himself in Germany rather than Birmingham. And so 'The German Connection' began.

Often referred to as Norton Spares Used, rather than NSU, by his former workmates back in Great Britain, Moore created a series of machines which bore an

THE GERMAN CONNECTION

uncanny resemblance to the CS1 Norton; these included the 501/601SS (Super Sport) racing machines.

Both the 501 and 601 were built between 1930 and 1935 and featured a single overhead camshaft driven by shaft and bevels, exposed hairpin valve-springs, dry sump lubrication, Bosch magneto, Fischer Amal carburettor and a four-speed, foot-operated gearbox.

The 501 had a displacement of 494cc (80 x 99mm) and put out 30bhp at 6,000rpm. Its bigger brother, the 601 displaced 592cc (87.5 x 99mm) and produced an extra 8bhp at the same engine revolutions.

Although both bikes featured a rigid full-loop tubular steel frame, a degree of springing was provided by way of central spring, girder front forks plus a single sprung saddle.

A double overhead cam version (also constructed in 348cc form) debuted in the middle of the decade, in many ways mirroring developments taking place at Moore's previous employer.

NSU's top rider at the same time was another Englishman, Tommy Bullus, who had joined NSU in 1930.

Probably due to Moore's influence there were several NSU entries in the Isle of Man TT during the thirties, their best years being 1931, 1935 and 1936.

After transferring his attention to the initial design and development of the new dohc supercharged parallel twin engine, Moore returned home to Great Britain on the eve of war in 1939.

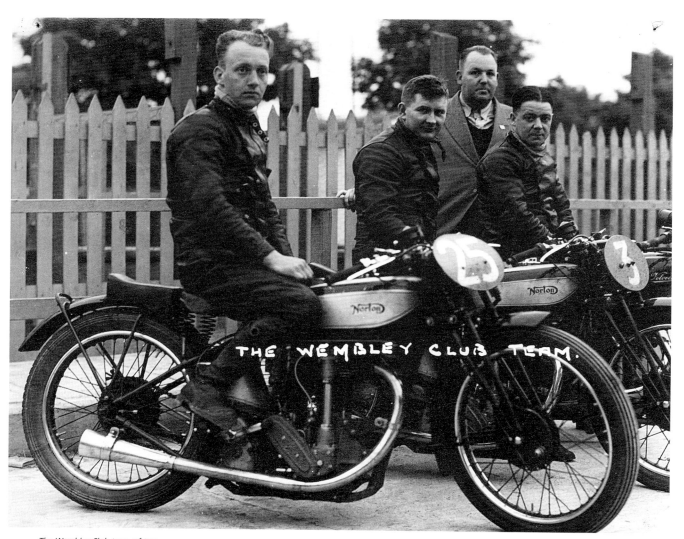

The Wembley Club team of two Nortons and a Velocette, for the 1937 TT. Sponsored by Bryants of Biggleswade (George Bryant standing).

It was around the same time that Norton faced financial difficulties. The firm lacked cash reserves and it was only through an association with R.T. Shelley, founder of R.T. Shelley Ltd (a well known neighbouring engineering company, which had been carrying out Norton machining work), that he was able to continue in business. The link with Shelley, completed in 1913, not only provided Norton with financial stability but also, perhaps even more importantly, allowed James Norton to concentrate his efforts upon designing models which combined Norton running gear and engines.

Sandy Kellas collecting his 350 Norton from George Bryant outside the Shortmead Street showrooms, 1937-38. There is a new BMW twin in the showroom window for £115.00.

Following the rescue operation a new company was formed, Norton Motors Ltd, with its headquarters in Samson Road North. R.T. Shelley was appointed Joint Managing Director together with James Norton, and C.A. Vandervell, of the CAV electrical concern, became Chairman.

1911 had seen Dan Bradbury, a great Norton enthusiast from Sheffield, record 70mph for the first time in a sprint. The following year, Jack Emerson rode his standard 3½ TT model from Hull to Brooklands, where he proceeded to clean up the prestigious 150-mile Brooklands TT, breaking three world long-distance records in the process, at around 65mph.

A Brooklands Special (BS) was offered in 1914 with a guaranteed Brooklands lap speed of 65mph. It was at this time that former Singer works rider Dr. 'Wizard' O'Donovan appeared on the scene. The brother-in-law of R.T. Shelley, he soon built up a reputation for his efforts both as a Brooklands record-breaker and ace tuner and set some 112 British and world records in the period prior to World War One. With this sporting success the Birmingham marque was very much in favour in the years immediately prior to the outbreak of hostilities in 1914.

Belt drive was still fitted in 1914 and while the 3½ TT and the BS models had single speeds, the touring bikes featured three-speed Sturmey-Archer hub-gears. The latter were the work of J. Cohen. By 1915 James Norton was beginning to seriously consider overhead valves, but had been hampered in his work because of a heart condition following an illness that he had contracted during one of his Isle of Man visits. Norton's poor health was one of the main reasons why his original company had faced liquidation before intervention by the R.T. Shelley organisation.

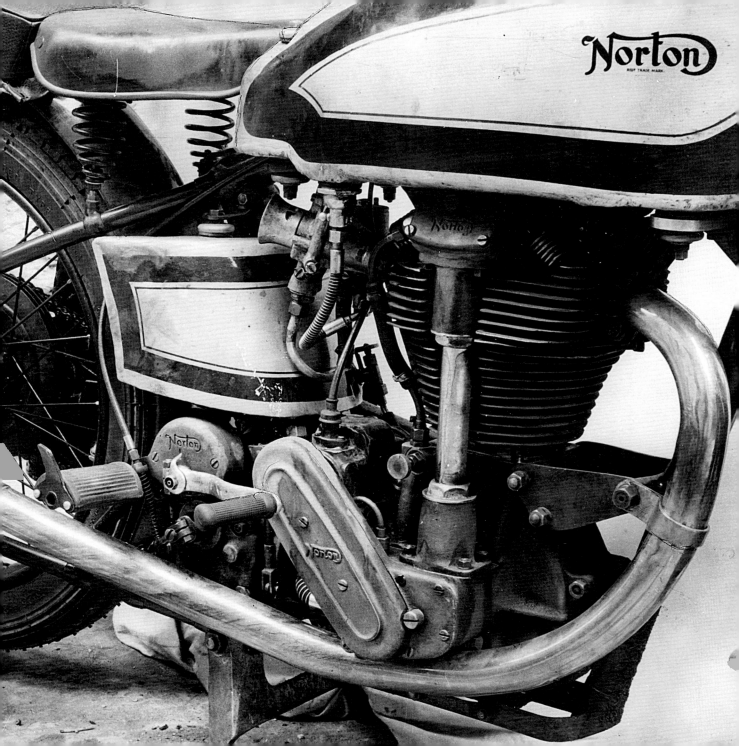

Freddie Frith on his way to victory in the 1936 Junior TT.

1915 saw the Norton frame modified to provide a lower seating position, and the three-speed countershaft gearbox, with final drive by belt or enclosed chain on the touring models. The racers, however, still retained single-speed belt drive and the BS was now guaranteed to achieve a genuine 70mph Brooklands lap (or 75mph maximum), with the road-going version, the BRS (Brooklands Racing Special), similarly guaranteed to attain 65 and 70mph, each machine coming complete with a signed certificate. The TT model with single-speed became the Model 9, and for 1916, with countershaft three-speed, the Model 16.

In 1916 the company moved once again, this time to a new location in Phillips Street that backed on to that of R.T. Shelley Ltd in Aston Brook Street. Subsequently, the now famous Bracebridge Street site was acquired, to bring the whole organisation between three streets in Birmingham.

When war was declared in 1914 Norton was in no position to bid for British Government contracts to supply motorcycles to the armed forces. But the move to the new and larger premises in 1916 brought about a substantial increase in manufacturing capacity, and with it the need for new customers, including the military. Strangely the first new contract was not to supply the home front, but the Russians! However, by late 1916 Norton were at last supplying machines to the British Army. Following the Armistice in November 1918, there was a huge civilian demand for personal transport, so Norton Motors did a healthy line in acquiring and refurbishing former service motorcycles for sale on the civilian market. Other manufacturers followed Norton's lead, such was the level of demand, with prices going through the roof. But of course this state of affairs could not last, and by 1920 things were getting back to a more normal state of affairs.

Harold Daniell rode for Norton before and after the Second World War. He is seen here as a spectator at the 1958 TT. By then Daniell was a leading Norton dealer in Forest Hill, South East London.

In 1920, the TT races were revived. Norton entered a five-strong team, including such diverse characters as Duggie Brown (a former works Rover rider) and the future editor of *Motor Cycling*, Graham Walker, the latter making his island debut. The machines were chain-driven versions of the 1916 Model 16, thereafter referred to with the H prefix and in vindication of the company's policy of racing what they sold. (No fewer than eight private owners competed on similar models.) Brown nearly won too, after the early pacemakers blew up, Tommy de la Hay ousting him from the lead a lap from the end, while Walker was one place off the leader board at the finish. The early 1920s saw men such as Victor Horsman and Rex Judd (both later to become leading dealers) record-breaking at Brooklands on Norton machinery tuned by O'Donovan, with speeds now pushing 90mph, with overhead valve engines.

Success in the TT was a bit longer coming, and the only ohv Norton entered in the 1922 Senior retired on the final lap. But the production version, the Model 18, which made its debut at that year's Olympia Show, benefited greatly from the racing and record-breaking adventures. The same venue saw the last belt-drive Norton, the Model 9, make its final bow at the Show, thus bringing down the curtain on an era in the company's history.

Opposite: Plunger framed works engine, 1936 Isle of Man TT. This is a single overhead camshaft - dohc did not arrive until the following year.

Winner of the 1938 Senior TT Harold Daniell was back in action on works Nortons during the immediate post-war period.

1923 saw the Bracebridge Street team and their latest ohv racers put up a much improved showing at the TT, gaining second, fourth and fifth places and in the process carrying off the Manufacturers Team prize. The factory also became the first recipient of the Maudes Trophy that year. If 1923 was considered a success, then the 1924 TT can only be called sensational! Not only did George Tucker win the sidecar event to gain Norton's second TT victory, the first being that far-off 1907 Fowler victory, but Alec Bennett took the all-important Senior at 61mph, the first time it had been won at over 60mph.

Of equal importance, in the light of later developments, was that an Ulsterman named Joe Craig took 12th spot in the Senior TT as a member of the Norton team, and Walter Moore (formerly the Douglas chief designer) assumed the role of passenger to George Tucker. Shortly after the TT, Moore joined Norton Motors.

Sadly the glorious events of the 1924 TT could not hide the fact that founder James Norton was by now a very sick man indeed, and the following spring, on 25th April, 1925, he died. Norton was a deeply religious person, and a leading figure with the Salvation Army in his native Birmingham. By the time of his death this devout Christian, known to his many friends and employees simply as 'Pa', had created a company which to many represented the very best in his chosen industry. In his memory the University of Birmingham created the Norton Scholarship in Motorcycle Engineering, a fitting tribute to one of that city's greatest sons.

Even with his passing, the influence of James Lansdowne Norton did not falter, and in the 1925 TT Norton machines once again challenged for honours. The 1924 winner, Alec Bennett, had trouble early in the race, and it was left to Joe Craig to chase Howard Davies on his own creation, the HRD. In 1926 Stanley Woods, a new recruit to the Norton team, won the race with Craig backing him up in fourth spot. This was the beginning of an era of the legendary Norton-Irish connection, when the team comprised Bennett, Craig, Shaw and Woods, all of whom hailed from the Emerald Isle.

1947 Belgian GP. The Norton team, left to right; Ken Bills (6), Joe Craig, Harold Daniell (2) and Artie Bell (4).

1927 saw a total redesign by Walter Moore (Tucker's 1924 TT sidecar passenger). The result was the real start of the Manx Norton story with Moore's creation of the first Norton overhead camshaft engine. Proof of just how good this 490cc (79 x 100mm) design was, is to recall that mounted in a cradle frame with saddle tank, and almost straight off the drawing board, this camshaft wonder provided team leader Bennett with an easy win, after similarly mounted Stanley Woods had set a new lap record. So the new ohc Norton was born, and known as the CSI (Cam Shaft One) it was listed as a production machine for the 1928 season, together with the smaller 348cc (71 x 85mm) known as the CJ (Camshaft Junior).

DONINGTON PARK.
EASTER. 1933.

Donington Park Easter 1933, left to right; Arthur Tyler, Arthur Prince (Donington official) and a journalist from the Nottingham evening post. Arthur won the Craner Bowl for the fastest lap of 1932 at Donington Park, on his Joe Craig prepared Norton.

Artie Bell crossing the finish line to win
the 1948 Senior TT at an average speed
of 84.97mph on his factory Norton.

Besides the camshaft engine, 1927 had seen one of the push-rod engines average over 100mph in the classic hour for the very first time, piloted by Bert Denly, and W. Mansell, who had been connected with the R.T. Shelley Ltd side of the business, became Norton Motors' managing director following the death of R.T. Shelley. Incidentally, Mansell's son Dennis became the top British Trials sidecar ace of the time, using a 490cc overhead cam Norton engine.

In the Isle of Man, Joe Craig retired while leading the 1928 Senior - his last TT. Craig thereafter concentrated his efforts on engine tuning and team management, almost exclusively for Norton, over the next three decades, as related fully in Chapter eight. 1928 also saw Nortons compete in the Junior TT for the first time, a tradition which was to be followed over succeeding years. In 1929 Jimmy Simpson and former amateur TT star Tim Hunt joined the Norton team, and although they were unlucky on the Island, Hunt won the 500cc class of the European Grand Prix, while Dennis Mansell made it a Norton double by taking victory in the sidecar race.

By 1930 Walter Moore had left to work for NSU in Germany, and for the TT that year, Arthur Carroll, who had succeeded him at Bracebridge Street, redesigned the camshaft engine, with a square, lower, bevel box and several other features which were to remain basically unaltered for many years thereafter. Carroll had come direct to Norton Motors immediately after an engineering apprenticeship, and had the great advantage of working directly under 'Pa' Norton himself. But 1930 was the heyday of Graham Walker's all-conquering Rudge team in the Senior TT. The best Norton could achieve to prevent a total Rudge whitewash that year was getting Jimmy Simpson home third behind Wal Handley and Walker.

The Australian J.H. Pringle who finished 12th in the 1932 Senior TT.

Although, like other manufacturers, Norton were now in the midst of the Great Depression, this did not stop racing, or for that matter changes to the standard production roadster models which came in 1931. That year also witnessed the start of a truly fantastic period in the company's history, with Norton machines winning every Senior and Junior TT for the next eight years, except the 1935 Senior and the 1938 Junior.

Tim Hunt won both races in 1931, Stanley Woods did the double in 1932 and 1933, Jimmie Guthrie did it in 1934 and just missed out in 1935, when Woods, now Guzzi v-twin mounted, pipped him by a slender four-second margin in the Senior. But Guthrie won the Senior again in 1936 (and so missed by four seconds becoming the first man in history to score the hat-trick), while Freddie Frith took the Junior.

In 1937 Frith won the Senior and Guthrie took the Junior, while in 1938 Harold Daniell beat Stanley Woods, now Velocette-mounted, in the Senior and also won the Junior. During this period the silver, red and black bikes from Bracebridge Street acquired hairpin valve springs (in 1934), a megaphone exhaust (in 1935), plunger rear springing (in 1936), twin overhead camshafts (in 1937) and telescopic front forks (in 1938). Even so, the original Moore/Carroll camshaft engine remained basically unchanged. Instead it was painstakingly developed by that engineering genius Joe Craig. Another important change came in 1938, when the bore and stroke were

JIMMIE GUTHRIE

On the Mountain Road of the Isle of Man TT circuit near the Cutting stands a simple stone monolith known as 'The Guthrie Memorial'. This is a tribute to one of the all-time racing greats, the Scot Jimmie Guthrie who not only won six TTs, but was, without doubt, the greatest Norton rider of pre-war days.

From Hawick in the Scottish borders, Guthrie was born on the 23rd May 1897 and made his first appearance on the Isle of Man in 1923 when he entered the Junior TT on a Matchless. He did not ride on the Island again until 1927, when he raced a New Imperial to a magnificent 2nd place in the senior event. From then until 1937 he competed every year, riding Nortons in 1928 and 1929, an AJS in 1930 and Nortons again from 1931 to 1937.

In 1934 he rewarded team manager Joe Craig's faith in him by joining the select band who had won two races in a week - becoming only the second man to accomplish this feat.

Freddie Frith, J.H. (Crasher) White and Jimmie Guthrie at the Isle of Man TT, 1937.

Probably the most heartbreaking TT in which Guthrie rode was the 1935 Senior, when after being hailed as the winner it was later announced he had lost to Stanley Woods (Moto Guzzi v-twin) by the narrow margin of four seconds.

Besides his TT successes, Jimmie Guthrie won many Continental Grand Prix races for the Norton team, and it was whilst racing in the German Grand Prix at the Sachsenring that he met his untimely death. His last race was reported by *The Motor Cycle* dated 12th August 1937 and he was described as 'a fine man, who has done more to spread the fame of the British racing motorcycle than anyone'. Guthrie's crash came on the final lap of a 214-mile long 500cc race which he was leading comfortably and he had actually lapped the third man, Kurt Mansfeld (DKW). Within a mile of the finish line, with the race in his pocket, he crashed at the last corner and died shortly afterwards from his injuries.

The Guthrie Memorial on Snaefell marks the spot where he retired in his last TT race, the 1937 Senior. On a clear day from the Vantage point can be seen Scotland, Guthrie's native land.

Start of a 500cc race at the Buenos Aires Autodrome, Argentina, September 1952; Number 1 and 50 are Garden Gate Manx models, number 31 is a Featherbed model, whilst 3 is a GP Triumph and 6 an Italian Gilera Saturno.

Opposite: Plunger-framed 'Garden Gate' Manx pictured in 1947 with Australian Ken Kavanagh aboard.

revised on both the 350 and the 500. The 350 now had a capacity of 348cc (75.9 x 77mm) and the 500, 498cc (82 x 94.3mm). The larger bike was now good for over 120mph. Proof of how effective the improvements were came in the 1938 Senior TT, when Harold Daniell set a new lap record at 91mph, which was to stand for twelve years.

Not only did Norton dominate world-class road racing during this period, they also produced the famous International model. With its single overhead camshaft engine, which was based on the Moore/Carroll racing unit, it was the envy of every 'Promenade Percy', as the cafe racers of the 1930s were called; it gained its name from its use in the ISDT (International Six Day Trial). Trials riders Vic Brittain and Jack Williams joined the Bracebridge Street company in 1933, and between them won almost every event of national importance over the next five years.

Because of the threatening international situation, Norton Motors spent most of 1939 carrying out military contracts, so they were unable to compete with the new supercharged Gilera from Italy, or the blown BMW flat-twin from Germany; even the Isle of Man Senior TT was won by BMW. For the private owner 1939 was a year of significance because Norton introduced the Manx Grand Prix model, which post-war, became the legendary Manx, the production racer par excellence.

So the final few months before the outbreak of the Second World War were devoted to producing the WD (War Department) models - and this was to set a pattern for the next six years. Some 100,000 of the side-valve 16H military models were to roll off the Bracebridge Street production lines, including several hundred of the 'Big Four'-type sidecar outfits, many with sidecar wheel drive. Although the works took quite a battering from German bombs during the conflict, somehow production was maintained throughout the war years.

After six long years, peace finally returned in 1945. Gilbert Smith (who had joined the company back in 1916) was now the man in charge at Bracebridge Street, setting the civilian wheels back in motion, not at first with any new machinery, but by concentrating on the existing pre-war designs for the transport-hungry customer. And, of course, with supplies unobtainable for such a long while there was an equally strong export demand.

THE INTERNATIONAL

Coded Model 30 (490cc) and Model 40 (348cc) the International series was derived from the new Model 30 designed by Arthur Carroll, who replaced Walter Moore when he left to work for NSU in Germany.

Carroll's basic layout followed that of the Moore-designed CS1. In otherwords an overhead cam single with shaft and bevel gears - and the traditional Norton long-stroke 79 x 100mm dimensions. However, in many other details there were significant differences. A number of them, a journalist once described, were borrowed from a successful rival, the KTT Velocette. In fact the original Model 30 was not simply an updated and improved CS1, but a new design in its own right.

The Model 30 didn't win the TT in its debut year as the CS1 had done, but in virtually every other aspect it was superior to its older brother. It achieved a famous

Johnny Lockett's 1936 three-fifty sohc Norton, which was used on the road and raced at Brooklands and the Manx Grand Prix with considerable success; now owned by Eric Kirk.

double TT success the following year gaining both the Junior and Senior events. Even more importantly it set a trend which was to continue for three decades - that of the overhead camshaft Norton reigning supreme on the race circuits of the World.

The production over-the-counter version of the Norton Cammy single, the International, made its public debut at Londons Olympia Show in 1931, and followed the works models splendid fifteen victories at international road races throughout Europe that Summer. Norton publicity referred to the newcomer as 'a genuine TT replica, incorporating all the Norton racing practices'.

The Inter, as it soon became known, was not only a pukka racer, but also one of the era's fastest road-going motorcycles, being able to achieve a genuine 90mph in standard (silenced) form. Customers could order the machine in either competition or roadster guises (the road version having full

Plunger-framed International, showing period oil tank, spring saddle/pillion pad and Brooklands 'can'.

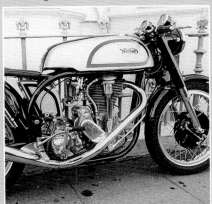

An International-engined, Manx-framed roadster special; beautifully executed and a credit to its enthusiastic owner. This photograph was taken in TT week, 1985.

lighting equipment costing just over £5 extra).

By 1939, four-speed foot-change and plunger rear suspension had been fitted; the 1949 Inter models being the first to feature telescopic front forks. By then the Inter was only available as a roadster, the Manx long since taking over its pukka racing role.

The 1957 model was the final version of the famous International line, with the redoubtable Featherbed frame, Roadholder forks and full width aluminium brake hubs. Alan Shepherd finished third in the 1956 Junior (350cc) Clubman's TT on a smaller-engined Inter Model 40 against a swarm of BSA Gold Stars.

Final production versions of the International featured a featherbed frame.

BEMSEE

This curious name, which is a contraction of the letters BMCRC (British Motor Cycle Racing Club) is the one by which countless thousands of racing enthusiasts have known the longest established specialist racing club in the world down through the years. It's emblem is the crossed Union Jacks and its objectives have always been the promotion of road races for the benefit of the sport in general and the enjoyment of its membership.

The club was founded in March 1909, at Carlton House, Regent Street, London, at that time the headquarters of the BARC (British Automobile Racing Club), who operated the Brooklands racing track at Weybridge, Surrey.

Bemsee's first race meeting was staged on Thursday, 18th April 1909, at Brooklands. And from then on until the outbreak of the Second World War in September 1939, the club continued to organise racing at Brooklands; which didn't reopen at the end of the conflict much to everyone's dismay.

The classic Brooklands racing in the 1920s and 1930s were the 200 mile solo and sidecar events and the Hutchinson Hundred handicap race first staged in 1925, but the mainstay of the programmes throughout the years that Bemsee raced at Brooklands were the short-distance and Lightning handicaps, held over three, five or ten laps of the outer circuit. As a variant of the outer circuit, the shorter 'Mountain' course was devised, and by means of artificial barriers and the steep slope of the banking, a more confined, tricky circuit was created where, unlike the full circuit, sheer

maximum speed was of a less importance than acceleration. Finally there was the 'Campbell Circuit', planned with the aid of the famous speedman Sir Malcolm Campbell. A road section linked the banking with the Fork by way of several corners and a bridge over the River Wey. The new circuit was thus half-road, half track.

The 1920s were the hey-days of the great tuners of the era, men such as le Vack, Temple, Marchant, Waters and of course O'Donovan, to mention a few and the racing machinery was not confined to three or four marques, but drawn from nearly every manufacturer in the country.

The era of the across-the-counter racing motorcycle was yet to come, but when it arrived, the character of Brooklands and racing began to change; the specialist and professional tuner less prominent than hitherto. It also meant that instead of concentrating their efforts solely in Brooklands, private riders began dividing their interests between track and road racing. Although it was not fully appreciated then, the character of Bemsee was also changing.

From then on Brooklands was not the be-all and end-all of racing as it had been before this new era, for many club members took in road racing on the Continent and on the Isle of Man – even sprint events.

Unlike Brooklands which was left in ruins after the end of World War Two, the club was reformed in the immediate postwar period and although without a permanent home anymore, they went to Haddenham, Dunholme Airfield in

Lincolnshire, Silverstone and finally Brands Hatch and Snetterton. Bemsee also organised meetings at Crystal Palace, Oulton Park, plus the famous Shelsley Walsh hill climb in Worcestershire.

The most well-known BMCRC meeting was always the Hutchinson Hundred (nicknamed the 'Hutch'). At Brooklands it was very much a speed bowl event, but after it was resumed in 1947 it became a road race – first at Dunholme for two years, then Silverstone for 17 years, and finally at Brands Hatch. The most famous of the 'Hutch' awards was the Mellano Trophy. From 1947 to 1952 the Mellano Trophy was awarded to the winner of a sealed handicap, the rider competing in a separate race. Afterwards this formula was abandoned, with a new formula being used until 1972 – the trophy being awarded to the rider whose average speed exceeded by the greatest margin the then present class lap record, or if no rider exceeded the class lap record, the rider whose average speed came closest to it. From 1973 to 1976 the Mellano Trophy was awarded in yet another formula, this time as the main race winner.

Norton riders won the coveted 'Mellano' seven times in 1950, 1951, 1952, 1955, 1971, 1972 and 1974.

Bemsee survives to the present day, running a full programme of club meetings at circuits all over Great Britain, but sadly no longer international events featuring the world's top stars.

On the competition front the situation was much the same. Joe Craig returned to the company early in 1946 and the FIM banned supercharging, but the Norton racing effort relied very much on pre-war machinery. The official Norton team reappeared with basically the same double-knocker bikes they campaigned with in 1938, while the private owners at home and abroad dug out their jealously guarded 1930s production single overhead cam models to do battle once again on the world's race circuits. The ban on superchargers was in fact Norton's biggest boost (as it was for all builders of unblown engines) rather than any development in the workshop during the 1946/47 period.

There was no Isle of Man TT in 1946, but the September 'amateur' Manx Grand Prix did take place. Although a Norton ridden by Ken Bills came home second, the Senior event was won by Ernie Lyons on a Triumph twin. Then Bills and Norton did have the satisfaction of winning the Junior event with a Bracebridge Street special.

The TT reappeared in 1947, and Joe Craig admitted to having to drop the compression ratios drastically from around 11:1 to 7.5:1 because of 'pool' low-octane petrol. Otherwise the engines were much as they had been in 1938. But changes to the running gear included Roadholder front forks and hydraulically operated dampers for the rear suspension. Factory riders for the event were announced as Harold Daniell, Artie Bell and the 1946 Manx Grand Prix winner, Lyons. The team were reported to be taking over to the Island six 1938 racers, three 350s and three 500s; and while there were various spares available, there were no spare bikes.

Englishman Tommy Woods riding his plunger-framed 499cc dohc Norton to victory at Erlen, Switzerland in 1948.

Trying to find somewhere (other than short circuits) to test the TT machinery was proving exasperatingly acute until Joe Craig found the French Montlhéry circuit to be in first class condition. Interestingly, from this requirement came the record stints for the marque in later years (see Chapter 5). Actual race testing prior to the TT (the first 'classic' event on the calendar) was confined to the North West 200 at the end of May, where all three works riders competed.

Straight afterwards came the start of TT practice. Joe Craig's comments following the North West 200 showed how important actual race testing was. It transpired that the Norton machines suffered from various troubles which, if they had not been tested, would have shown up on the Island. The event also illustrated, said Craig, that materials that had proved eminently suitable in wartime aircraft engines did not necessarily prove so suitable in air-cooled racing motorcycle engines!

1952 Bryants TT team, Harry King (73), Bob King (48), Les Dear (45), two Clubmans Gold Stars and a 7R, unknown riders. George and Elsie Bryant standing.

In the Junior TT it was Velocette, not Norton, that dominated and took the first four places. But in the Senior TT the Bracebridge Street marque struck back by scoring an impressive one-two (Daniell and Bell), although Velocette's Percy Goodman had the honour of sharing the fastest lap, of 84.07mph, with race winner Daniell. Due to his personal preference, Daniell chose to race without the new rear dampers.

When the 1948 TT came around a year later the works engines showed the benefits of a winter's work. The new features included, for the first time, a common crankcase for the 350 and 500. This employed a larger capacity oil sump and was a more rigid assembly. The pistons were of an improved design, while the cylinder finning was increased. The cylinder barrel (Wellworthy Al-fin) was considerably more effficient than before, while a number of smaller, but still important, modifications were also introduced. Although the frame remained unchanged, the rear wheel size was reduced (from 20 to 19 inches), providing not only improved handling but also a lower seat height. Other changes included a new clutch and twin leading-shoe brakes front and rear.

By now the factory team were beginning to notch up a string of wins and places, not only in the British Isles but also in Europe. Other riders who had joined Craig's elite team included Johnny Lockett and Bill Doran.

1949 saw even more success, but notably, not in the World Championship Series, which was introduced that year. In this, except for Eric Oliver's three-wheel title, Norton only scored one solitary class victory, the Senior TT, won by veteran Daniell at 86.93mph. Even this would not have come about had not the magneto of race leader Les Graham's AJS Porcupine twin expired a few miles from the finish.

But perhaps that penultimate year of the decade is most notable because of the success of a young rider called G. E. Duke, who won first the 500 Clubmans TT and then, three months later, added the Senior Manx Grand Prix, after finishing second in the Junior event - all on Norton machines.

As the new decade dawned it was to be this up-and-coming star, by now a Norton works rider, plus a radical technical leap in frame design that were to spearhead a Norton revival on the race circuit and bring World Championship glory to Bracebridge Street.

Opposite: Close-up of the Garden Gate Manx model's plunger rear suspension.

2 The Featherbed

Rex McCandless, the brains behind the world famous Featherbed frame.

By the end of the 1949 racing season it was patently obvious to all concerned at Norton, from Joe Craig down, that something drastic was needed if the company was to have any real chance of winning either the 350 or 500cc World Championships.

Strangely the answer to the company's prayers was not destined to come from within the Bracebridge Street factory but from across the Irish Sea in the backstreets of Belfast, Northern Ireland. Back in 1944, while the war was still raging, *Motor Cycling* carried a two-page story detailing how a well-known 29-year-old Irish rider, Rex McCandless, had come up with an interesting new frame design and rear wheel suspension system which had been in the process of development in Ulster over the previous couple of years. In fact, as long ago as 1942 *Motor Cycling's* Belfast correspondent, who was then serving in the RAF, had visited the journal's London offices and talked with 'immense enthusiasm' of a new type of suspension that a couple of his fellow citizens had been 'playing around with'. One of these was McCandless and the other Artie Bell, who in 1939 was just beginning to attract factory interest as a rider of great promise - Bell was signed up post-war by Joe Craig, as related in the previous chapter.

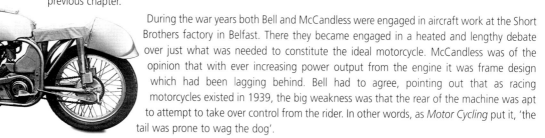

Rex McCandless' 1949 Norton Featherbed prototype pictured in Belfast late that year.

During the war years both Bell and McCandless were engaged in aircraft work at the Short Brothers factory in Belfast. There they became engaged in a heated and lengthy debate over just what was needed to constitute the ideal motorcycle. McCandless was of the opinion that with ever increasing power output from the engine it was frame design which had been lagging behind. Bell had to agree, pointing out that as racing motorcycles existed in 1939, the big weakness was that the rear of the machine was apt to attempt to take over control from the rider. In other words, as *Motor Cycling* put it, 'the tail was prone to wag the dog'.

Artie Bell in action during the Senior TT when he finished second behind team-mate Geoff Duke on 9th June, 1950.

Unlike the majority of designers, Rex McCandless had one big advantage; he was also a topclass competitor in the Irish racing world. When, because of the war, competition events had come to an end, he had to his credit a lengthy list of wins and places, both on grass and tarmac. Rex McCandless could lay claim to being the winner of the very last pre-war road race staged in the British Isles, the 1940 Dublin 100, and he was the holder of the 100 Miles Championship of Ireland, together with the 500cc class Hill Climb Championship. It had been experience in events such as the last-named that had provided the spark of an idea which was to see him create his own racer, incorporating certain features which he realised were lacking in the conventional motorcycle of the era.

One of the major problems with the average motorcycle of the late 1930s was overhard or nonexistent rear suspension, which meant that the machine and rider were subjected to an awful pounding and the roadholding and handling were badly affected, particularly on uneven surfaces. McCandless therefore reasoned that if he could smooth out the bumps, and thereby obtain improved roadholding, he would be able to make far greater use of the extra power he had managed to extract from his self-tuned Triumph Tiger 100 engine.

So he set about designing what *Motor Cycling* described as a 'spring heel'. This proved so successful that he decided to add to it an equally special frame. And perhaps this was the most vital development of all, for certainly it establishes that Rex McCandless was not only a successful rider but also a gifted designer.

McCandless was strongly of the opinion that frame design had not kept pace with power output. Although there had been spring frames before, to obtain the best results he believed that the main-frame and rear-wheel springing had to be designed as a whole. After much consideration he conceived an idea to achieve the correct combination. McCandless then laid this out on paper, and for some 12 weeks the concept was, as *Motor Cycling* commented, 'drafted, modified, studied and amended' until finally he was satisfied that it was ready to proceed

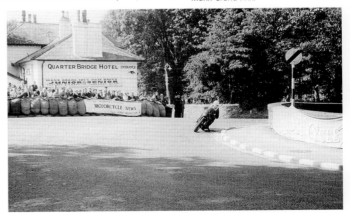

Action at Quarter Bridge as an unidentified Norton rider negotiates the famous landmark during the 1959 Manx Grand Prix.

to the workshop. By 1942 McCandless had produced the first suspension units (from a Citroen car, which at the time was the only ready source of telescopic struts, and was fitted with Salter springs) and had actually built and tried them on his Triumph twin (nicknamed 'Benniel') before the visit of the Belfast *Motor Cycling* correspondent that year. He was therefore able to demonstrate how 'the dog was showing distinct signs of exercising more control over the tail'. The Triumph engine was not only highly tuned but also inclined in the frame at an angle of 45 degrees.

Because of the war years there was very little in the way of technical advancement in the two-wheel world, a notable exception being Rex McCandless. By the cessation of hostilities he had all but perfected his theories, so that in the immediate post-war years various riders were to chalk up some impressive results thanks to his work.

The Motor Cycle's George Wilson tests Geoff Duke's Senior TT winning Norton, June 1950. Note the registration number and the tax disc!

One such competitor was fellow Irishman Bill Nicholson (later to win fame as a BSA works trials and scrambles rider). *The Motor Cycle* of 4th July, 1946, carried the following report: 'Riding with brilliant consistency, W. Nicholson, from Belfast, comfortably won the 350cc and unlimited cc events in last Saturday's open Cotswold Scramble organised by the Stroud Valley MC.

'In consummate style Nicholson vanquished some of the finest scramble exponents of today, and at the same time showed the advantages of rear-wheel springing over rough terrain. His 348cc BSA was fitted with McCandless rear suspension, which worked to perfection on a course distinctly tough for men and machines.'

The Motor Cycle had this to say in their issue of 18th July: 'Telescopic forks have now been almost universally adopted for scramble work and many a well-known rider has been heard to say he wouldn't dream of using girder forks again, so distinct are the advantages of telescopics. Will the same situation arise over rear-wheel springing? Without disparaging in the least Nicholson's magnificent riding in the Cotswold Scramble, it is fair to say that he appeared to have a considerable advantage over other competitors - his McCandless rear suspension worked beautifully, and he obviously got better rear-wheel traction and had a less fatiguing ride than anyone else.' A little known fact is that Nicholson was at that time an employee of McCandless and Bell, who had by then entered into a business partnership, based in Belfast.

Meanwhile, a month later, the first major post-war road racing event was held in Ireland. This was the Ulster Road Race on Saturday, 17th August. This event, which took the place that year of the pre-war Ulster Grand Prix, was held over a course that included part of the former Grand Prix circuit. The 'new' circuit was some 16½ miles in length, four miles shorter than the Grand Prix course. The entry included Artie Bell (Norton) and Rex McCandless, who were by then busy supplying McCandless rear springing conversion sets to local riders as well as to competition riders from the mainland, for it was a feature of the suspension system that it could be incorporated in practically any make of motorcycle.

The 132-mile 500cc class of the Ulster Road Race was notable for only one thing, Bell and McCandless, together with all but one of the entry failing to reach the finishing flag! However, Bell had the satisfaction of setting the fastest lap, at almost 89mph. Artie Bell did manage to put up some excellent results at other venues that year, so much so that 1947 saw him invited to join the Norton racing team. This was ultimately to lead to much greater things for both Bell and McCandless.

1950 works Norton Featherbed as raced by Geoff Duke.

Following public demonstrations, on both sides of the Irish Sea, of the McCandless springing in action, many riders, both competition and touring, had noted its seemingly effortless performance and many began to put aside prejudices generated by years in the saddle. During the latter part of 1946 and early 1947 enquiries by the score were forwarded to the Bell-McCandless establishment. Satisfied customers of the relatively simple and inexpensive conversion generated even more customers, and of course the previously rigid-framed machines attracted attention, including that of certain 'trade' gentlemen. One of the latter was James R. Ferriday, Chairman and Managing Director of Feridax Ltd, the Birmingham wholesalers. Mr Ferriday despatched his Ariel Square Four to Belfast, and when it returned with its tail spring he proceeded to personally test it around England, often at high speed. Among these activities were a number of fast laps of the recently opened Olivers Mount racing circuit, Scarborough, this time in the hands of travelling marshal Arnold Moore. Moore was so impressed that he attempted to purchase the McCandless-Ariel, but James Ferriday simply laughed and said 'no'. Ferriday visited McCandless in Belfast, the result being the formation of Feridax-McCandless Ltd.

This company, launched in July 1947, carried out the McCandless spring-frame conversion for £25 from a small factory in Albion Street, Cheltenham. Involved in the management was Fred Anning, one-time West Country trials specialist. The Feridax operation was divorced from McCandless himself, who had sold the manufacturing rights of the conversion to the Midland businessman.

Artie Bell with the original McCandless prototype, Spring 1950.

Meanwhile, Rex McCandless had set himself another goal, and kept it a well-guarded secret; that of applying his new creation to the Norton racing machine. This proved neither easy nor straightforward. McCandless produced ideas aplenty; Bell tried them out and, often enough, convinced his friend that a 'little more work was needed'. However, Rex McCandless was not one to give up easily, and in any case, each new experiment produced better results. But of course none of this hard work would have been of any use if the management at Norton had not taken any notice. And credit must be given to Norton's Bill Mansell, who invited McCandless to work 'freelance' for the Birmingham company. Mansell was not only interested in the Belfast project but also gave active assistance and support, so that McCandless was able to undertake a period of long, exhaustive tests of a suitable chassis to house the double-knocker, Norton single-cylinder racing engine. But his first job for Norton was designing the 500T trials machine; and, like all McCandless's practical work for Norton, the bike was built in Belfast. But obviously it is the road racing side which is the subject of this chapter, and it was there that McCandless came into contact, and sometimes conflict, with race supremo Joe Craig. Both were Ulstermen and both were skilled engineers, so perhaps it was inevitable.

But even though relations did not always run smoothly with Joe Craig, Rex McCandless was still kept on the payroll and kept up to date with the development of the latest racing engines, with their output, dimensions, weight and other relevant factors all taken into account.

Geoff Duke leaps his 500 Norton at the infamous Ballyhill Jump during the Ulster Grand Prix, August 1950.

Following a truly dreadful year, which had seen the Norton team almost totally out-paced by Velocette, AJS and Gilera, McCandless told Norton he could produce a much superior frame to replace the breakage-prone plunger 'Garden-Gate' device that Norton had favoured for many years. After an intensive development programme, which commenced in the autumn of 1949, Bell and McCandless brought the completed prototype to Birmingham in early 1950, where, under a veil of great secrecy, the new racer was subject to another period of rigorous testing. This included being taken to the Isle of Man in January, thrashed round Montlhéry at high speed (some 400 miles were covered), and then at MIRA (the Motor Industry Research Association establishment) near Nuneaton, Warwickshire, and finally around the Silverstone circuit. It must be said that Joe Craig was a hard man to win over to the new development, but even he realised just what an improvement it was. It was at Silverstone that Harold Daniell commented that he felt it was like riding a 'featherbed' - hence the name.

Geoff Duke about to push his works Norton into life at the start of the 1950 Junior TT.

After the successful completion of tests a full complement of 'Featherbed'-framed works racers was assembled by the Norton race shop during April and May, but only after the frames themselves were built by McCandless and his employee, Oliver Nelson! The works racers used by the team incorporated very few modifications from the original prototype.

The Featherbed's baptism of fire came at Blandford Camp, at the first post-war International road race staged on the British mainland, on Saturday, 29th April, 1950. And what a debut it proved! In front of a crowd of 40,000 spectators Duke, riding the new Featherbed-framed machine (the only one at the meeting), slaughtered the star-studded opposition, which included the 1950 works AJS twin, in the 500cc race. Duke was mounted on a 'Garden-Gate'-type Norton in the 350cc event. The test of the Featherbed was thorough since, in spite of high winds, Duke lapped the 3-mile 247-yard course in 2 minutes 7.2 seconds, a speed of 88.88mph; not only easily the highest speed of the day, but a record for the track. Duke expressed his complete satisfaction with his new mount.

Geoff Duke giving the new Norton 500 a race-winning debut at Blandford Camp, 29th April, 1950.

The 4th May issue of *The Motor Cycle* commented: 'At last the news has broken! For many months rumours have been circulating of an entirely new Norton frame and a modified power unit. At Blandford the cat metaphorically jumped out of the bag when Joe Craig lifted the all-enveloping cloth cover from Geoff Duke's 500cc model. There, most definitely, stood a new frame and one, moreover, devoid of lugs and equipped with swinging arm rear suspension!'

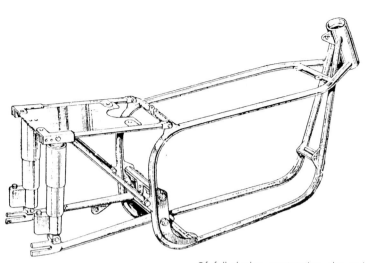

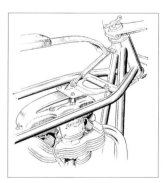

The McCandless Featherbed frame in its original guise with bolt-on sub-frame and remote reservoir rear shocks. Detail view displays head steady and tank strap.

Of full duplex construction, the main frame consisted of two continuous lengths of tubing. Sif-bronzed to the base of the large-diameter steering head, each curved outward and then ran horizontally to the saddle peak, dropped vertically, ran forward to form the cradle for engine and gearbox, then tapered upward, passing between the top rails to be Sif-bronzed to the top of the steering head. The frame was braced at strategic points by Sif-bronzed cross tubes, and a large gusset on each side provided support for the rear engine plates, footrests, gear-change, brake pedals (the rear brake was cable operated) and the swing arm. A pair of adjustable oil-damped coil spring units provided the rear suspension. These, like the vast majority of earlier McCandless rear units, were mounted vertically, not slightly angled, as on later models; the swinging arm was supported by Silentbloc bushes. Norton Roadholder forks with the upper shrouds removed completed the frame assembly and the separate clip-on handlebars were of the 'swan-neck' variety. The front wheel was equipped with a 3.00 x 20in tyre, with the rear being a wider 3.25 section, but of smaller 19in diameter. Both were of Dunlop manufacture, and the tyres were soon to show up as one of the new machine's few really serious failings. Rex McCandless had been involved in a fierce battle to get these smaller wheel sizes accepted, as previously Norton had used 21in front and 20in rear tyres, which were obviously outdated for the new frame technology.

The massive four-gallon capacity alloy fuel tank, with its recesses for the rider's arms and knees, was held in position by a broad, longitudinal steel strap running the full length of the tank. The matching oil tank was housed neatly between the rear frame tubes, and the saddle nose was cut away to provide access to the filler cap. A small platform at the front of the tank carried a rubber mounting for the remote float chamber feeding the downdraught Amal racing carburettor.

A new-style gearbox, essentially the old one tidied up, was attached to the engine by light-alloy plates, and the complete assembly was bolted to the frame at three points, one at the front and two at the rear.

It was not only the running gear that had been improved. The 1950 works double-knocker engine had also been updated. Most notable was that the cambox base had been enlarged, with increased rigidity in its mounting of the cylinder head, and there was now continuous finning surrounding the vertical shaft tunnel on the offside

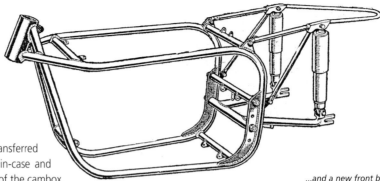

The 1951 works' Featherbed frame featured an integral tail member and new hydraulic rear shock absorbers...

of the engine. The tacho drive had been transferred from its former position on the magneto chain-case and was now tucked out of harm's way on the left of the cambox.

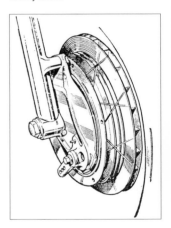

...and a new front brake for the Norton factory effort.

But of course it was that McCandless-designed frame that was all important. He had used Sif-bronzed welding, which made it possible to join tubes together without lugs. Not only this but the frame was much easier to manufacture than the 'Garden-Gate' type.

The older design needed 96 separate machining operations per frame. Sif-bronze welding had been developed in the war years, using an alloy that melted at a lower temperature than steel; and unlike brass, which was previously used on motorcycle frames, Sif-bronze could be built up into fillets.

Assisted by his right-hand man and chief welder Oliver Nelson, McCandless had constructed the original prototype frame, but not just the bare frame, as was often believed: a complete machine was delivered to the Norton factory in early 1950. The basic layout was to remain virtually unchanged during the life of the Featherbed Manx. Clip-on handlebars, a cowled front number plate and an alloy central oil tank were all features of the Belfast-built prototype. An alloy fairing behind the seat forming a rear mudguard was one of the few features that were soon dropped. Another item that was changed, in this case even before the bike's first race, was the leading axle front fork sliders, which McCandless had been asked to incorporate by Craig. These were replaced by the now familiar central axle-type Roadholders. McCandless was also required to sign a document in which he agreed not to seek publicity for himself... it is often thought that the man behind this move was none other than Joe Craig.

On Saturday, 6 May, Johnny Lockett gave the 350 Featherbed its first race outing, and victory, at the Leinster 200 at Wicklow, Eire, while Artie Bell comfortably won the 'Senior Class' on another of the new Nortons. More success was soon to follow a week later when Nortons swamped all the opposition in Ireland's International North West 200 held over the popular 11.1-mile Portstewart-Coleraine-Portrush course, before a reported record crowd and beneath a blistering sun on Saturday, 13th May. The *Motor Cycling* headline read: 'Fastest Ever North West 200. With race and lap records broken in all classes, Artie Bell (500) and Geoff Duke (350) made it a Norton double.' So superior was the new Featherbed that during practice Duke, with the 350, had lapped faster than Bell's 1949 record 500 lap!

The 1952 works Nortons at their Isle of Man headquarters for that year's TT races.

With these race victories under its belt, Norton turned its attention to the Isle of Man TT. When practice got under way on Thursday 25th May, Johnny Lockett was fastest Senior at 84.38mph and Geoff Duke the quickest Junior with a lap of 82.49mph. But the following morning practice session saw both these times beaten by AJS riders Graham and Doran. Much of this early Norton practice was carried out with either older works mounts or even, in the case of Artie Bell, a single-knocker, over-the-counter racer! But later during practice the new Featherbed machines started to appear, and Duke showed his hand by lapping on his Senior mount at just over 90mph during the early morning period on 31st May, the fastest speed of the entire practice week.

The Junior TT took place on Monday, 5th June, with *Motor Cycling* reporting: 'What a magnificent morning for the 1950 Junior Tourist Trophy race. The Island has done us proud. There is still a sea mist in the bay and as the crowd begins to assemble between 9 and 10am the mournful wailing of "Moaning Minnie", the Douglas Bay fog horn, can be heard. This year her warning carries no threats, for inland the conditions are marvellous and when the fog lifts off the water later in the morning the heat will be almost tropical.'

And so it proved, with absolutely ideal racing conditions. At the end of lap 1, Les Graham had his AJS a mere second ahead of Duke in second spot, on adjusted time, and Bell in third. But at the end of lap 2 the positions were reversed - Bell, Duke, Graham - and so it remained until lap 6. As the chequered flag fell at the end of the seventh and final circuit a great cheer greeted Bell, Duke and also Graham, who, it seemed, had held on to his third place. But with a very quick final sprint it was Daniell who grabbed this position, so completing a resounding one-two-three for Norton. Lockett had brought the fourth Bracebridge Street model home in sixth and Rex

First of the production Featherbed Manx; this photograph shows a 1951 348cc 40M model.

McCandless's younger brother Cromie was eighth, on a 'Garden-Gate' model, after his machine suffered problems on the final circuit when he was lying sixth. *Motor Cycling* reported: 'In a long experience our reporter has never seen three machines finish in better order.' And when interviewed after the race, all the Norton riders had been full of praise for the new McCandless frame.

Once again Senior TT day, Friday, 9th June, was held in perfect weather conditions: dry and warm. And once again it was to prove an impressive one-two-three for the Norton team. But in place of Bell it was Duke who out-rode the opposition. In the process he pushed the average for the seven-lap race up from 89.38mph to 92.82mph, and raised the lap record from 91 to 93.33mph! Bell was second, with Lockett third and Daniell fifth. AJS team leader and 1949 World Champion Graham once again had to settle for fourth place.

The Editorial in *Motor Cycling*, dated 15th June, 1950, was full of praise for the 32nd TT, commenting: 'Those who believed the days of the single-cylinder racing machine to be numbered are surely silenced. So, too, must be those critics who believed the TT races could no longer serve any useful purpose in the development of production machines. How much of the Norton performance is due to improvements in the power unit and how much to the new frame is still open to debate, but it may safely be assumed the industry as a whole will now be spurred to further research in the fields of controlled combustion and machine suspension to the ultimate benefit of the ordinary, everyday motorcyclist.' But that Editorial was both right and wrong with the following comment in the same article: 'The supremacy of the single will probably be short-lived, but it will provide data which should make British multi-cylinder machines unbeatable in the world's classic events in due course.'

A 1956 Manx; from 1954 there had been short-stroke engines. 1956 saw further improvements including a hollow exhaust valve, hinged double-row ball race timing side main bearing and full ring clutch plates.

If the TT proved a great success for Norton, the Belgian Grand Prix, which followed on Sunday, 2nd July, was a disaster. First came the 350cc race. The Circuit of Spa Francorchamps in the Belgian Ardennes was to blunt the Bracebridge Street factory's World Championship challenge, as at the finish it was Foster and Velocette who were the victors, even though Bell and Duke came second and third. Although Geoff Duke had the satisfaction of setting the fastest lap at 103.84mph in the 500cc, the Blue Riband was to see all the works Nortons retire! There was no hint of the drama that was to follow as the 42 starters began the 14-lap 500cc race. The start was spectacular, for the four-cylinder Gileras and the solitary MV Agusta of Artesiani shot off at a fantastic rate. Slower away, but soon on the heels of the Italian multis were the Norton singles and AJS twins. At Masta it was Pagani, Bandirola and Masetti, all on Gileras, who led, but at Stavelot Duke was up into third, and as they sped down from La Source it was a duel between no less than eight riders, with Bell second and Duke fourth.

On lap 2 Bandirola was in front by one second from Duke and the other two Gileras, and then came Johnny Lockett, another two seconds astern. Others went by, but there was no sign of Bell or Graham. Then the French rider Georges Houel toured in with Graham on his pillion; the AJS star's leathers clearly displaying the signs of a high-speed tumble.

The bad news filtered through from the pits that Graham, on the tail of Bandirola entering the 100mph left hander before the hairpin, touched the rear wheel of the Italian's machine; Graham came off and, in falling, collided with Bell, who was also closely behind the leading pair. Both men and machines slid into the broadcasters' hut, and while Graham escaped with some bruising, Norton teamster Bell was badly injured (he never raced again). Meanwhile, his team-mate, Duke, probably several miles down on maximum speed compared with the 135mph Gileras, outrode the Italian team and had taken the lead, only to lose it when he was forced to slow down by an ambulance, which was on the course attending to the Bell accident. On the fifth circuit Masetti moved ahead of Bandirola, a mere second behind Duke. On the seventh lap Lockett disappeared, soon to tour into the pits and retire with streaks of bare canvas showing on his Dunlop rear tyre.

A 1953 works Norton 350cc.

At half-distance Pagani, Masetti and Duke came through the line abreast, but Duke got through the bridge first and disappeared in the lead. From then on the Italian fours could not touch him. On lap 12, just as everyone thought he had victory in the bag, Duke retired with exactly the same trouble as Lockett. This left Gilera first, second and fourth, with AJS third.

A week later, another race and an almost carbon copy result - *Motor Cycling* called it 'the Dutch debacle'. Norton again experienced tyre failure, as did AJS, in the 500cc Dutch TT at Assen. But before this Bob Foster (Velocette) had once again defeated the Norton team in the 350cc race, with Duke second and Lockett fourth; Bill Lomas, on another Velocette, was third.

By the end of lap 8 of the 18-lap 500cc Dutch TT only one British works rider was left circuiting. The problem centred around the tyre tread coming adrift, caused, said a report at the time, 'by a lack of a high-speed circuit like Monza or Montlhéry in Britain'. In reality Dunlop had simply not produced tyres capable of matching the performance. Those (from a different manufacturer) fitted to the Gileras and MVs did not give the same problem and, following an accident to Duke, Joe Craig pulled out all his team from Holland.

This left Gilera in a dominant position. However, Australian Harry Hinton, on a private production Garden Gate Manx, had other ideas. Hinton, with a race average speed of over 90mph, split the trio of Gileras to finish third in front of Bandirola, a truly superb piece of riding!

On 20th July, *Motor Cycling* carried a report saying that Artie Bell, injured a fortnight before in Belgium, had been flown by air ambulance to London. He had suffered multiple injuries, but thankfully, although seriously ill, he was off the critical list. Constantly at his bedside had been his wife, sister and his friend and business partner Rex McCandless.

A huge Bank Holiday crowd had seen Geoff Duke back in action and smashing records at the 3-mile Blandford Camp circuit on Monday, 7th August. They also saw the last event of the year to be staged at this popular track, for, following a spate of accidents, the military authorities had decided not to permit further racing at this venue (this decision was later relaxed to allow racing the following year). In the last race of the day Duke bettered his own track record of 88.88mph on every one of the 16 laps. All his laps after the third were over 90mph and his fastest was 91.03mph.

Barry Sheene (seated) and Geoff Duke with a 1962 499cc Manx, Earls Court Show, London, 1977.

The next round in the World Championship series was in Ireland, and prior to the start of the 500cc Ulster Grand Prix, everyone firmly believed that Umberto Masetti and his four-cylinder Gilera were unbeatable in the Championship. But 15 laps and 247½ miles later on that Saturday, 19th August, the Italian star had suffered the humiliation of being lapped by Geoff Duke. This meant that the Norton star and second finisher Les Graham had suffficient points to stand a sporting chance of winning the 500cc Championship at the final round to be staged at Monza during early September.

A strong westerly wind was blowing, an advantage on the punishing 7-mile Clady straight, but a handicap on the remainder of the 16½-mile circuit and occasional sharp showers made the going tricky; yet Duke came within three seconds of Graham's 1949 lap record of just over 98mph on his opening lap and shattered it on each of the subsequent circuits of the race, which he won at an average speed of 99.56mph. Both Graham and third finisher Lockett covered the full distance at higher average speeds than that of the previous fastest lap, while Duke's two best circuits were made at 101.77mph. Dickie Dale, making his debut as a works Norton rider, secured fourth spot.

After his superb showing in Holland, 41-year-old Australian Harry Hinton was also given his first outing on one of the 1950 works Nortons in the 350cc race, coming home third behind the Velocettes of Foster and Armstrong. Harold Daniell on another Featherbed was sixth.

So to the final classic of the year, the Grand Prix des Nations, which took place at Monza on Sunday, 10th September. The previous season Norton did not even bother to contest the final round of the Championship series, but they now sent four team riders; Duke, Lockett, Daniell and new boy Dickie Dale, plus Hinton on a 350.

The 350cc race was a 24-lap, 93.7-mile affair and proved to be a very close race, with Duke finally winning from Graham (AJS), Hinton, Dale and Lomas (Velocette). Hinton made fastest lap at 97.15mph. But it was the 500cc event that most people had come to see. One hundred and twenty-five miles of almost flat-out riding was to decide the 'Senior' 1950 Championship. If Masetti and his Gilera struck any trouble, Duke (and Graham) were close enough on points to benefit. Of the British riders, only Duke seemed to be able to stay with the flying Italian fours from Gilera and MV. After four laps Duke had extended his lead at the front of the pack, with champion Masetti in second spot. And except for lap 10, when Masetti screamed his Gilera four to the front, Duke maintained his lead to the very end, which came by mistake at the end of lap 31, not the scheduled 32 as per the programme. Yes, the mistake had been made, but the organisers stood by their decision and, despite an appeal, it was confirmed by the international jury that the positions of the riders at the end of the 31st circuit constituted the final result.

The next Norton (or for that matter British) machine home was Dale in sixth, with Graham seventh and Lockett eighth. All other riders were lapped, including Daniell in tenth place. Daniell then finally hung up his leathers and 'retired' to his London motorcycle dealership - trading in Nortons of course.

The real star of Monza was Duke, even though Masetti's second spot had given him the Championship. *Motor Cycling* said: 'In winning the 500cc race at Monza, Geoffrey Duke put up the most remarkable performance in his phenomenal career. By defeating the Italian aces on their home circuit he scored a victory of incalculable value to British prestige in Europe.' Even with the mid-season tyre problems, Duke was second in both the 350cc and 500cc World Championships - no mean achievement!

The Hintons, famous Australian racing family, left to right: Harry Junior, Harry senior, and Eric.

And so the 1950 classic racing season came to an end, but with great hope for the future at Norton, as even with their undoubted disadvantage, the single-cylinder Featherbed-framed Nortons had beaten the best Italy could put up in their own backyard. This new-found pride was shown to the full when Geoff Duke was received enthusiastically by the Sports Writers' Association at its dinner in London's Press Club on Thursday, 14th December. He was one of five sportsmen, guests of the Association, chosen as the men who had contributed most to Britain's international prestige in 1950. The others were: Reg Harris (cycling); Jack Holden (athletics); Colonel Harry Llewellyn (show jumping), and Reg Parnell (motor racing).

A month earlier the injured Artie Bell had been flown home to Ulster, and although still in hospital at Christmas was reported to be making steady progress towards recovery. When recovery finally came, it left him with a disabled right arm, ruling out not only road racing but his other sporting love, horse jumping.

Artie Bell's 'other half', Rex McCandless, was still with Norton and was to prove that his innovative mind could still be of great benefit to the old-established Birmingham marque. In any case, the Featherbed-framed double-knocker Norton single was still to score its finest achievements, as the 1951 season was to prove .

1960 saw a whole host of changes including higher comp. pistons, stronger big-end, reinforced clutch, glass-fibre seat base and number plate with perspex flyscreen.

3 Grand Prix Exploits

The German Grand Prix on 28th August 1951. This is the start of the 350cc event, won by double World Champion Geoff Duke (60). Other Norton riders are Kavanagh (70) and Lockett (65).

Although 1950 had seen the arrival of the Featherbed and the emergence of Geoff Duke as a world class rider, not everything had gone according to plan for the works Norton racing team, led by Joe Craig. Firstly, there had been the dramatic mid-season tyre problems, which had no doubt cost the team one, if not two, World Championship titles. And behind the scenes the hoped-for development of an all-British four-cylinder Grand Prix engine had not progressed as Craig had hoped. But the Norton team manager was not one to give up; and there was no denying that he was the driving force behind the Norton racing effort. Over the years certain individuals had tried to lessen Craig's authority, but the majority defend his record. A Craig admirer, Ken Kavanagh, puts it like this: 'The great Joe Craig... Joe Craig with his blunt pigheadedness and four faithful mechanics, Frank Sharrit, Ivor Smith, Harry Salter and Charlie Edwards... these were the real heroes who kept British motorcycle prestige at or near the top from 1930 till 1954.' It is true to say that Craig got on well with anyone... who he thought would be of benefit to his ultimate aim of winning races.

1951 - The works team solo riders, when announced during that close season, were to be Duke, Lockett and Dale. The first classic of the new season was the Spanish Grand Prix, held at Barcelona in early April. Although the Gilera, Moto Guzzi and MV Agusta teams were out in force, there were no works Norton entries (Eric Oliver was 'officially' a private entry). And it was not until the following May, at the Irish North West 200, that the public first saw the latest works machinery in action.

In the Junior race Dale won at an average speed of 87.70mph, while Duke set the fastest lap at a speed of 89.19mph before retiring - his time bettered the existing 500cc lap record! Duke took the Senior race, averaging 88.71mph, from Lockett and Dale, twice breaking the lap record; his first was recorded at 90.19mph and the second raised it to 92.29mph; the latter represented a chop of 18 seconds from the 1950 figure set by Artie Bell.

For 1951 the 350's bore and stroke were changed to 75.9 x 77mm, while the 500cc engine's became 84 x 90mm. The cambox was modified to fit directly into the cylinder head, with more finning for the head itself. Other changes included a new type of remote float chamber for the Amal carb, and the 350's megaphone was shortened and given a reverse cone to improve low-down pressure. The earlier 'swan-neck' clip-ons were replaced by a simpler straight type, while the wheel rims, front and rear, were reduced to 18 inches and the tyres changed from Dunlop to Avon.

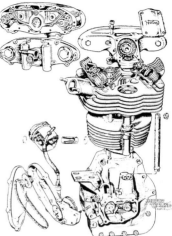

1950 factory five-hundred engine with diagonal head fins and integral bevel housing.

Before the TT came the Swiss Grand Prix, held over the 4¹/₂-mile Bremgarten circuit, Berne, on Saturday and Sunday 26th and 27th May. Although the days prior to this had been hot and dry, the race period was staged under treacherously wet conditions.

The 350 race saw two works Norton entries; Geoff Duke and the popular local rider Georges Cordey. Although Les Graham initially led on a Velocette, Duke soon took over at the front, with Cordey a safe third, the new 350 Nortons appeared considerably faster than the previous year's machines. Duke was lapping at around 81mph, by no means a record-breaking speed, but as *The Motor Cycle* said in its report, 'absolutely superb on the wet roads'.

Close-up of a 1951 works Norton at the North West 200.

On the fifth lap Cordey was out because of magneto trouble. On the next lap fate struck at Duke, and he too was reported as a retirement due to magneto trouble. Graham went on to an easy win, and gained eight more points in the World Championship to add to the six won at the first classic of the year, the Spanish Grand Prix the previous month. So the Velocette rider led the 350cc title hunt comfortably.

By the time the 500cc race had started (it was the last of the two-day meeting) the rain, rather than easing up, was teeming down. True to form Duke and Cordey were both forced to retire with yet more magneto trouble after being well placed! So ended a thoroughly dismal weekend for the Norton team, with two rounds gone and not a solitary solo World Championship point to their name, although for the final outcome it did not matter, as only the best four results counted.

Cromie McCandless at Creg-na-Baa during the 1951 Senior TT. Besides race winner Geoff Duke, McCandless was the top scoring Norton rider finishing in 3rd position.

Australian Harry Hinton was drafted into the Norton team for the 1951 TT, he is seen here airborne at Ballaugh Bridge in the Junior race.

With the TT practice so close to the Swiss event, most of the top riders who intended competing in both arrived on the Island by air. Duke was soon in the groove, obviously putting the disappointments of Switzerland behind him, with an early lap during the Junior practice of 25 minutes 29 seconds (88.85mph), surpassing Artie Bell's class record of 25 minutes 56 seconds (87.31mph) with ease. But if anyone thought these speeds were quick, the Junior TT itself was something else... Run under perfect conditions before very large crowds, Duke broke the lap record from a standing start in 25 minutes 14 seconds (89.75mph). On his second, third and fifth circuits Duke exceeded 90mph, with the second lap the fastest at 91.38mph (24 minutes 47 seconds). He went on to win comfortably in 2 hours 56 minutes 17.6 seconds at an average speed of 89.90mph (he had averaged 90.40mph up to the end of six laps, but slowed down when he knew the race was in his pocket). Works Nortons were also second, Lockett, and third, Jack Brett (Brett had taken over from Dale, who was ill with pleurisy). Other notable features of the race were the form shown by Aussie Harry Hinton, who lay a superb second for two laps, and TT newcomer Ray Amm, of Southern Rhodesia, who finished ninth - a clear hint of things to come.

After his winning ride Geoff Duke said that he 'had ridden to orders, changing up at between 6,800 and 7,000rpm, whereas the engine peaks in the region of 7,500rpm'. He also stated that he had been rolling the grip back when passing the pits and on several other sections of the course.

In practice for the Senior TT Duke had circulated in 24 minutes 13 seconds (93.52mph), which boded well for the race itself. And so it proved, when, shattering all existing records, Duke scorched round the famous Mountain circuit to follow up his Junior success by winning the Senior at an average of nearly 94mph and setting a new outright lap record at 95.22mph. Until the last lap it appeared that a Norton would also take second place, but it was not to be, for Johnny Lockett struck chain trouble and was forced to retire a dozen miles from the finish. This let Bill Doran with his works AJS Porcupine into the vacant second berth, and Rex McCandless's younger brother Cromie into third spot.

After the racing was over *The Motor Cycle's* George Wilson had the happy task of testing both Duke's winning mounts... and he was impressed. Not only did he call the handling and braking 'superb', but followed this by saying, 'I could scream the 350 right up to over 7,000rpm from 2,000 with it hardly missing a beat.' And it was this feature which he considered contributed most to Duke's record-breaking Junior race, commenting, 'On a circuit such as the Isle of Man, which has innumerable slow corners, clean and rapid pick-up on the throttle is a tremendous advantage. I am told that Geoff can come out of the dip at Governor's Bridge with his hand away from the clutch lever. Bottom-end power is something which has barely been considered by racing engineers in the past, but it is becoming increasingly realised that acceleration between corners must be as dynamic as it possibly can be.' Wilson also considered that in the handling department the latest bikes were even better than the 1950 mounts he had tested a year earlier. 'The

The 1951 double world champion, Geoff Duke pictured with his factory Norton at one of the Grands Prix that year.

machines this year had 18in rims, and while I may be wrong about this, I did feel that the steering was improved over last year's.' These were the first engines modified by Leo Kusmicki, and the first with squish heads. *The Motor Cycle* man also remarked that 'the new five-hundreds, probably because of the shortened stroke, are now fitted with much smaller megaphones than previously, and "megaphonitis" is not nearly so pronounced as it was, for instance, on last year's Senior winner'.

Sunday 1st July saw the Norton equipe return to the fastest circuit on the classic trail, the famous 8.8-mile Spa Francorchamps track, scene of the Belgian Grand Prix. Spectators had been impressed when, in 1950, the 500cc class was won at an average speed of over 100mph. Yet 1951 saw that magic three figure speed exceeded by the winner of the 350cc race! His average for the 96.4 miles was 100.52mph and he accomplished a fastest lap at 101.28mph. Who was he? None other than Geoff Duke! Not only this, but in a highly impressive display of skilful riding and machine reliability the same rider came home first in the 500cc event, this time averaging 106.66mph and establishing a new lap record at 107.8mph, which was the highest speed ever achieved up to that time on a classic road-race circuit. It should be noted that the 500cc race saw works teams from not only Norton, but also AJS, Moto Guzzi, Gilera and MV Agusta! After Duke the next best Norton rider was Lockett in sixth, followed by Brett in seventh. In the Junior event Brett had finished in an identical position, but Lockett had managed to make it a Norton one-two, with runner-up spot behind race winner Duke.

Six days later and the venue was the Dutch Grand Prix, the 20th meeting over the 10.2-mile Van Drenthe circuit, near Assen. Among the 35 who came to the grid for the 350cc race on Saturday, 7th July were three works Norton riders with Duke, Lockett and Brett occupying the front row. They made the most of this advantage. Duke and Brett, side by side, headed the booming, weaving pack as they approached the first corner. The order at Oude Tol, four miles out, was Duke, Lockett and Brett. Another four miles on, at Laaghaleveen, Doran (AJS) was among the Norton threesome, but some 100 yards behind the irrepressible Duke.

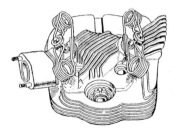

The 1950 factory cylinder head with diagonal fins on top and vertical above the exhaust port.

DICKIE DALE – THE FORGOTTEN NORTON STAR

A works rider during the glory days of the 1950s for MV Agusta, Gilera, Moto Guzzi, BMW and Benelli, Dickie Dale began and ended his career on Norton singles; he also rode briefly for Joe Craig as an official Norton works rider.

Born at Wyberton, near Boston, Lincolnshire on the 25th April 1927, Dickie Dale was drafted as a flight mechanic into the RAF during 1945 and served for three years. He worked on a wide variety of aircraft from Tiger Moths to Meteors. Whilst stationed at RAF Cranwell he purchased his first motorcycle, a 1939 AJS Silver Streak, for transport between the base and his home.

But like many before and since, he soon found bikes more than a means of getting from A to B and started competition in grasstrack events organised by the local Boston Motorcycle Club.

His first roadrace came at Cadwell Park in 1946, on a Norton single, and his successes that season caught the eye of Austin Monks, himself a four-times Manx Grand Prix winner. Then came more help from Monks' friend and racing colleague

Sam Coupland, whose house was in the middle of the 7-mile Frithville straight, and this section of road was used for unofficial testing with the local policemen turning a blind eye!

Dickie won the 1948 Lightweight Manx Grand Prix (on a Monks-entered Moto Guzzi) at record speed. He also rode a Monks-tuned 500 Norton and a Coupland-owned KTT Velocette that year.

Dale's first TT rides came in 1949, when he rode a Moto Guzzi in the Lightweight and a Velocette in the Junior, and although he retired in both, he had caught the eye of Norton's team manager, Joe Craig. The result was an offer of a team ride in 1950. His best results that year were two 4ths – on the 350 at Monza and on the 500 in Ulster.

The following season was a write-off racing wise, after contracting tuberculosis and spending most of the year in a sanatorium in Dorchester. Many riders would have given up, but not Dickie Dale who by 1953 was back in the saddle, first with Gilera, followed by an MV contract for 1954. Then in 1955 he joined Moto Guzzi, whom he stayed with until they quit racing at the end of 1957. Probably his most famous Guzzi performance was bringing home a very sick V8 to 4th place in that years Senior TT.

In 1958 he rode a BMW Rennsport (together with Geoff Duke) and in 1959 (again with Duke) a 250 Benelli dohc single. For 1960 he went back to being a privateer with a pair of Manx models, having ridden the same bikes for Bob Foster of Parkstone, on the occasions when the BMW and Benellis were not available.

Then came 1961 and whilst racing at the demanding Nürburgring on the 30th April, in wet conditions, he crashed fatally (caused, it is believed, by oil on the track). After a cremation ceremony in Bournemouth, his ashes were put under Sam Coupland's lawn.

The Motor Cycle of the 4th May 1961 commented: 'No road racing man will be more missed by fans the world over than Dickie Dale. His fatal accident while leading the 500cc Race at the Nürburgring in Germany last Sunday robs the game of one of its most likeable gentlemen. He was popular in Britain and on the continent, and equally so farther afield – in South Africa and Australia'.

Dickie Dale back in Lincolnshire with the family dog.

Dickie Dale at the Nürburgring,
30th April 1961.

Opposite: Johnny Lockett in action during the 1951 North West 200 in Northern Ireland.

As the leaders went past to complete lap 1, the shock announcement came over the loudspeaker system that the Norton team leader had crashed on the next corner! Eyes strained along the road to the bend just after the start. Yes, Duke had come down and both he and his machine had skated luridly at high speed. Although he was up in a flash, his machine was too badly damaged to continue. Shortly afterwards Duke walked back to the pits nursing his elbow and announcing sheepishly that 'I just fell off.' It was not only Duke of the Norton men who had hit the tarmac, Brett had too. But at least he had been able to remount and had therefore begun to climb rapidly back up the field. By the eighth lap Reg Armstrong (AJS) and Lockett were fighting for the lead. This battle came to an end when Armstrong, leading by a few yards, dropped his machine at Hooghalen and brought down Lockett; both had to retire. But this was not all. On the same lap, Brett and three other riders all came off because of oil on a corner near Laaghalen. The whole Norton team was sidelined by crashes! So it was left to privateer Ken Kavanagh to uphold Bracebridge Street honour on his production Manx. He finished an excellent third behind the works AJSs of Doran and Petch.

Showing no signs of his high-speed exit in the earlier race, Duke was soon in the thick of the action in the 500cc event. By half-way round lap 1, Fergus Anderson and Bruno Ruffo on Moto Guzzis had forged ahead, with Duke third, followed by the Gilera fours of Pagani and Milani. Duke managed to displace Ruffo before the end of the lap, but could not catch the flying Scot. Only yards separated the first six at the end of lap 2. Duke was just ahead of Anderson; then came Pagani, Masetti, Milani and Ruffo - 'a snarling, screeching crocodile that passed in a flash' as *The Motor Cycle* reported. About 25 seconds behind the leaders came Lockett and Brett, then Graham and Artesiani on the first of the MVs. Not very far to the rear of the MVs came the leading privateer, Ray Amm. Masetti overhauled Pagani and Anderson on lap 3 and in so doing recorded the fastest lap of the race at 97.28mph. After two more laps he and Pagani were ahead of Duke. Then Duke led; then Masetti again; then Duke again. Anderson was fourth behind Pagani and losing a few yards each lap. A mere two seconds covered all four men. The crowds were on their toes, for it seemed impossible that the pace could last. And sure enough, lap 10 saw the quartet broken as Anderson fell at low speed at Bartelds Bocht. Although he quickly remounted, his race was run, and he retired a few miles further on.

Shortly after this came a spate of mechanical retirements - but the leading three were not affected. The Italians were close, but could never get past Duke. It seemed that with their superior speed on the straights they must be playing a waiting game, but in reality Duke was just too good. By lap 13 the Norton rider had a 100-yard lead over Pagani, who by then had a 300-yard lead over Masetti. Both Gileras sounded less crisp than previously and Masetti's engine was definitely misfiring. On the next lap, Pagani's motor was reported to have cut out at Bartelds Bocht and he retired before Hooghalen. The Gilera challenge fizzled out when Masetti also failed to appear. The excitement was by now largely over, and so at the end of 18 laps and 185 miles, Duke crossed the line to take the chequered flag at an average of 95.55mph. Milani on the surviving Gilera four came in second, while Lockett just missed third on the line to a strong-finishing Enrico Lorenzetti (Guzzi). Brett was fifth.

Nearly 20 years had elapsed since a road-race meeting with FIM classic status had been held in France. But this long period came to an end on Sunday, 15th July, 1951, when the French Grand Prix took place over the 5½-mile Albi circuit. A problem during the practice period centred around unsuitable fuel, but eventually this was solved, only for the meeting to suffer a fatal accident in the Friday practice period, when Benelli's 250cc World Champion Dario Ambrosini skidded on tar melted by scorching sunshine, collided with a telegraph pole and died almost instantly.

Yorkshireman Jack Brett was a works Norton rider for several years, but his only classic victory for the marque was in the 1957 500cc Belgian Grand Prix.

Johnny Lockett, who provided reliable back-up to the likes of Duke and Bell rather than race-winning performances.

The triangular Albi circuit consisted in the main of very fast straights and very slow corners and there were few high speed curves. A violent thunderstorm on Saturday night, with rain so heavy that roads were temporarily flooded, reduced the torrid heat experienced during the previous days. Early Sunday morning, race day, and the rain continued to fall sporadically. The result was a much smaller than expected crowd and a road surface that looked decidedly slippery. A 10-lap race for French nationals on 350cc and 500cc machines got the programme under way, and by the time the first Grand Prix riders were warming up their bikes, for the 350cc race, the rain came down heavily again. At 10.30, when the start was scheduled, the air was still and the flags hung wet and limp against their poles, a forlorn sight indeed.

On the front row of the 27 starters was the New Zealand AJS star Rod Coleman in company with the works Norton trio. But all the four front men were caught out by the quick start of Pierre Monneret (AJS). The star men were soon overhauling the young Frenchman. All three works Norton riders, Duke, Brett and Lockett, in that order, swept past him well before the end of the first lap. Duke's time was 4 minutes 6 seconds (around 81mph). His second-lap time of 3 minutes 50.8 seconds gave him a 200-yard lead, which he increased to an even longer gap, 15 seconds, after three laps. Lap speeds were over 86mph, and the rain had stopped. Speeds were going up, and Duke was already lapping the tail-enders. And so it continued, the Norton star coming past the pits to complete ten laps and at the same time equalling the 350cc class lap record of 89.15mph - set by Les Graham in 1950 - on wet roads! Next time around he recorded 89.54mph - would he beat 90mph? Duke and Brett were way out in front and had only to keep going to be placed first and second, while Lockett was involved in a raging battle with the leading AJS riders. In spite of his commanding lead, Duke went faster and faster lap by lap. And on the last lap, still on wet roads, he lapped in 3 minutes 38.6 seconds (91.02mph), a remarkable time in such awful weather conditions.

Between the 350cc and 500cc races came the 250cc and sidecar events. By the time the big bikes came out there was welcome blue sky between the patches of billowing cloud. As in Holland, it was Fergus Anderson on his Guzzi who made a flyer at the start to lead the field away. But soon the Gileras of Pagani and Milani had forged ahead. Duke was in fourth place, close behind Anderson. The two Gileras were going exceptionally quickly, Milani turning in a fourth lap of 100.15mph. And although Duke had finally got the better of the Guzzi rider, the Gileras were now over 50 yards in front. Brett was eighth and Lockett, on the third works Norton, 11th. On lap 6, Anderson got back ahead of Duke for third. The big Nortons seemed to lack their usual turn of speed. And so it proved at the end of the 23-lap 127-mile race, with Duke fifth, Brett sixth and Lockett tenth. The victor's spoils went to Milani (Gilera).

It was wet again for Duke's return to the British scene at Thruxton in early August, when he won the Festival of Britain Invitation Race - second-place man was a certain John Surtees on a Vincent Grey Flash. Two weeks after Thruxton came the Ulster Grand Prix. An innovation for the Ulster was racing on two days. Past practice had seen

1952 Senior TT winner Reg Armstrong at May Hill, Ramsay during his victorious ride. His average speed for the 7-lap, 264-mile race was 92.97mph.

all classes run concurrently. However, this traditional arrangement was not possible under the new 1951 FIM ruling for World Championship meetings, whereby the programme had to be such that a rider could take part in at least one race in each of the groups: (a) 125cc, 250cc and 350cc solo; (b) 500cc and 500cc sidecar. The 350, 250 and 125cc classes were staged on the evening of Thursday 16th August and the 500cc (and sidecar) two days later. The weather was overcast with threatening clouds completely obliterating the sky. Flags in the starting area were at half-mast in tribute to the Italian riders Sante Geminiani and Gianni Leoni, who had been killed in an accident the day before on the circuit when the roads were open to the public.

Seventy-eight bikes were ready to go (52 350cc, the rest 125cc and 250cc). When the flag fell to let loose the 350s, Australian Ken Kavanagh, competing for the first time on a works Norton, streaked into the lead. He was chased by the other factory Nortons of Duke, Lockett and Brett. Kavanagh's orders were 'to forget Geoff Duke and learn the circuit'. As the riders came thundering along the straight to complete the first lap it was Duke in the lead, followed by Brett, Kavanagh and Lockett, in that order. Then there was an appreciable gap before the AJS team; with none of the works Velocettes offering much opposition.

Duke's opening lap had been completed in 10 minutes 24 seconds; his speed of 95.07mph meant he had improved by over two miles per hour on the fastest 350cc lap of 1950 - and Duke had done it from a standing start! A speed of 98.24mph on his second circuit meant that Duke had a seven second lead over the best of his team-mates, Kavanagh, who was leading Lockett and Brett. Meanwhile, they in turn were over half a minute ahead of the AJS riders. But Brett rather spoiled things by falling at Nutt's Corner on lap 4, and although he was able to continue, he had surrendered his position to the AJS team and the Velocettes of Foster and Sandford.

The Australian Tom Phillis (1961, 125cc World Champion on a Honda), rode Nortons early in his career. This startline shot was taken at the 1959 German Grand Prix.

Opposite: At Monza on 19th September, 1952, are the Norton trio of Armstrong (20), Kavanagh (22) and Amm (standing on the extreme right of the photograph).

With the sky even more overcast, Duke commenced his final lap; the rain held off and he kept the lead to not only win the Ulster at record speed but also to become the 1951 350cc World Champion. A great result was made even greater, as this win put Norton in an unassailable position in the manufacturers' contest. The race also saw another star born: Kavanagh had finished second to Duke in his debut ride for the team.

If Thursday's race had escaped the downpour that had threatened, Saturday's certainly did not. At 11.30, just as the engines were being warmed up ready for the off in half an hour, rain spotted down and soon afterwards settled into a torrent, which *The Motor Cycle* reporter stated 'could scarcely have been worse'.

Among the 38 riders who appeared on the starting grid there were works teams from Norton, AJS and Gilera, but no MV Agustas or Moto Guzzis. The latter had withdrawn because of the double fatality mentioned earlier. As on the Thursday, there was a brief silence in memory of the two Italian riders, then the flag dropped and the pushing began. At the end of the first lap it was Kavanagh who led. His time from the standing start was 10 minutes 32 seconds, a speed of 94.04mph in rain that saturated clothing and almost obliterated vision through goggle lenses. Team-mate Duke was almost abreast, then, a full 400 yards behind, was the next man, Milani! With only two laps gone Duke was 100 yards up on Kavanagh, but both were a full half-mile ahead of Milani, who then stopped at his pit for 20 seconds to change goggles. With the majority of the field struggling just to keep going, let alone mount a challenge, Duke and Kavanagh simply cleared off into the distance. Lockett was sixth, while Brett was advised to retire after suffering severe cramp.

The rain continued relentlessly. The massed spectators were thoroughly soaked and chilled to the bone, yet they strained forward whenever the Norton pair passed, for they knew that this day Duke was well on his way to gaining the 500cc World Championship to add to his 350cc crown won two days before. After over 247 miles, which included two refuelling stops, Duke received the flag as the first man in the history of the World Championships to be double champion in one year. New boy Kavanagh had also performed remarkably by gaining a brace of runner-up positions at his debut meeting. Lockett finished fifth behind the Gileras of Masetti and Milani. Truly the 1951 Ulster Grand Prix was a massive test of courage, stamina, skill and machine reliability, which the Norton team had passed with flying colours.

With the new double World Champion on display, 400,000 spectators trekked to the Solitude circuit to see the German Grand Prix, the first classic staged by that country since the end of hostilities some six years before. Held eight days after Duke's 500cc Ulster Grand Prix victory, the press claimed, probably correctly, that this gathering 'was the largest ever present at any motor cycle meeting in Europe, if not the world'.

The 7.1-mile circuit was situated in hilly, wooded country west of Stuttgart, and long stretches had gigantic natural grandstands formed by the wooded hillsides, where thousands of spectators gathered. Without doubt this huge crowd had not only come because the Norton team was entered but also to see how Germany's latest racing machines, in their first year of unsupercharged form, would fare against the world's best. The result gave the answer in full measure... Nortons ridden by Duke, Kavanagh, Brett and Lockett took the first four places ahead of the BMW works riders Georg Meier and Walter Zeller in the 500cc class. Moreover, the fastest lap by Kavanagh, at exactly 86mph, was an absolute record for the circuit, and bettered the speed achieved previously with supercharged machines.

In the 350cc class Duke, Lockett and Brett took the first three places and almost certainly Kavanagh would have been among the leaders to give Norton one, two, three, four if he had not suffered a spill on one of the fast, tricky s-bends just over 5 miles from the start and had to retire near the end of this 12-lap 85½-mile race. But perhaps the most amazing aspect of the whole meeting was the vast crowd that lined the circuit, right to its very edges.

The last of the classic races in 1951, the Gran Premio delle Nazoni, was staged on Sunday, 9th September at Monza, just outside Milan. In the 350cc race Kavanagh (only following 'team orders') once again displayed his worth by following Duke home, only 1.1 seconds behind after almost 94 miles of wheel-to-wheel dicing for the lead. Brett was third, while Lockett had been forced to retire after cruising into the pits with an inoperative rear brake. According to practice times it looked as if the 500cc class would be a walkover for Gilera. It seemed as though Duke's only chance would come if he could slipstream one of the Gileras and be 'towed' round, after proving to be the fastest 'Senior' Norton rider in practice. But all hopes of this happening were soon dispelled. From the drop of the flag, the leading Gilera rider, Milani, howled off on his own and by the end of the 32-lap 125-mile race was well clear of his teammates Masetti and Pagani, with Duke fourth. Brett finished eighth only completing 31 laps, and 11th-place man Lockett completed 30 laps. Kavanagh had retired when his rear chain came off. The rubber had collapsed in one of the swinging arm Silentbloc bushes. And so the curtain fell on what had been a memorable season for the Bracebridge Street singles; but as Monza had proved, in terms of speed, Norton was likely to find things much more difficult in 1952.

Less than a week after Monza, on Friday, 14th September, the 1951 350cc and 500cc World Champion Geoffery Ernest Duke was married to Patricia Ann Reid, second daughter of the Reverend Reid, Chairman of the Manx Motor Cycle and Automobile Clubs. Held at St George's Church, Douglas, the ceremony was performed by the bride's father, assisted by the Reverend Canon Stenning, president of the Manx Motor Cycle Club. The wedding proved so popular that over 1,000 people could not even get into the church. After the wedding the couple left for a honeymoon in Paris, and thereafter Switzerland.

Dave Chadwick, second man home in the 1954 Junior Manx Grand Prix, approaching Cronk ny Mona.

But there was still racing at home. With record crowds, record speeds and perfect weather, Scarborough's first international meeting at the Olivers Mount circuit proved a double success for Jack Brett and Norton, with both the 350cc and 500cc races going to the popular Leeds rider. Joining Brett and Lockett was Len Parry, not an official team member, but 'on trial', who scored a couple of third places. Johnny Lockett had a miserable two days, however; in the Junior he retired with a broken chain, whilst in the Senior event he fell at the Memorial and broke his collarbone.

Duke was back in action for the final meeting of a thrill packed season - at Silverstone on Saturday, 5th October. This saw not only Duke but also Brett and David Bennett (making his works debut) on factory 500cc Nortons, a trio of riders on works AJSs and Les Graham with the four-cylinder MV Agusta. Duke took victory in both 500cc races, with Brett scoring a second and third and Bennett a fourth and fifth.

The Norton stand at the important London Show that November had one of Duke's 500cc works racers sharing pride of place with the new Dominator 88 De-Luxe, which featured a Featherbed-type frame, the first time that it had been used on one of the company's roadster models. At the same time it was confirmed that Duke and Kavanagh would be members of the 1952 Norton racing team, but no final decision had been taken about other riders.

The first appearance by a Featherbed Manx in Australia came when Ken Kavanagh scored a double victory in the Victoria TT, held in November 1951 at the Ballarat circuit in New South Wales.

Kavanagh was soon in action 'down under', where he won the Junior and Senior TT races at Ballarat, Victoria, New South Wales, on 13 November. The Manx Nortons he rode were being seen in Australia for the very first time. After Ballarat orders came from Birmingham not to race again in Australia.

1952 - Norton's advertising during the winter of 1951/52 usually showed a picture of Duke in action with the words 'World Champions - The Unapproachable Norton, Upholder of British Motor Cycle Supremacy Throughout The World'. As the new 1952 racing season dawned expectations after the double world titles the previous year were obviously high. When the team made its bow at the Leinster 100 on the Irish Wicklow circuit with the 1952 racers, it was the weather conditions that proved the biggest opposition. The only record made during the day was by new team member Reg Armstrong, who knocked three seconds off Johnny Lockett's 1950 figure in the 500cc class with a lap of 83.40mph.

Externally the 1952 Nortons featured new rear hubs with the brake drum on the offside (right), except for Armstrong's 350, and modified rear suspension units. Geoff Duke was a non-starter and the 'official' explanation was that he was unable to make the journey to Ireland. Armstrong, at his debut meeting, won both the 350cc and 500cc races and made fastest lap in each; Ken Kavanagh was runner-up in both races. The rear brake had been changed over on the insistence of Renold Chains. Renold insisted that heat from the brake was the cause of chain trouble... but the real trouble was the chains themselves.

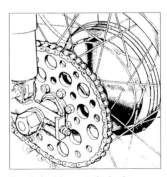

Rear hub with remote brake drum; tested in 1951, but not introduced until the 1952 season.

Typical 1950s Manx Grand Prix action, a Senior rider with the number one plate flashes past the camera. Note the rare Bristol 403 car in the background and the spectators sitting almost in the road.

Technically the 1952 500s were claimed to attain higher rpm in top gear than their predecessors, gaining in the process, as Joe Craig put it, 'increased liveliness in the indirect gear ratios'. This was achieved without any increase in piston speed by making the bore and stroke of the 500 almost square. The measurements were now 84 x 90mm. Cooling was claimed to have been slightly improved by extending the cylinder barrel fins around the bevel shaft tube, which was now in light alloy. This was retained at its upper end by the trapping of the tube flange, together with a suitable oil sealing ring, between the cylinder head and barrel. At the lower end the tube was secured in a gland nut containing rubber oil seals. Oil flowed down the inside of the bevel shaft tube, and the use of light alloy for the tube resulted in the oil losing a certain amount of heat at this point. A large-radius rim had been incorporated in the Amal carburettor air intake bell mouth to minimise eddying at this point. Entirely new was the Lucas rotating-type magneto, which came at the insistence of Joe Craig himself. This type was not new in itself, however, having previously been widely used on aircraft and stationary engines. Advantages over the conventional rotating armature type were that the windings, the condenser and the contact breaker did not rotate. Norton also stated that this type of magneto was both stronger and better balanced. As already mentioned, a new rear hub had been fitted; this featured a duralumin sprocket and the 2LS (two leading shoes) were cable operated from the usual rear brake pedal.

Supporting the racing seat and forming the top anchorage for the rear suspension units, the subframe was now integral with the main frame. Where before it was bolted up, now it was Sif-bronzed into position. The cross-tube, which formed the upper fixing for the central oil tank and carried the ears for the fuel-tank strap, was now also Sif-bronzed integrally with the frame. The metallistic rubber bushes in the swinging arm pivot were replaced by phosphor bronze components, which offered zero flexing - and resulted from Kavanagh's retirement in the 1951 Italian Grand Prix. The rear units themselves had to be redesigned and were now inclined slightly forward from the vertical, cast alloy being used in part of their construction to further reduce weight. To facilitate chain adjustment, abutments formed at the ends of the bolts securing the suspension legs to the frame and swinging

Brought in mid-way through the 1952 season, Syd Lawton's stay with the Bracebridge Street équipe was short-lived. A crash during TT practice the following year put him out of the reckoning. Lawton is pictured here in Nobles Hospital, Isle of Man, with his wife Beryl.

arm, enabled a suitably drilled jig-plate to be slipped into position when the legs were depressed. This provided the maximum possible chain centres for the rear chain so that it could be set tight and was automatically in correct adjustment when the suspension unit legs were released.

A minor alteration to the simplex primary-chain oiler was that the delivery pipe now ran almost parallel to the lower run of the chain. This was an attempt to solve the problem of excess oil reaching the rear tyre as it had on occasions the previous season. But the chains still acted 'like rubber bands', as Ken Kavanagh put it recently. All these modifications applied equally to the 350 works Nortons except that in their case the bore and stroke measurements remained unchanged

A final development - which was ultimately shelved - was a new 4.00 x 16 Avon racing rear tyre. This was tried by Ken Kavanagh in the Leinster 100, but was found only to lower the machine fractionally and not to help the handling. It was claimed, however, that its main advantage was improved adhesion when cornering. It also called for the use of a wider WM3 wheel rim. This idea came from the fertile mind of Rex McCandless.

Future Honda team leader Jim Redman with the Norton on which he finished fourth in the 1958 500cc Czech Grand Prix at Brno, then a non-championship event.

The first classic meeting of the year was the Swiss Grand Prix. There was a panic during practice when the wrong fuel was supplied to both the Norton and AJS teams by the Swiss Federation - this resulted in what *The Motor Cycle* called 'serious damage' before special supplies of the correct 80 octane type were obtained. Joe Craig was not a happy man that day.

In contrast to the event of a year ago, the weather of the 1952 Swiss Grand Prix weekend - staged over Saturday and Sunday, 16th and 17th May - was superb. The 250cc race got the proceedings under way on the first day. And as the 28 starters in the 350cc race wheeled their machines from the pits to the starting grid there was bright, uninterrupted sunshine to bathe the scene. There was also no doubt as to who was the favourite. Geoff Duke had achieved record-breaking times in practice, and the crowds showed their feelings with cheers and hand-clapping. Armstrong and Kavanagh were also Norton mounted. Opposing this trio were the new triple-knocker AJS models and the equally new three-cylinder German DKW two-stroke of Siegfried Wunsche.

Duke sped to the front soon after the start and remained ahead throughout the 21-lap 95-mile race. His fastest lap was 93.27mph, comfortably better than the outright circuit record of 91.4mph, held since 1937 by Freddie Frith on a 500cc Norton. The following day the weather was more overcast. But this didn't stop vast crowds coming in the expectation of seeing exciting machinery... On the grid were three works Nortons (Duke, Armstrong and Bennett), three AJS Porcupines, three Gilera fours and two MV Agustas, plus 14 others to make up a field of 25. The true potential of the various 1952 Blue Riband class contenders was about to be put to the test.

Though Brett (AJS), Armstrong and Duke were fastest away, it was Graham's MV which chased the double Norton World Champion at the end of lap 1. Armstrong was fifth and Bennett, making his first appearance in a continental race, several places behind him. Although Duke was circulating at around 95mph, Graham's new five-speed four-cylinder MV was showing a remarkable turn of speed and keeping within striking distance of the Norton. After 5 laps the gap had increased to 9 seconds, and behind Graham came the AJS pair of Coleman and Brett, then Milani (Gilera) followed by Doran (AJS); next came Armstrong and Bennett. Soon after experiencing rear tyre problems (a thrown tread, as in 1950) Graham was out. Armstrong was also in trouble, making two pit stops before finally giving up owing to the engine persistently cutting out. Two of the Gilera riders were also making repeated halts. Then Coleman had to make a prolonged pit visit.

The Scot Alastair King (348cc Manx) led the 1956 Junior Manx Grand Prix for four laps before retiring with big-end failure. He also set the fastest lap at 91.07mph – a new class record.

Meanwhile, Duke continued to circulate with almost monotonous precision. But this was the calm before the storm. When crossing the finishing line to start his 20th lap his engine called enough - the exhaust valve had broken! This let the new AJS rider - former Norton man Jack Brett - into the lead. By the 24th lap the order was Brett, Bennett and Doran, the Norton rider packed like a sardine between the two AJS Porcupines - a towel could almost have been thrown over the trio, they were that close. It stayed that way until lap 26. On the last lap but one - lap 27 - it was Brett, Doran- and no Bennett. As he passed Doran appeared to signal that Bennett had crashed. The signal proved all too true. Sadly the Norton rider had suffered fatal injuries. *The Motor Cycle* showed the grief felt by saying: 'Few young men had ridden with such impressive style on their first appearance in a continental race - and this was an unusually tigerish initiation. The racing world is poorer for the grievous loss of so promising a rider.' A native of Birmingham, David Bennett had previously won the 1951 Senior Manx Grand Prix and was 23-years-old when the accident happened. Previously employed by the Ariel experimental department, he had only recently begun work at Norton.

After the Swiss Grand Prix the Norton team journeyed to the Isle of Man to commence practice for the 1952 TT series. There were no real surprises, except that the fourth slot in the Norton team had been taken over by Len Parry. Technically the most interesting feature was the reappearance of 19-inch front wheels; both 348cc and 499cc machines now sported 3.00 x 19 components. On the rear wheels the tyre sizes were 3.50 x 18 on the 350s and 4.00 x 16 on the Senior mounts. Up until midweek practising had been strictly to instructions, with Joe Craig and his mechanics forming an unoffficial reception committee at a suitably secret vantage point on the course (this 'secret' vantage point was at Ballaugh Bridge), so non-stop laps (and, therefore, speeds) had meant that the pundits had been kept guessing. But on the evening of Thursday, 5th June, Duke took his Senior mount round at 94.4mph from a standing start - only 12 seconds outside his 1951 lap record. Privateer Ray Amm of Southern Rhodesia had been impressive in training, culminating in his sharing with AJS works star Coleman the honour of second fastest, at 92.07mph. Over the following weekend it emerged that Norton were to provide Amm with factory machines for both the Junior and Senior races...*The Motor Cycle* headline told the story: 'Another Junior TT win for Geoff Duke.' The Norton star led from start to finish, with team-mate Reg Armstrong in second place. However, what of the other three team members? Newcomer Amm had set off at a fantastic pace - and was lying third at the end of lap 1, two places in front of Armstrong! But on the fourth lap, when lying fifth, Amm crashed at Braddon Bridge. Lap 6 saw Kavanagh (then fourth) compelled to retire with machine trouble, while the unfortunate Parry suffered a similar fate on the last lap. Their retirements stemmed from the discs coming out of the sodium-filled exhaust valves. Although staged in perfect conditions, Duke did not set any records, averaging 90.29mph, with a fastest lap of 91mph.

If the Junior TT lacked excitement, the same could not be said of the Senior - it was dramatic! Not only was it watched by what was claimed to be a record crowd, but after oppressive heat and sea mists which threatened thunderstorms, Friday, 13th June proved a perfect day for racing.

Geoff Duke had been receiving treatment in an attempt to cure the cramp that had affected his Junior ride. He had won the last two Senior TTs, and most observers expected him to complete a hat-trick. And so it looked at the end of lap 1, when Duke led from Graham's MV. Then came the Norton works trio of Amm, Armstrong and Kavanagh. Sixth spot was held by Cromie McCandless on a private Norton. The end of lap 3 saw an identical set of positions - with lap 4's only change being Armstrong swapping places with Amm for third spot.

The luck of the Irish. Reg Armstrong's primary chain broke as he crossed the line to win the 1952 Senior TT.

Another newcomer to the Norton team, Ray Amm at La Source hairpin in the 500cc Belgian Grand Prix on 5th July, 1952. He finished third behind Duke and race winner Masetti (Gilera).

The end of the lap drama was of the highest nature. The first warning of the impending trouble for race leader Geoff Duke was when the red light that told spectators in the start/finish grandstand that Duke was at Governor's Bridge was not followed by the usual shattering Norton bellow. Instead, his approach was slow and silent. He stopped at his pit for the second lap running (the previous lap had seen the double World Champion refuel). His pit attendant Steve Darbishire (who had been Duke's best man at his recent wedding) inspected the bike and, after a couple of words with its rider, Duke handed over his machine and removed his crash helmet, his race over. The problem was later revealed as a seized clutch centre bearing. This left Les Graham on the lone MV four in front of the field. But it soon became obvious that Armstrong's Norton was catching the Italian machine. And sure enough, at the end of lap 6 Armstrong led by four seconds. Amm was still holding third and Kavanagh fourth. The seventh and final lap was to prove lucky for one member of the Norton team, and unlucky for another. The lucky man was the race winner. Reg Armstrong, who, leading Graham by 26.6 seconds, had his primary chain snap as he crossed the finish line. How more fortunate could a man be? Meanwhile, team-mate Ken Kavanagh also suffered primary chain trouble at the Bungalow on that final lap - but pushed in to finish 32nd. Ray Amm was third. Armstrong's average speed was 92.97mph, with the fastest lap going to early leader Duke in 23 minutes 52 seconds, a speed of 94.88mph (on his second circuit).

The maestro Geoff Duke. He won three world titles in three years as a Norton factory rider (1951 350 and 500cc, 1952 350cc).

After the TT came the Dutch and Belgian classics (now in reverse order). Both the 350cc races went to Geoff Duke, while Gilera's Umberto Masetti took both 500cc events - with Duke second on both occasions. Amm continued his excellent showing in the TT, with Kavanagh and Armstrong providing the back-up.

Then came the German Grand Prix over the 7.1-mile Solitude circuit, held by many to be among the most difficult of any used in classic racing at that time. It required many, many practice laps before it could be ridden with full abandon. But in July 1952 the hazards were increased. Part of the circuit had been resurfaced with a smooth type of tarmac, with the result that it was more slippery than it first appeared, several riders being caught out in practice; Ray Amm sustained a broken leg and two cracked vertebrae. This meant that the Norton team was without Geoff Duke (who had crashed at a non-championship meeting at Schotten the previous weekend) and Amm. Without two of his stars, Joe Craig brought in Syd Lawton, who was given Amm's bikes.

Other teams were also in trouble and without some of their leading riders, notably Gilera, who had both Masetti and Milani walk away from bent machines during the practice period. The former was virtually unhurt, but his teammate suffered a broken collarbone. With all these practice problems Norton still managed to score an impressive 350cc and 500cc double - although it was generally agreed that Kavanagh, who had dominated both races, 'allowed' Armstrong to win by easing off right at the end of both events; team orders, rather than riding ability, winning the day... For the record, Armstrong's average speed for the 350 was 81.07mph and 83.10mph for the 500, both up on the 1951 figures.

The latest news of Geoff Duke was that his most serious injuries were torn ligaments in his right ankle. In addition to this he had sustained a broken big toe on his left foot, a cut thigh and a torn shin. And he quashed press reports that his accident had been caused by chain breakage by saying, 'It was down to misjudgement on my part.' He also had the satisfaction of knowing the 1952 350cc world title was his - as the rider's best four performances counted, and with four wins in a seven-race series he couldn't be beaten.

Back in Britain Kavanagh continued to display fine form at the end of July by winning both his races (and becoming 'British Champion') at Boreham, where he also shattered the lap record. A mere week later the same rider was back to score another double at the same circuit, this time having the satisfaction of beating second-place man Les Graham and his mighty four-cylinder MV. However, the circuit came in for heavy criticism for being liberally coated with oil and rubber, the result of it being employed usually for car events.

The 1952 Ulster Grand Prix was, except for a win by Ken Kavanagh in the 350cc race, not a happy event for the Norton team, all three works machines being forced to retire with mechanical troubles in the all-important 500cc clash. First a sheet of flame came from Kavanagh's megaphone and the engine died, with a broken exhaust valve. Next Lawton's oil return pump was playing up, pumping oil on to the rear of his machine - eventually he was forced to quit with an empty oil tank. Finally, after leading the race by almost three minutes, Armstrong was forced out on the 13th lap of the 15-lap race with, of all things, yet another broken primary chain! His TT luck had not held this time. The race was won by none other than Cromie McCandless on a Gilera four . . . The only satisfaction Armstrong gained was his earlier second place behind Kavanagh in the 350cc race. In this, Lawton's engine had seized on the 7-mile-long Clady Straight near the end of the race.

At the end of August Ken Kavanagh completed his hat-trick of double victories at Boreham when he won both the 350cc and the 500cc events at the Essex track's end-of-season meeting. In the process he yet again beat Les Graham's MV four.

GEOFF DUKE

Geoff Duke was born in St. Helens, Lancashire in 1923, the son of a baker. He first caught the motorcycle bug when he was a very small boy, watching races on the sands at Southport and Wallasey – and riding pillion behind his brother, Eric, some nine years his senior.

Later Geoff, with a school friend, clubbed together to buy his first motorcycle when he was only thirteen. They could not ride it on the public highway, but learned to ride on farmland. Geoff had to keep all this secret from his parents!

After beginning work as a mechanic at a telephone exchange, at the age of sixteen, he purchased a Dot two-stroke. Then at eighteen Geoff volunteered to be an army despatch rider, but found he could only be accepted as an insrument mechanic. However, this did get him into the Royal Corps of Signals, so Geoff joined and subsequently made such a nuisance of himself that he was transferred to DR (Despatch Rider) duties. This led to the chance of riding for the army's display

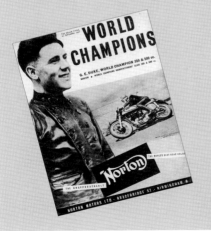

After winning the 1951, 350cc Italian Grand Prix ahead of team-mate Ken Kavanagh.

team – and meeting a certain Hugh Viney (a famous AMC trials rider and winner of the Scottish Six Days).

When Duke was demobbed in 1947 he used his gratuity to purchase a BSA single and got a job at the same factory preparing trials bikes – and riding them. His trials results were noticed by Norton teamster

Artie Bell the Belfast rider, who after seeing him ride in Yorkshire introduced Geoff to the Norton management. This resulted in the offer of a job – which the St. Helens man accepted. After riding the 500T in trials for his new employers, Geoff switched to road racing.

During the 1948 Manx Grand Prix (his first ever race) he was leading when forced to retire with a split oil tank. The following year he returned for the Senior Clubman's race and won at a record speed of 82.97mph. Three months later he won the Senior Manx Grand Prix and was runner up in the Junior race. Geoff was then promoted to the full Norton works team, managed by Joe Craig, for the 1950 season.

A series of tyre problems meant that Norton didn't have a very good 1950 – even though it debuted the Featherbed class. But from then on, until he left in the Spring of 1953, Geoff and Norton could do no wrong; winning the 350/500cc world titles (the first time this had been achieved) in 1951, followed by the 350cc championship in 1952.

But by now the four-cylinder Italian models were at last outpacing the double-knocker Norton singles, so Geoff signed for Gilera, winning the 500cc title for the next three seasons, 1953, 1954 and 1955.

Politics and accidents did much to restrict his efforts in 1956 and 1957, and Gilera quit. Geoff followed two years later after racing a mixture of Norton, BMW and Benelli machinery. He will be best remembered as one of the smoothest riders of all time – making racing seem as much an art form as ice skating was with Torvill and Dean.

Graham, however, was to get his revenge in the much more important Grand Prix arena. The setting was the Italian Grand Prix at Monza on 14th September. Before the start of the 500cc race, Armstrong led the points chart with 19, followed by Masetti (Gilera) with 16. Both Armstrong and Kavanagh had earlier spilled while dicing for the lead in the 350cc event, which was won by Ray Amm, who was making his comeback appearance after his German Grand Prix practice accident. This had meant that Lawton had lost his team place. In the 500cc race Kavanagh was a non-starter, so Norton's hopes rested with Armstrong and Amm. In the event the British singles were totally outclassed in terms of speed by the Italian fours. While Monza demanded some riding skills, it most definitely favoured outright speed above all else.

Graham and MV at long last lived up to their potential by walking away with the race, in which the MV rider set new race and lap records; the best Armstrong could manage was sixth, whilst Amm retired after his rear chain broke on the 28th of the 32-lap race. Graham's victory produced scenes of enthusiasm which had never been witnessed at the end of a classic road race. Hundreds of excited Italians surged into the road and a police escort was necessary to escort him to the dais for the presentation ceremony. The 1952 500cc Italian Grand Prix also witnessed the beginning of the end of the British monopoly in the 350cc and 500cc classes at world level. From then on things were on a downward spiral.

On to the final round in the 1952 World Championship, and Barcelona on Sunday, 5th October, where the 500cc (and sidecar) were finally to be resolved. The all-important race was to be staged over no less than 48 laps - 125.3 miles of the super-tight Montjuich Park circuit. Surely here, unlike Monza, the Norton single would be at an advantage compared to the more powerful, but heavier, Italian multis. But it was not to be. Almost from the start Les Graham screamed his four-cylinder MV into a lead that increased with every lap. Then came Gilera Champion-elect Umberto Masetti, with the Nortons of Kavanagh and Armstrong way down the field. Towards the end Kavanagh started to improve his position and by dint of some hard riding eventually came home third, with Armstrong fifth. But the world title had gone to Masetti and Gilera. The real problem for the Norton team was the ultra-high bottom gear, which meant that they lost valuable seconds on a steep hairpin bend each lap.

That the writing was on the wall was first hinted at publicly when, in an article in *The Motor Cycle* dated 13th November, 1952, the following was stated, concerning Norton's star rider Geoff Duke: 'His plans for 1953 are vague. It is not yet certain that he will be physically fit and he has signed no contracts. It is known that he has had tempting offers to ride foreign machines. But he is intensely pro-national, and it is doubtful whether he will accept.' Duke's own viewpoint was that 'irrespective of the type of circuit, the multis have finally arrived'. Barcelona, he felt, was the case in point. A circuit where previously the singles were unbeatable was now one on which in 1952 the fours at last displayed the superiority of the type.

Duke also revealed that on the Isle of Man, a 350 Norton was capable of covering some parts of the course faster than the larger version 'because of its handleability and because of its different, more suitable engine characteristics.'

1953 - Just as the London Show at Earls Court was in full swing during mid-November, the national newspapers drew attention to the fact that Geoff Duke would not be a member of the official Norton team in 1953. It was suggested (correctly as events were to turn out) that he was likely to go car racing or accept an offer to ride a foreign machine. Also disclosed was the news that other famous riders were considering, or had signed, contracts with foreign manufacturers. *The Motor Cycle* commented: 'This situation has arisen for a variety of reasons. By far the most important is the shortage of top ranking riders in Italy for 500cc racing at a time when Italian multi-cylinder machines promise great success. Italian manufacturers know that the few riders who can do full justice to their machines hail from Britain, the Commonwealth and Eire. Hence their determined effort to ensure success by engaging the best riders, irrespective of nationality.' The editorial went on to say: 'The turn of events is viewed with concern in Britain. If, in fact, Italian machines gain overwhelming victories next year (1953), at a time when sales competition in world markets is increasing, proud British prestige will receive a serious setback. For many years this prestige has been upheld by comparatively few factories, yet its dividends have accrued to the industry as a whole.'

Close up view of the Norton Kneeler. It was used by Ray Amm and Eric Oliver to set up a number of new world records at Montlhéry, near Paris, on 8th and 9th November 1953; including the coveted one hour 500cc record at 133.7mph.

This statement is of particular interest. For one thing, no other British factory had put the amount of money and effort into racing that Norton had. Yet at the same time it had not developed a multi to challenge the Gileras and MV Agustas - why? Was it race chief Joe Craig's reluctance to pension off his long-serving singles, or the simple fact that the money didn't exist at Norton to mount a new challenge? In my opinion it was probably mainly for the latter reason. But the inevitable result was that by early 1953 it had become all too evident that many British stars - including Armstrong and Dale - had gone abroad in search of more competitive machinery, these two signing to ride for Gilera. So the Norton team for 1953 was to be Kavanagh, Amm and Lawton. At the same time it was rumoured that the Bracebridge Street factory was experimenting with a rotary-valve engine. This in fact proved true, as is described later, together with other developments that did not pass the prototype stage. In addition, Craig was a development engineer rather than a designer, and was, therefore, happier patiently developing an established engine rather than designing a new one. But ultimately it was Norton's financial position that dictated its future - both on and off the tracks.

By the end of 1952 Norton were struggling, as, although they had gained much glory for the marque and for the British industry in general, their only modern design was the Dominator twin. It should also be remembered that Norton was an assembler, much of the machining being done outside. But, even though they were about to lose their star riders and with all the other problems that have been mentioned, Norton were not short of ideas. One was the 'streamliner', which, using Manx parts and 350 double-knocker engine, was built by Rex McCandless in the summer of 1952 and tested by Ken Kavanagh at Montlhéry that October. The streamlined shielding (in alloy) comprised a nose-piece, which extended from a point about hub level ahead of the front wheel to (at the top) just above handlebar level in line with the steering axis and, at the bottom, to the cylinder-base joint-face level. The nose was sufficiently wide to allow the front wheel to turn within it. To the rear of the nose, separate shields extended rearwards and were profiled to the rider's thighs and arms. The rider adopted a semi-prone riding position, that is to say, his shins were horizontal and his feet braced against the footrest adjacent to the rear-wheel spindle. In other words, the rider was kneeling. The rear of the machine was enclosed in a streamlined pressing.

But perhaps the most dramatic news - certainly as regards the future of Norton - was made on 25th February, 1953, at the annual general meeting of Associated Motor Cycles Ltd, when it was revealed that a plan existed for AMC to acquire the issued share capital of Norton. It was also revealed at the same time that the company would continue as a separate organisation under the existing managing director, Gilbert Smith (who had been with the Bracebridge Street company since 1916), and that, in the words of AMC Chairman S.R. Hogg, 'the Norton factory team will continue to compete in the major events'. However, the real truth was somewhat different. The share capital and financial control of Norton had been acquired by the Pearl Assurance Company and put under the day-to-day running of AMC.

A month later The Motor Cycle carried a story that in view of 'the new streamlined Norton' Geoff Duke might still be mounted on British machinery in the 1953 classic road races.

Kavanagh and Lawton were both in action during early April at Thruxton on Easter Monday, but it was young John Surtees (now with a production Manx model to replace his Vincent) who impressed. Kavanagh did manage to equal the lap record in the 500cc final after a poor start, which Surtees won. But at Thruxton and the big Silverstone meeting held later that month the Norton works riders were on production Manx models, not works machines. Most interestingly, not only were Kavanagh and Amm entered by Norton Motors but also Geoff Duke,

having his first outing since his Schotten crash the previous July. In the event none of these three riders finished in the first three in any race.

When the full works team and bikes made their 1953 debut Duke was not among them. This was because certain other contracted team members objected, saying that Duke would have to sign a contract too... he did not and the rest is history. As already issued, the team comprised Kavanagh, Amm and Lawton, these three riders filling the first three places in the 500cc event of the International Circuit de Floreffe, Belgium, on Sunday, 26th April. Nortons also finished first, second and third in the 350cc event. But this time it was the turn of Lawton to taste victory, with Kavanagh second and Amm third. When the Isle of Man TT entries were announced it was seen that in both the Senior and Junior, four riders were specified: the Floreffe trio plus old hand Jack Brett. Meanwhile, although still linked with various firms by the popular press, Geoff Duke's entries were 'unspecified in the choice of machine'.

The first the public saw of the 1953 works Norton was at the Irish North West 200 on Saturday, 9th May, when Lawton and Kavanagh scored an impressive one-two in the 500cc category. Lawton averaged 93.01mph, a new record for the race, and he also made fastest lap in 6 minutes 54 seconds (96.20mph) as he came round for the final time, thus knocking no fewer than 18 seconds off the record set by Geoff Duke in 1951. It should be noted that resurfacing had improved riding conditions on part of the course.

Traditionally, since the first meeting in 1929, the North West 200 had been used by Norton as a proving ground for their new-season's TT models, and that Saturday in May 1953 found Ray Amm piloting the experimental streamlined 350 in its first race. It made a slow start, firing only after a 50-yard run, and stayed in the race for only three laps, but this period was sufficient to give Amm the fastest lap in the class: 88.5mph. Although the streamlined Norton - nicknamed 'Silver Fish' - had made its debut, no firm decision had been made whether to use it in the TT. A query in the minds of many observers was whether the shell made it difficult to mount and dismount. This point was settled by the stewards of the North West, who met Joe Craig, Artie Bell and Rex McCandless on the Friday afternoon prior to the race day, to witness a demonstration by Amm. Officials were satisfied that the 'kneeler' was perfectly safe, its rider being able to start the engine and get aboard without undue difficulty, and it was considered that the bike was not likely to cause any inconvenience to fellow competitors. There was not only controversy concerning the possible use in the TT of the new streamliner, but also what would be the destiny of Geoff Duke, who first nominated an AJS 7R, then flew to Italy to test Gileras at Monza in mid-May.

Technical changes to the 'conventional' works Nortons that year saw a further small increase in bhp on the 500cc model - achieved by shortening the stroke still more, so the even higher crankshaft rpm could be obtained for a given piston speed. Bore and stroke measurements of the 1953 500s were 88 x 82mm respectively. Other modfications included a special float chamber, which provided more stable carburation as far as the fuel level was concerned, and attention to the lubrication and cooling of the exhaust valve.

On the 500cc engines, a reduction in the running temperature of the exhaust valve (to prevent the previously mentioned disc problem) was obtained by providing a circulation of oil around the outside of the valve guide. Oil under pressure was taken from inside the cambox to an annular compartment concentric with the valve guide. A small quantity of oil was forced through a bleed in the guide on to the valve stem. The main volume of oil, however, was piped via a finned oil cooler located on the front down tube to the finned lower bevel housing, whence the oil was returned to the oil tank by the pump. To facilitate heat radiation from the oil tank, the external sides and rear of the tank were painted black. The oil capacity, at one gallon, remained as before. The original idea, which came from McCandless, had a battery-driven pump, but was modified to mechanical operation by Joe Craig and Ernie Walsh. Designed to obviate as much as possible any variation in bank angle, the newly designed float chamber incorporated a fuel weir. The overflow from the weir was returned to the petrol tank by means of a pump driven by one end of the inlet camshaft. The tank itself was modified slightly to allow more room for the rider's knees, but capacity remained unchanged at a shade over five gallons.

While the front tyre size of 3.00 x 19 remained unchanged, interestingly the rear was increased from 18in to 19in (3.50) section. This was stated to provide slightly improved handling and longer tyre life. The Lucas rotating magneto introduced the previous year was retained. After the spate of primary chain breakages, increased lubrication for this component was provided by means of a larger-capacity chain-oiler tank. At the same time the decision was taken to use handmade Perry chains. From a single metering tap in the tank (mounted directly above the chain cover) parallel twin delivery pipes were taken to the lower run of the chain, the oil being directed at the inner faces of the chain link side plates. The capacity of this chain oiler was approximately one pint. The oil supply for the rear chain was contained in the nearside diagonal tube of the rear subframe instead of in the nearside rear swinging arm fork as previously, the supply being controlled by a metering tap set into the lower end of the tube; the supply pipe was clipped to the fork arm, hence unsprung weight was slightly decreased.

Nortons were also experimenting with a new five-speed gearbox incorporating a mainshaft torque-carrying capacity. As the clutch did not incorporate a shock absorber, it had to be used in conjunction with an engine shaft shock absorber. Another experimental project was an interesting trailing-link front suspension and modified mudguard used by Ray Amm at Floreffe in the 500c race, in which he finished second behind team-mate Ken Kavanagh. As it was not used again it was obvious that it did not offer any advantage over the conventional telescopics, and in any case was considerably heavier. With the exception of the changes to bore and stroke measurements on the larger engine, the innovations noted above applied equally to the 350cc model.

At this time (May 1953) Norton management were remaining tight-lipped about the McCandless-conceived streamlined kneeler. Officially the line was: 'One of deliberation. It is felt that we are, to quite an appreciable extent, pioneering into the unknown.'

Back in 1950 the small tail fairings on the original Featherbed racers had not proved a success. But Rex McCandless still believed in aerodynamics, and in 1952 came up with a pannier-framed prototype which was fitted with a comprehensive rear enclosure. To prove his theories McCandless sought the advice and facilities of the Short Brothers aircraft plant in his native Belfast. McCandless hit a major snag with this first machine. Quite simply, with its standard frame, the rider's arms and chest were fouling his knees, and as he revealed before his death: 'I realised that I'd gone as far as I could with an orthodox frame without cutting my legs off, and I wasn't about to do that!' The solution was the kneeler concept, with its lower build and comprehensive streamlining. The new extra-low chassis was then built in the McCandless workshop, with a basic-layout Featherbed but lower, and 'with the top frame tubes raked sharply down to the swinging arm gusset', as Mick Duckworth described it in an article on Rex McCandless in the December 1984 issue of *Classic Bike*. No top fuel tank was employed, instead the fuel was contained in two tanks alongside the crankcase and gearbox. Channels were provided on top of these for the rider to kneel on (hence the kneeler title) and foot controls placed accordingly. The fuel was raised to the carburettor by a pump driven by the inlet cam; the fuel level was controlled by an instrument with special weir-type float chambers (as on the conventional works bikes that year).

The main problem that McCandless had to watch carefully was the potential 'lifting' at speeds in excess of 140 mph - which engineers at Shorts had warned him about. Ken Kavanagh, who carried out the original factory testing at Montlhéry, claims 'no one ever told me this at the time'. But in typical McCandless fashion he incorporated a simple device to warn the rider that the machine was becoming front-end light. This was also a reason why it was first race tested with the smaller double-knocker engine.

Opposite: Inventor of the Featherbed chassis, Rex McCandless was also a part-time racer as this photograph taken before the start of the 1952 North West 200 shows. Former Norton factory star and fellow Ulsterman Artie Bell is looking on (next to McCandless with hat).

One of the 'conventional' 1953 works Nortons; unlike the 350 shown, the 500 featured new bore and stroke measurements.

After the North West outing it was only ever used during practice for the 1953 TT, and the successful record-breaking spree later that year at Montlhéry (described in Chapter 5).

Why then wasn't the kneeler developed further in the Norton race team effort? Of the four men most concerned with it - Amm, Craig, Kavanagh, McCandless, only Kavanagh is alive today. When I spoke to McCandless in 1988, his version was that, 'it wasn't Joe Craig's idea, so he was against it from the start'. Backing this up is the fact that this was his final project with the Norton factory (but AMC's involvement may have featured in the real truth). That same year the McCandless brothers moved their business to new, larger premises in Belfast's Limestone Road and ceased their involvement with motorcycle racing, to concentrate upon other, probably more profitable, engineering work. But Kavanagh disputes this, saying that the reason was inferior handling and roadholding.

Without doubt, the 1953 series of TT races were the most hotly contested since the war. In the 500cc category there were works teams from not only Norton and AJS but also from BMW, Gilera and MV, whilst even in the Junior there were foreign entries from DKW, Moto Guzzi and MV!

The Junior race came first. Five works Nortons were scheduled to start, but two of these, Syd Lawton with arm and leg injuries and young John Surtees, robbed of his works Norton debut because of injuries sustained while practising on a 125 EMC two-stroke, were non-starters when the newly appointed Isle of Man Governor inspected the proceedings before the first of the 99 starters was duly launched.

As the field passed along the Glencrutchery Road, to start their second lap, the first times were posted. These showed Kavanagh 42 seconds ahead of Graham's four-cylinder MV Agusta. It then became apparent that Amm had lapped in six seconds less than Kavanagh, at 88.99mph. As *The Motor Cycle* said: 'Wizard Joe Craig appears to have done it again, and the flying Italian four will have no walkover.' But after everyone had gone through it was revealed that the first-lap leader was Rod Coleman on an AJS, with Amm second, Kavanagh fourth and Brett sixth.

Lap 2 ended with Coleman and Amm joint leaders and Kavanagh third. Almost at the start of the next lap the AJS rider was out with a split oil tank, letting the Norton pair into an impressive one, two placing. By the end of lap 3 the only foreign machine still circulating was Anderson's Moto Guzzi, which was in third place - with Brett now fourth. By the end of lap 6 Amm was leading Kavanagh by seven seconds, with the Moto Guzzi rider over a minute and a half in arrears.

Then came the final circuit, and at the end it was Amm's race by 9.6 seconds, with Kavanagh an excellent second, Anderson third and Brett fourth. A truly superb showing for the Norton team of speed and reliability on what was without doubt the toughest road race circuit in the world. Amm's time vvas 2 hours 55 minutes 55 seconds, an average speed of 90.52mph. Both Amm and Kavanagh had the added satisfaction of beating Geoff Duke's lap record (made in 1951) on their final circuit; Amm was the faster in 24 minutes 40 seconds, a speed of 91.82mph.

'Who will win the Senior?' asked Michael Kirk in *The Motor Cycle*. His prediction was: 'A titanic Duke (Gilera) Graham (MV) battle foreshadowed, with Duke probably gaining top honours'. But in the Senior TT race report in the same journal the headline told a very different story: 'Singles Victorious in Dramatic Senior TT.' It was that man Amm who was very much the hero, winning, and so making it a memorable Norton double, in 2 hours 48 minutes 51.8 seconds, a speed of 93.85mph and setting the fastest lap (a record) of 97.41mph.

At the end of lap 1, however, it had all been so different, with Amm third behind race leader Duke's Gilera and Graham's MV. But then tragedy. Lap 2 had barely started when Les Graham, the veteran of so many hard-fought battles down the years, was fatally injured when he crashed the MV at the foot of Bray Hill. From that time on the rest of the race was that of 'vanished joy' as *The Motor Cycle* described the feeling.

At the end of lap 3 it was Duke, Amm, Armstrong (Gilera), Kavanagh and Brett - Norton in three of the top five places. Just after this, as the leading Gilera sped down Bray Hill, Duke's dreams of winning on the Italian machine ended when he crashed at Quarter Bridge. But, unlike the unlucky Graham, Duke was completely unscathed from his mishap, even if his motorcycle was not. So, confounding the experts, a Norton led the 1953 Senior. But lap 4 saw Kavanagh's machine expire at Creg-na-Baa with engine trouble. This left the order Amm, Armstrong (Gilera), Coleman (AJS) and Brett. On the final lap there was more drama. First Amm fell, breaking a footrest clean off, though he managed to restart. Then Armstrong's chain jumped off, but he managed to put it back on and restarted too. So what was the final order to be? Amm won, deservedly, after a brilliant performance that included breaking the

Amm with his 1953 Senior TT-winning factory Norton. He also set a new lap record for the 37 3/4-mile Mountain circuit in 23 minutes 15 seconds, a speed of 97.41mph.

RAY AMM

Ray Amm with his wife, mother and his 1953 Senior TT mount. He rode valiantly to keep British hopes alive until he joined MV Agusta at the beginning of 1955. Sadly he was killed in his very first race.

Ray (William Raymond) Amm was the last of Joe Craig's many stars to claim TT and Grand Prix glory for the Bracebridge Street works.

Born in Salisbury, Southern Rhodesia (now Zimbabwe) in 1927 he first raced in grass track events in his homeland and later in South African road events, such as the Port Elizabeth 200. Ray was by profession a draughtsman, although just before coming to Europe in 1951 he had entered into a partnership with his brother, in the motorcycle business.

In December 1949, he married Jill, who accompanied him throughout his travels and who was a familiar figure in the race paddocks of the world in her own right.

First arriving in Great Britain for the TT races in 1951, he was known for his especially aggressive style and as *The Motor Cycle* once said was 'probably one of the most courageous riders ever to appear in racing circles'.

At first Amm was a private entrant, riding production Manx models, until he joined the official Norton works squad soon after the 1952 TT. He remained with Norton until their retirement from full-blown factory support at the end of 1954.

As well as many international victories, Ray Amm is best remembered for achieving the TT double in 1953 and his controversial victory in the 1954 Senior race. He also set a new lap record for the 37.73 mile Mountain circuit in 1953 of 97.41mph.

When his beloved Norton factory quit, Ray Amm finally signed for a foreign marque, in this case MV Agusta (who had, with other factories, been trying to gain his signature for some considerable time).

His first big race for his new team came at the International Shell Gold Cup at Imola, Italy in April 1955. He was riding a dustbin-faired four-cylinder model when he crashed in the 350cc event. Ray Amm suffered a fractured skull and died some 20 minutes after reaching hospital.

With his passing went one of Norton's hardest riders - in later years some would say he tried too hard at times. But the fact remains that Ray Amm was the man who succeeded the legendary Geoff Duke and did the task well - no mean feat.

Ray Amm flat on the tank during his record-breaking victory in the 1953 Junior TT.

lap record, from Brett, with Armstrong third and Coleman fourth. Norton had scored a one-two to add to their duplicate result in the Junior. What a week for the marque! But what if the rulebook had been obeyed? Amm would have been disqualified - he had received help to restart his machine from marshals - and Brett would have won!

When the 'circus' travelled to the first of the European world championship rounds - the Dutch TT at Assen - things were more as the pundits had pronounced at the beginning of the year, with Italian victories in both the 350cc and 500cc classes... Guzzi/Lorenzetti and Gilera/Duke respectively. Amazingly, in the larger class Ray Amm set the fastest lap, only to retire a mile or so from the finish while in second place. This let in the second Gilera four of Armstrong, with Kavanagh third and Brett fifth. With less opposition, Norton claimed second, third and fourth in the 350cc race (Amm, Kavanagh and Brett).

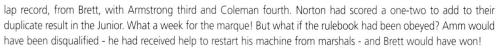

Again it was Amm who was the leading Norton rider the following week in Belgium. Third in the 350 (behind a pair of Guzzis) and a gallant second in the middle of a Gilera sandwich of race winner Milani and Armstrong. Again Amm took a lap record, but this time in the smaller category.

The German Grand Prix - scheduled to be staged at Schotten on Sunday, 19th July - created history for all the wrong reasons. The bulk of the factory teams, Norton included, deemed after inspecting the circuit before practice that the surface was so slippery that it would be courting disaster to run a complete championship meeting there. Faced with the absence of most of the top riders, the FIM officially ruled that the meeting could still take place but that neither of the major classes would count towards that year's championships.

The next port of call was Les Essarts, some half a dozen miles south of Rouen, for the French Grand Prix. In general everyone, unlike at the German debacle, was full of praise for the finely surfaced, 3.2-mile circuit, which ran through wooded terrain, and, unlike the previous years, this venue was a permanent circuit with well-constructed headquarters, pits and grandstand.

With the threat of the Italian fours in the 500cc class, it appeared that Norton's best chance of honours rested in the 350cc race. However, it was soon clear that the new 345cc Guzzis (Anderson had used a 310cc model in the TT) had a definite speed advantage over the heavier British singles. Undaunted when the flag fell, the Norton pair of Amm and Kavanagh tore off into an immediate lead, pursued by Anderson. By half-distance Amm was still in the lead, having set the fastest lap, but Anderson was now in second place and closing. On the 18th lap of the 30-lap race the Guzzi rider took the lead. However, the courageous Rhodesian fought back and by the 25th lap, by dint of some superb riding, retook the lead after setting a new lap record at 79.79mph. But already Kavanagh and then Brett had been forced to retire with engine seizures. So Norton hopes rested squarely on Amm. (The seizures had been caused through the wrong gearing - practice week was run in foggy conditions!) It appeared that he had the race in the bag as he built up a 12-second advantage by the 27th lap, but on the next lap, only two from the end (a little over seven miles) and with the chance to consolidate his world title lead, the Norton star overdid things and came off on the Nouveau Monde hairpin, breaking his collarbone in the process. In this fleeting second Norton and Amm had flung away the chance to bring the championship back to Birmingham once again. The crash put paid to Amm's season, and Anderson went on to win the first of his and Guzzi's two successive 350cc crowns.

With Amm out for the rest of the classic racing season, Norton were left with only Kavanagh and Brett to fight off the Italian challenge, which at some events was awe-inspiring. Witness the seven Gilera 500 fours in the French Grand Prix, for example... But as in the past, just when everyone was ready to write off the Norton single as a dead duck, Joe Craig's boys pulled something special out of the hat.

Opposite: Geoff Duke receiving the spoils of victory after yet another Grand Prix win.

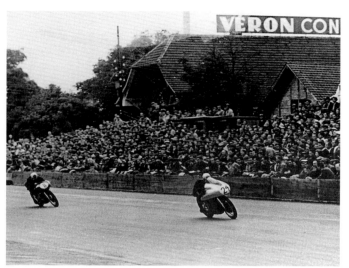

The 1954 Swiss Grand Prix: Amm leads Geoff Duke during their great battle in the 500cc event, with victory finally going to the Gilera star.

After the French meeting came the 25th Ulster Grand Prix, and the first to be staged over the Dundrod circuit, following criticism of the old Clady course and its over-long, seven-mile, bumpy straight. Thursday, 13th August saw the first event, the 125, followed by the 350cc race. With the non arrival of the smaller MV fours it was virtually a three cornered scrap between AJS, Moto Guzzi and Norton, whose squad now had a third member, New Zealander Ken Mudford. When first Brett and then Kavanagh (who was leading) were forced to retire it was up to Mudford to justify his inclusion in the team, which he duly did by outpacing the opposition to take victory. The man who finished second was none other than Bob McIntyre, the first time he had displayed his potential against world-class opposition. Mudford's time for the 28-lap 208½-mile race was 2 hours 28 minutes 18 seconds, a speed of 84.01mph. He also put in the fastest lap, at 88.11mph.

Sunday, 15th August, after a day and a night of rain, saw the promise of bright weather for the sidecar and 500cc races. This time the race distance was 30 laps - 223 miles. Without any MVs or Guzzis it appeared a straightforward battle between the Norton trio of Brett, Kavanagh and Mudford and the three Gilera riders, Armstrong, Duke and Milani.

When the flag dropped it was Duke who broke away from the remainder of the snarling pack, which was led by Brett. Duke led all around that first circuit, but Brett and Kavanagh were reported hard on his heels at the Hairpin. After ten laps Duke led by almost five minutes, but thereafter Kavanagh began to pull out all the stops and put in laps equal to Duke's quickest. At exactly half-distance Kavanagh refuelled - in under 20 seconds, including a change of goggles - but when Duke came in to refuel on the 19th lap things did not go so smoothly, his clutch would not free off, and before he could get back into the action Kavanagh thundered through to take the lead. The Aussie star was now leading the race by ten seconds from Duke, with Brett no more than that behind the Gilera rider. At two-thirds distance the order was Kavanagh (who was increasing his advantage), Duke, Brett and Armstrong, on the second Gilera. Mudford was back in sixth place. And so the order remained to the end, with Duke and Kavanagh sharing the fastest lap at 91.74mph. Even though Duke was troubled with his clutch, Kavanagh's performance was still outstanding and made up for the considerable amount of bad luck he had experienced earlier in the season.

Next stop was the Swiss Grand Prix, over the traditional treelined Bremgarten circuit, on Sunday, 23rd August. For once this was bathed in brilliant sunshine, in stark contrast to the two previous years' depressing rain soaked meetings. The 350cc race saw three works Guzzis, four DKWs, a pair of Horex singles and two AJSs lined up against a pair of Nortons (Amm still being unfit). Although Anderson and Guzzi won (to take the 350cc crown), Kavanagh finished a fine second. But in the 500cc race both Nortons retired, overwhelmed by a massive array of opposition, which included no less than six Gilera fours, three BMWs and a whole assortment of machinery from Italy and Germany.

Although no official statements were issued by Norton and AJS as to their absence from the Italian Grand Prix at Monza, it confirmed rumours circulating at the conclusion of the Swiss Grand Prix that it was the intention of the two factories to withdraw from racing for the remainder of the 1953 season. Was the reason the heavy expense when the titles had all but been settled at Berne, the need to prepare for the following season, or quite simply the fire and passion, when every single meeting had to be contested to the final yard of the race, beginning to crumble? Certainly the injury to their star rider had been a disappointment, but was the real reason that the purse strings were now being controlled from south of the Thames in Woolwich? Whatever the reason, for the rest of the season Norton riders Kavanagh and Brett had to content themselves with action on the British short circuits; perhaps the most notable performance was Kavanagh's Silverstone success in winning the coveted Mellano Trophy in late September - his last race as a Norton rider.

The spill that cost Amm and Norton the 1953 350cc World Championship. This happened in the French Grand Prix when, with the race in the bag, the Rhodesian crashed, breaking his collarbone in the process.

At the end of the year rumours started flying round that Ray Amm, now fully recovered, would be joining MV Agusta. However, in early December, Amm issued the following statement to the press: 'As a Rhodesian and British national, I want to support the Old Country. If I am losing on the fire that is too bad, but I am staying right here with Nortons to do what I can for British prestige.' (Not strictly true, as Amm received £3,000 paid into a Swiss bank by one of the trade barons, organised by Gilbert Smith.) Coupled with this statement came one from Gilbert Smith: 'I know that in deciding to stay with us Amm is making a big financial sacrifice. Taxation makes it utterly impossible for British manufacturers to offer riders anything like the inducements that are held out by continental manufacturers, who make no secret of the fact that they will pay almost anything to attract men who have made their reputations on British machines. I am delighted that Amm has decided to stay in the British camp and I know that his decision will hearten the thousands of friends he has made since he came to this country a couple of years ago.' *Motor Cycling* commented: 'Count me as one of those thousands who have been heartened, Mr Smith!'

1954 - Norton announced that their 1954 race team, at least as regards the Isle of Man TT series, would be Amm, plus Bob Keeler and Jack Brett. Ken Kavanagh had signed for the Italian Guzzi team during the close season and Mudford's contract had not been renewed.

Racing got under way earlier than usual, at least for Ray Amm, who was the sole British factory representative to be entered for the international races to be held on the tortuous Interlagos circuit at São Paulo, Brazil, over two

Ray Amm crosses the finishing line three-fifths of a second ahead of Gilera-mounted Alfredo Milani to win the 500cc event at the São Paulo, Brazil road races, 21st February 1954. The poor track conditions can be seen from the dust thrown up by Amm's machine.

weeks in mid February. The meetings were being staged to celebrate the four hundredth anniversary of the foundation of the city of São Paulo. Now it was a city of 2½ million inhabitants and the largest industrial centre in Latin America. An aircraft was chartered by the organizers which flew from Rome, stopping at Paris to pick up riders from Britain, Eire, Belgium, Sweden, Austria, Switzerland and Finland. The machines were sent by sea.

Even with factory opposition from Moto Guzzi and Gilera, Amm managed to win all the 350cc and 500cc races he contested. However, after the racing there were a host of problems for the organisers. These not only centred around complaints about the poor conditions of the course but were also financial. The latter was caused - or so the organisers claimed - by the relatively small number of spectators that attended. Many riders claimed they received no money at all. Things were so bad that many were also forced to pay their own hotel bills!

The 1954 350 and 500 factory Nortons were given their first race test (Amm had used 1953 models in Brazil) at Floreffe, Belgium, on Sunday, 2nd May. Amm rode them into second place in both 350cc and 500cc classes. At first glance the new bikes looked very similar to the previous year's models, but there were actually a number of important differences. In search of still higher rpm, to try to combat the latest Italian machines, the bore of both engines had been increased and the stroke shortened. The dimensions were now 90 x 78.4mm (499cc) on the larger engine and 78 x 73mm (349cc) on the smaller unit. As a result of the shorter stroke, the connecting rod length was reduced on both engines.

To minimize crankcase size and oil drag, internal flywheels were no longer employed. Instead, a single external flywheel was mounted behind the engine sprocket. This had been decided by Joe Craig following a visit by Kavanagh to Moto Guzzi. The resulting increase in loading had necessitated modifications to the double-row roller bearings. Previously a single-row roller bearing and a single-row ball race were fitted. The larger the diameter of a flywheel, the lighter it can be for a given flywheel effect. Consequently the adoption of an outside flywheel - at least in theory - offered a useful saving in weight because the flywheel diameter was no longer limited by the need to keep the overall engine height (and hence the crankcase size) down sufficiently for easy (and as low as possible) installation in the frame.

1954 developments saw the introduction of a three-fifty outside flywheel engine.

Although, obviously, the cylinder barrel and head were new, the oil cooling of the exhaust valve guide, which had proved entirely satisfactory the previous year, was retained. The only real modification to the cylinder head and valve gear was the redesigned cams and larger valves to make use of the higher rpm obtainable. That engine speed had, in fact, been increased, was evidenced by the reduced exhaust pipe length. Although a fuel weir was still embodied in the carburettor, the float chamber was no longer scavenged.

A crankcase breather of the tap valve type was located in the upper front of the crankcase. From the breather the discharge pipe led back to the neighbourhood of the primary chain. By then Craig was planning a full 'Guzzi-type' horizontal layout (to emerge later as the 'F' type). Changes in the transmission included the adoption of an engine-shaft shock absorber - intended to improve the chain life - and the introduction of a five-speed gearbox (made specially for Norton by the Burman Company), which featured a five-plate clutch and a short, direct-operating gear pedal in place of the linkage arrangement employed previously. The twin-pipe drip lubrication of the primary chain was again featured, but its oil reservoir had been moved to the left top tube of the frame. Oil for the rear chain was now carried in the suspension sub-frame tube.

Frame dimensions had been slightly modified because of the altered engine proportions, and in addition the lower run of the nearside mainframe tube had been modified to clear the flywheel. Rigidity of the rear sub-frame had been improved by the use of $^7/_8$in-diameter 18-gauge tube throughout. Some additional weight had been saved on the 350 mainframe by a reduction in the tube thickness from 16 to 17 gauge.

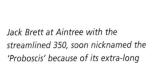

The rear brake assembly (on the right, separate from the sprocket) was the same, but its operation was changed. Instead of the long cable, which led from the brake over the wheel to the brake pedal on the other side of the machine, a much shorter cable had been substituted to a lever on a cross-shaft incorporated in the swinging arm pivot. The pedal was on the other end of the cross-shaft. Front brake cooling was now of the forced draught type; the inclined air scoop on the shoe plate was still fitted, but the outlet was through vanes disposed round the hub, between the two sets of spokes. As the wheel revolved, these vanes acted as a centrifugal extractor fan and drew air from the inlet scoop across the interior of the brake.

Although the elimination of the dust covers from the rear suspension units saved a certain amount of weight, the main purpose of the change was to improve the cooling of the damper units. Previously an excessive rise in temperature of the damper fluid had occasionally caused a reduction of viscosity and consequently a loss of damping, an obviously undesirable occurrence on a racing machine. In addition, dual-rate springs were now utilised on the units so that a more sensitive response to small road irregularities was ensured. But in all other respects the bikes remained unchanged.

Team leader Amm spent most of the pre-TT period racing abroad in Italy and Germany. In addition none of the Norton team attended the opening classic of the season, the French Grand Prix at Reims, as it took place a mere three days before the start of the TT practice. In the bigger classes only Gilera and AJS officially took part. The Junior TT saw a surprise victory for AJS star Rod Coleman - after it first looked set to be a Guzzi win - followed by a period in the middle of the race when Amm was in front, only to drop out with mechanical problems near the end. Brett retired on the first lap, while Keeler kept going to finish third. But the most noteworthy feature was the amount of streamlining on the factory bikes (of all makes). For example, Ray Amm's machine (and his Senior mount, too) sported a steering head-mounted fairing (soon nicknamed the 'Proboscis') that tapered forward to a point vertically in line with the foremost limit of the front wheel. Side panels, rubber-mounted on the twin tank tubes and front down tubes, boxed in the

Jack Brett at Aintree with the streamlined 350, soon nicknamed the 'Proboscis' because of its extra-long nose section.

The other side of the 1954 works 350cc engine, showing the outside flywheel.

The twin-leading shoe front brake introduced for the 1954 season.

power unit, except at the front, and extended rearwards as far as the rider's legs. During practice, observers noted that although it seemed to handle well down Bray Hill, it did not seem as stable as the unstreamlined models on some corners in the Mountain area. At the Gooseneck during one practice session, Amm struck a greasy patch of tarmac and slid into the bank, but in typical fashion carried on unperturbed - with various vegetation growing from the bike! On another practice lap Amm lapped at 95.77mph on his Senior mount, only a shade slower than the quickest of the week, put up by Duke and the Gilera.

After the excellent weather during practice and all races up to the final day everyone was fully expecting a record-breaking Senior TT, some even talking of a 100mph lap for the first time. But it was not to be. Owing to poor visibility, the Senior start had to be postponed twice. Reports, subsequently proved unreliable, of a slight improvement in the weather induced the stewards to permit a noon start, a full one-and-a-half-hours after the scheduled time. But even before the halfway stage had been completed these same stewards were forced to admit they had made a serious error - the weather was getting worse by the minute! - with the result that it was hurriedly agreed to proclaim the leader at the end of lap 4 the winner. Under these unparalleled conditions the victor proved to be Ray Amm, whose time of 1 hour 42 minutes 46.8 seconds for the four laps represented an average speed of 88.12mph. Second man was Geoff Duke at 87.19mph and third Jack Brett at 86.04mph. But as *The Motor Cycle* commented: 'Of the entire entry Amm was probably the only rider trying everything he knew. Duke decided that the laurels were not worth the risks and rode cautiously.' Also, there is no doubt that under the prevailing conditions the Norton single was a more suitable tool than one of the Italian fours.

Maybe luck was on the British factory's side that day, as after the race was abandoned the weather changed rapidly: first the mist was blown away, then the rain stopped and finally the sun shone out in all its glory. For the rest of that Friday in June 1954 the weather was perfect! The press was up in arms with *The Motor Cycle* going as far as to say: 'Its the Senior TT lustre that has been sorely tarnished by last Friday's debacle.' In addition many pundits openly complained that whereas Duke had had to take on fuel, Amm had not - some even going as far as saying the stewards had virtually fixed the result by stopping the race after Duke had refuelled. However, this overlooks the fact that the race-winning Norton combined top and pannier tanks (one of McCandless' ideas) to enable it to complete seven Senior laps non-stop. This also meant that for the early laps this put the British bike at a disadvantage with the extra weight of fuel, which, because the race was much shorter, did not allow the Norton the advantage it would have had later. So on balance Norton's 1954 Senior TT victory was, in my opinion, gained on merit - and Ray Amm's determined (hard!) riding.

The atrocious weather of the Senior TT followed the Grand Prix circus over the Irish Sea, where the Ulster Grand Prix was staged on the following Thursday, 24th June (350cc), and Saturday, 26th June (500cc). Unlike previous years the Irish event was staged much earlier - it was said to enable 'foreign' teams to make only one visit to the British Isles instead of two. But the awful weather throughout the practice and race periods, and the non-entry of the Gilera riders and non arrival of the Guzzi and MV entries conspired to take much of its interest away, which was reflected in sparse spectator attendance. The 250cc and 500cc events shared Thursday, with the smaller bikes going out first. It was wet for the 250s, but weather conditions had deteriorated still further by the time the 500s came out to start. Mindful no doubt of the uproar that characterised the Senior TT the previous week, the organisers adopted the unusual course of inviting three riders to carry out a lap of inspection to determine whether conditions were suitable for racing. Ray Amm was one of those selected and, together with another works competitor (Rod Coleman), Amm reported slippery roads but good visibility, whereupon the

Amm chases Guzzi star Ken Kavanagh in the 350 Belgian Grand Prix, July 1954.

officials decided to run the race, reducing the distance from 27 to 15 laps. The rider nominated to represent the 'privateers' did not bother going out.

South African Rudi Allison had been the latest recruit to the official Norton team, but he had put himself out of the running after injuring his back in a practice crash; his place was taken on the third factory Norton by the Australian Gordon Laing. Laing's subsequent display by finishing third (AJS star Coleman was second) seemed to justify his inclusion in the team. In the race no one could challenge the winner Amm, who won as he pleased.

Two days later things were different - at least to start with - and it was not until the eighth lap of the 350cc race that Amm was able to force his Norton into the lead, where he remained until the end. The early leader had been young John Surtees, who, riding a production Manx brilliantly, led the factory models for the first four laps; for the next half dozen circuits he lay third behind Amm and Laing to display the potential that would later carry him to the very top. Surtees was forced to retire with engine trouble after first overshooting his pit during refuelling midway through the race. At the end it was Amm from Brett, McIntyre (AJS) and Laing in fourth spot. So with three rounds gone Amm led the 500cc title chase by a clear margin.

But then came the continental events. The first was the Belgian. In the 350cc race Amm's clutch sleeve disintegrated and he spilled at high speed. However, the tough Rhodesian turned out for the 500cc, and after getting up to second behind Duke his clutch expired at Stavelot on the sixth lap. The other official Norton entry was Gordon Laing, who was killed on the second lap trying to stay with Amm. Ken Kavanagh believes it was 'Manxie' Laing's accident that was to bring to an end the official works Norton effort. A week later at the Dutch TT, Amm was once again the solitary works Norton entry. But the gremlins that had played havoc with his chances in Belgium were still with him, and after an engine blow-up in the 350cc race, he ran out of fuel in the larger-capacity event after his tank split. With two wins to add to his second place in the Isle of Man, Duke and Gilera now led the 500cc Championship.

Half a million spectators turned out to see the 1954 German Grand Prix, back at Solitude once more. Amm's luck had improved and after winning the 350cc race he rode superbly to finish second in the 500cc behind Duke, but ahead of Armstrong (Gilera) and the Guzzi pair of Anderson and Kavanagh. And it was no easy victory for the Gilera team leader, with Amm exchanging the lead and breaking the lap record before Duke finally set an even higher speed and took the flag from the hard riding Norton ace. Brett was back on the scene to record a third (350cc) and sixth (500cc).

The Swiss Grand Prix saw Duke score his fourth successive classic win in the 500cc category - but not without a massive fight in which Amm led for 14 of the 28 laps and finished a mere 3.7 seconds behind the Gilera rider at the finish. And it was only three laps from the end that Duke was able to make a decisive move that led to his win. Prior to that it was tooth and nail all the way. Brett was fourth behind Armstrong on the other Gilera. Meanwhile, Guzzis dominated the 350cc race, with Anderson and Kavanagh beating Amm and Brett under wet conditions. By now it was all too apparent that a Guzzi was going to win the 350 title, while Gilera would take the larger class. There was absolutely nothing that Ray Amm or the Norton team could do about it.

It was the 1954 Grand Prix des Nations at Monza in September - the eighth and penultimate classic meeting of the year - that must in retrospect be regarded as the occasion on which streamlining finally became accepted as essential equipment for road-racing machines (even if the FIM were later to ban the fully faired type at the end of 1957).

An interesting development on one factory 499cc Norton was the addition of coil ignition. The contact breaker was concealed by a cover on the bottom bevel box. Two coils were mounted in place of the magneto and there were also two spark plugs - one in the orthodox position and one under the cambox. The 12-volt current was supplied from two small batteries mounted pannier fashion each side of the rear wheel. In fact, although taken out in practice, this machine was not used in the race, where both Amm and Brett reverted to their conventional magneto-sparked machines.

After leading for the first lap on his smaller bike, Amm was forced to give way to the flying Guzzis, headed by Champion Fergus Anderson. At the end three other Guzzis, plus race-winner Anderson, meant that Amm was back in fifth, with Brett a place behind. The 500cc race was even less of an event for Norton, with Amm down in seventh place and Brett 11th! MVs, Gileras and Guzzis packed the leaderboard placings.

Back home in Britain, late September saw the first ever motorcycle race meeting on the Aintree circuit - and Amm's last Norton race. Norton were represented by Amm, Brett and privateer John Surtees (who had finished second behind Duke's Gilera at Scarborough the previous weekend). While riding one of the streamlined Nortons in the 350cc race, Amm was unfortunate enough to crash at high speed; happily his injuries, though including a

Opposite: A paddock full of Manx Nortons at Brands Hatch, circa 1955. Number 152 is Alan Trow with his mechanic Peter Goodwin; the rider in the centre background is none other than John Surtees.

broken collarbone, were not serious. Even so, the Norton rider did have the satisfaction of setting the fastest lap in the class at an average speed of 78.37mph. In the 500cc event Surtees rode like a demon on his own Manx to split the Gilera fours of Duke and Armstrong. The same weekend it was announced that Norton (together with AJS) would not be contesting the final classic of the season in Spain the following month. With wins at several venues throughout Britain John Surtees had laid claim to a place in the Norton team. He was rewarded with the use of a works 350 at the final Brands Hatch meeting in late October - and he subsequently won not only this event but also the 500cc race, to score a memorable double.

The Norton stand at the Earls Court Show in mid November saw the company display the streamlined racer ridden to victory in the 1954 Senior TT by Ray Amm, together with the gleaming Senior Tourist Trophy. But less than a month later came the bombshell that team leader Ray Amm had signed for the Italian MV Agusta concern and would be riding that company's four-cylinder machines in the 1955 Grand Prix series. Sadly he was to lose his life at Imola during his first race on one of the Italian multis the following April.

Although Craig remained with Norton for another year before retiring, the 1955 race effort was with specially prepared production Manx models and not with fully blown works specials. Quite simply, even the pro-British, pro-Norton Amm had finally realized that Norton's days as a factory team on the race track were over, as the Norton directors had been forced to accept the financial facts that the company could no longer afford the luxury of a full Grand Prix racing effort - and this included Joe Craig. In future, what racing Norton did back would be connected with the sale to the public of the production Manx models. In fact, all Norton could offer Amm for 1955 was the sale of two Manx models at a special discount.

Other projects - Why had Norton not pushed forward earlier with the design of a new machine themselves? Well, they had... but ill fortune and eventually AMC policy were to cramp their style. As far back as 1949 Joe Craig had spent considerable time at the BRM factory in Bourne (see Chapter 8) in pursuit of a four-cylinder racing engine. Then, at the 1951 London Show, he had seen a rotary-valve cylinder head adapted to a JAP speedway engine. This was the work of Laurence Bond (later to win fame through his range of Bond Minicars). Craig signed an option on behalf of Norton, but confessed he was none too keen on the project. He was proved correct, as even though power output was raised from its initial 35bhp to 47bhp during 1952 and 1953, it never overcame seizure problems and was ultimately discarded from Norton plans.

Next came the four-cylinder concept. Craig favoured a transverse layout after the abortive co-operative venture with BRM, and Norton negotiated to purchase the rights for such an engine from the French designer Henri Nougier, but this fell through when the company that employed Nougier would not play ball. At the same time (late 1951) Rex McCandless put forward the idea of an in-line four - and even went as far as mounting a twin-cylinder Sunbeam S7 engine in one of his Featherbed frames to prove the concept would work.

Craig's 'co-operative' agreement with the design team that had been responsible for the BRM racing-car engine did, however, give birth to one concrete result. They supplied Norton with information to enable the Birmingham company to produce a transverse water-cooled four. But this got no further than the building and testing of a single-cylinder 125cc unit during November 1953, to prove the concept, and some basic castings for the 500cc four-cylinder itself. This would have been of unit construction, with gear drive to the dohc, wet sump and geared primary drive and was expected to produce around 65-70bhp in its final form.

CLASSIC RACING VICTORIES

COUNTING TOWARDS WORLD CHAMPIONSHIP POINTS FROM 1949

1949:	Senior TT	H. Daniell
	Swiss GP	E. Oliver, Sidecar
	Belgian GP	E. Oliver, Sidecar
1950:	Junior TT	A. Bell
	Senior TT	G. Duke
	Ulster GP	G. Duke, 350cc
	Italian GP	G. Duke, 350cc & 500cc
	Belgian GP	E. Oliver, Sidecar
	Swiss GP	E. Oliver, Sidecar
1951:	Junior TT	G. Duke
	Senior TT	G. Duke
	Belgian GP	G. Duke, 350 & 500cc
	Dutch TT	G. Duke, 500cc
	French GP	G. Duke, 350cc
	Ulster GP	G. Duke, 350 & 500cc
	Italian GP	G. Duke, 350cc
	Spanish GP	E. Oliver, Sidecar
	Belgian GP	E. Oliver, Sidecar
	French GP	E. Oliver, Sidecar
1952:	Swiss GP	G. Duke, 350cc
	Junior TT	G. Duke
	Senior TT	R. Armstrong
	Dutch TT	G. Duke, 350cc
	Belgian GP	G. Duke, 350cc
	German GP	R. Armstrong, 350 & 500cc
	Ulster GP	K. Kavanagh, 350cc
	Italian GP	R. Amm, 350cc
	Belgian GP	E. Oliver, Sidecar
	German GP	C. Smith, Sidecar
	Spanish GP	E. Oliver, Sidecar
1953:	Junior TT	R. Amm
	Senior TT	R. Amm
	Ulster GP	K. Mudford, 350cc

	Ulster GP	K. Kavanagh, 500cc
	Belgian GP	E. Oliver, Sidecar
	French GP	E. Oliver, Sidecar
	Ulster GP	C. Smith, Sidecar
	Swiss GP	E. Oliver, Sidecar
	Italian GP	E. Oliver, Sidecar
1954:	Senior TT	R. Amm
	Ulster GP	R. Amm, 350 & 500cc
	German GP	R. Amm, 350cc
	Isle of Man TT	E. Oliver, Sidecar
	Ulster GP	E. Oliver, Sidecar
	Belgian GP	E. Oliver, Sidecar
1956:	Ulster GP	J. Hartle, 500cc
1957:	Belgian GP	J. Brett, 500cc
1958:	Swedish GP	G. Duke, 350 & 500cc
1960:	Ulster GP	J. Hartle, 500cc
1961:	Junior TT	P. Read
	Senior TT	M. Hailwood
1964:	Ulster GP	P. Read, 500cc
1965:	Ulster GP	D. Creith, 500cc
1969:	Yugoslav GP	G. Nash, 500cc

World Champions

350cc	1951	G. Duke
350cc	1952	G. Duke
500cc	1951	G. Duke
Sidecar	1949	E. Oliver
Sidecar	1950	E. Oliver
Sidecar	1951	E. Oliver
Sidecar	1952	C. Smith
Sidecar	1952	E. Oliver

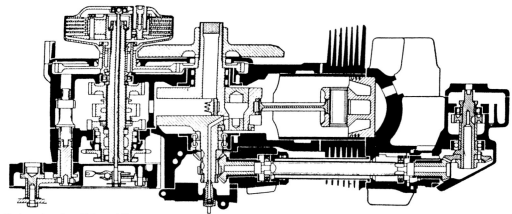

Horizontal engine which would have been raced in 1955, had the factory continued its world championship challenge.

The project that was most likely to have been used if Norton had continued into 1955 and beyond was the 'F' type. This was almost ready for track testing when the decision came that the factory was pulling out in the winter of 1954/55. The 'F' stood for Flat and was in direct response to Moto Guzzi's World Championship-winning horizontal single, which had been the machine finally to take Norton's title in the 350cc class. The Norton flat singles would have been produced in both 348cc and 499cc versions. The power units were revised factory 1954-type engines with a built-in gearbox (which would have allowed five or even six speeds) and clutch unit. One difference was that the engines ran backwards because of the two-pinion internal straight-cut primary gears. Another major change was that no separate crankpin was used in the crankshaft. The drive-side mainshaft and bobweight were manufactured as a one-piece assembly with the crankpin itself, while the timing-side shaft and bobweight were also integral. The idea of this was to provide additional stiffness at higher rpm.

Lucas had specially developed a coil ignition system (tried in practice during the 1954 Italian Grand Prix). There were obviously many smaller differences to the upright works motors, including the oil pump, larger-diameter big-end and various other smaller details. But it was the frame that saw the major change - and owed nothing to the Featherbed. Manufactured in Reynolds 531 tubing, its main backbone was a 4½in OD tube, which also doubled up as an oil tank. At its front it was Sif-bronzed to the steering-head block, whilst at the rear plates were welded to it to form a box section to support the engine. The cylinder head was also supported by a pair of thin tubes that ran downwards from the steering head.

With the horizontal engine mounting, the wheelbase had grown by an extra 1½ inches. Conventional 1954 works Roadholder forks and brakes were used laced to 19in rims. During bench testing, the larger version of the horizontal single produced as much power at the rear wheel as the 1954 works model had given at the crankshaft, but whether this would have given, together with its lower centre of gravity, a fighting chance against the latest Italian machinery is open to question.

Opposite: Horizontal single, the F (Flat)-type works Norton, which would have been used in 1955. Moto Guzzi influence is clearly evident.

With that final project died the saga of the fully fledged Norton Grand Prix challenge, to be replaced by the occasional sortie abroad by works-prepared versions of the existing production Manx models from 1955 onwards. A glorious chapter in the history of British motorcycle racing was over... and the start of a new era was about to begin.

4 Daytona Beach

The Daytona Beach circuit, essentially a
pair of straights comprising the sandy
beach and a tarmac road a few yards
inland, linked by a pair of hairpin bends.

As it still is today, the Daytona 200-mile classic was the premier American motorcycle race back in 1949. Then there were two big differences: the 'beach' circuit and the fact that it had not been won post-war by a British-made machine, victory instead going to home-grown products such as Indian and Harley-Davidson. Billy Mathews had taken first place on a Norton in 1941, the only previous British victory. But in March 1949 American riders, astride British Nortons, monopolised the honours in both the 100-mile National Amateur Championship race and the Blue Riband 200-mile National Experts Championship event. The Nortons that scored first and second places in the 100-mile race, and all three leading positions in the prestigious '200', were production Garden Gate Manx models, fitted with a specially produced kickstarter to meet AMA (American Motorcycle Association) rules for the meeting.

Dick Klamfoth, a 20-year-old from Ohio, soared to instant fame, winning the 1949 200-miler. This was his first ever appearance as an expert, and astride his 500 Manx, with which he had obtained second position in the 1948 100-mile amateur event, he established a new record for the famous 4.2-mile Daytona Beach, Florida circuit, situated on a peninsula 11 miles south of Daytona itself. Unlike the purpose-built Daytona Raceway used today, the circuit in those days featured a course that combined sand racing and road racing, with a two-mile straight on the sands flanked by the sea, whilst inland the other straight, of the same length, ran parallel. This latter part was tarmac surfaced. The two straights were linked by steep sand-bank turns with extremely tricky approaches and exits. In each race there was an entry of up to 150 machines. 1949 saw 124 entries in the

Opposite: The Daytona paddock – more
like a beach party than a race meeting.

Daytona 1950, the start of the 200 miles.

100-miler and 149 for the main event. At the start Harley man Floyd Emde was the hot favourite, having won on an Indian the previous year. Norton-mounted Klamfoth had different ideas.

Before the main event got under way the 100-mile amateur race was run. In this, Norton-mounted Don Evans, a 19-year-old from San Bernardino, California, won top honours for the second year in succession, in what was described by *The Motor Cycle* as, 'the most sensational finish ever seen in American motorcycling'. With some 30,000 spectators watching, the amateur classic got under way, with 103 of the original 124 entries starting the race but only 41 surviving to take the chequered flag. The most sensational part of the 100-miler was at the end. As Evans came down the back stretch over the paved road, which extended some 20 feet in width, and rounded the turn, he began to slide just as the flagman was waving his chequered flag for the finish. The Norton skidded over the finishing line and in the process headed straight for the unfortunate official, who tried to get out of its path. Luckily it only clipped his leg, then rolled over the bank. The organisers ruled that the young Californian had completed his 25 laps and he was declared the winner, finishing 30 seconds ahead of second-place man Ted Totoraitis (also on a Norton) of Grand Rapids, Michigan, with only six seconds to spare over Harley-Davidson rider Robert Chaves. Evans set a new record for the 100-mile race with a time of 1 hour 15 minutes 14.38 seconds, an average speed of 79.73mph, compared with the previous record for the amateur event, established in 1948, of 78.6mph.

The 200-mile expert (professional) classic got under way with 135 machines starting in rows of 15 at ten-second intervals. For 35 laps it appeared as if Jack Horn, riding a Triumph Grand Prix, was well on his way to victory. The Triumph rider had set a terrific pace at the front, leading the entire entry of old hands and younger riders alike, but engine trouble developed, forcing him to retire with 12 laps to go. Old-timer Ed Kretz, on an Indian, then took up the challenge for a short time before he too was forced out with engine problems. This left Klamfoth in the lead, where he was joined by Billy Mathews of Hamilton, Ontario, also with a Norton. During the last ten laps the race developed into a real dingdong between these two. With three laps left, Mathews came around the south turn a mere three seconds behind the leader, but he then lost time and finally finished 16 seconds adrift at the flag. Third place went to Ted Luse of Burbank, California. He was 2 minutes 8 seconds behind the winner. All three were on Nortons.

Pilots-eye-view of the plunger-framed Manx used at Daytona. The Featherbed-type was not allowed.

Klamfoth made one stop for fuel and his pit was so well organised that he was stopped for only 18 seconds, which many observers thought a record for the Daytona race. Mathews, who had lost the previous year's 200-miler solely through an over-lengthy pit stop, was much faster in 1949, but still could not match Klamfoth's time. He did, however, have the satisfaction of making the fastest lap at 88.3mph. In winning the first prize of $2,500 Klamfoth had completed the distance in 2 hours 18 minutes 53.5 seconds, an average of 86.42mph. This bettered the previous best set in 1948 by over two miles per hour. Pre-race favourite Emde and his Harley v-twin finished way down in 17th. All in all the 1949 Daytona races were great for Norton and British prestige, but disastrous for the American factories.

The following month many of the British motorcycle industry's leaders attended a lunch at the Savoy Hotel, London, in honour of Norton's Daytona triumph. After proposing the traditional toast to His Majesty's Government, C.A. Vandervell, the Chairman of both the Industry Association and Norton Motors, paid special thanks to the services of tuner Francis Beart, who had gone to Daytona to look after the Norton bikes, and later presented him, as a mark of appreciation, with a brand new International Norton sports roadster. Also at the luncheon was the Minister of Supply, G.R. Strauss, the vice-president of the Manufacturers Union, F.A. Kimberley, the managing director of the James concern, and Gilbert Smith, managing director of Norton.

1950 saw the Daytona races run a month earlier, in February, and even though a Triumph won the amateur 100-mile event, Norton took first, second and fourth in the all-important 200-miler. The one-two finishing order was reversed over the previous year with Mathews taking victory and Klamfoth runner-up. Bill Tuman on another Manx was fourth. All three machines were tuned by Francis Beart. Mathews's average speed of 88.87mph was faster than the 1949 record lap. This second Daytona victory ensured much publicity for Norton - and British bikes generally - on both sides of the Atlantic.

Norton machinery once again dominated the famous American meeting in 1951. But in place of the Indians and Harleys it was now BSA and Triumph that provided the main opposition. The amateur race saw Robert Michael take his Manx to victory after crashes and mechanical failures eliminated two-thirds of the field. Michael's winning time of 1 hour 12 minutes 41.22 seconds, a speed of 82.54mph, was a new record. Nortons filled six of the first ten places.

For the 1951 200-mile Experts race the ruling concerning compression ratio limits for 500cc ohv or ohc engines was relaxed. Riders could now use 8:1, instead of the previous 7:1 limit. The capacity rules, 750cc side-valve or 500cc ohv or ohc still favoured the home-grown v-twins. There was a formidable array of racing talent for the 1951 main event. Riders had come from every one of the 48 States and represented the cream of North American speedmen. The entry comprised eight Nortons, 15 BSAs, 44 Harley-Davidsons, 16 Triumphs, nine Indians, three AJSs, one Vincent and one BMW, a total of 97, which although down on previous years, was of an exceptionally high standard.

Right from the start the 1949 winner, Dick Klamfoth, went to the front of the field, but Bobby Hill, also Norton mounted, provided a stiff challenge throughout the race, and for a short period in the middle even led the field. For a long time it looked like another one-two-three for the Manx singles, but on the 31st lap Bill Tuman, the third Norton rider, got his timing wrong on one of the turns. Out of control, he ended up half buried in a sand-bank. After this mistake his only choice was to walk back to the pits, for his machine was too badly damaged to continue. So Klamfoth took the chequered flag, followed by team-mate Hill, with a Triumph twin making up the third rostrum position. Klamfoth had set another record, completing the 200 miles in 2 hours 9 minutes 15.71 seconds, an average speed of 92.81mph.

Opposite: 1950, Billy Mathews (98) took the win with Klamfoth (2) second. Bill Tuman (51) was fourth.

Manx Nortons dominated the 1949 200-mile Experts race; the winner was 20-year-old Dick Klamfoth from Groveport, Ohio. He went on to record a trio of victories, winning in 1950 and 1951.

Once again the man behind the scenes who helped all this happen was that master of tuning Francis Beart, but even though the 1951 production Manx models featured the new Featherbed frame, AMA rules had meant that 1950 Garden Gate machines had to be used yet again.

An interesting comment after this third year of American rider/British bike success was the following extract from *The Motor Cycle* of 22nd March, 1951: 'Caps off to the lads who did it. I still wonder on the precise significance of these Daytona wins. I should like to see what Geoff Duke would make of them against Klamfoth and Co. We all hope to see the American aces at Douglas before we die.' Well, the man who made that comment was none other than Harry Louis, who died in 1988. I wonder if he thought back to this statement when the likes of Roberts, Lawson and Spencer started cleaning up the World Championships during the late 1970s and early 1980s? But of course by then Douglas was no longer the centre of the road racing world.

The following year, 1952, extremely bad weather over the weekend of 23/24th February made racing impossible at Daytona Beach. Conditions were so poor on both these dates that the turns at the end of the beach straight, which linked up with the road section, were covered with water. In consequence, it was decided to postpone racing until the Monday and Tuesday. Crews worked all through the night with pumps and bulldozers and by the Monday morning the turns were in reasonable condition. However, they were still far from ideal, with the result that speeds were expected to be considerably down on previous years.

Because of the uncertain weather it was decided to run the 200-mile Experts event on the first day, and as zero time, 1.00pm, approached the spectators began to get into position. The crowds were well down, because thousands of enthusiasts had already left for home.

After all the pre-race problems, Dick Klamfoth really turned on the style to win a brilliantly judged race and thus complete a trio of wins (1949, 1951 and 1952) for himself and Norton. His speed was 87.88mph, some 5mph lower than the record he established the previous year, but none the less an excellent performance considering the conditions. The fastest lap, of 88.5mph, was made by Al Gunter riding a BSA Gold Star. Of the 103 starters only 47 finished. Although the conditions were so bad, the race was still an exciting spectacle to observe and there were very few crashes. Shortly after the last man was flagged off, the rain restarted and continued. So waterlogged did the track become that it was decided for that year to abandon the 100-mile amateur event, which had been re-scheduled for the following day.

When details of the 1953 Daytona races became known it was announced that for the first time since 1949, Francis Beart would not be assisting Norton riders, even though rival factories were supplying staff and had new machinery on display. 1953 was also to signal the end of the road for the single-cylinder Nortons in the premier American meeting.

When triple winner Klamfoth crashed heavily and Hill retired with mechanical trouble, both early on in the race, the way was clear for the brand-new, side-valve KR750 Harley v-twin to take the first American victory for five years: rider Paul Goldsmith averaged 94.45mph for the 200 miles, which beat handsomely Klamfoth's 1951 record of 92.81mph. And that was truly the end for the Manx at Daytona, because the AMA changed the rules - effectively banning the Norton single. Thereafter, Harley, BSA and Triumph machinery dominated, before the Stateside classic was relocated to an all-new tarmac raceway a few years later. But for a glorious four-year period, the Norton single had dominated an event that was, and still is, an American institution.

5 Record Breakers

Norton factory rider Jimmie Guthrie, raising the hour record to 114.09mph at Montlhéry 1935.

Even prior to World War I Norton had a reputation for setting new speed records and, as related in Chapter 1, had even offered for sale replicas of their Brooklands machines, complete with certificates guaranteeing a specified performance. The man behind much of this early record-breaking success was Dan O'Donovan, who was not only a skilful rider but also a gifted tuner, very much in the same mould as Joe Craig in later years.

In 1915 O'Donovan broke the world kilometre record on one of 'Pa' Norton's machines at 82.85mph, the same year in which the curly 'N' tank logos first appeared. O'Donovan's first major success after the end of hostilities in November 1918 was when he, Victor Horsman and Rex Judd set a new world 12 hours record at 60.7mph, in 1921, on a 500cc side-valve Norton. Horsman had also set a new one-hour record the previous year at 71.68mph, using a chain-drive side-valve Norton.

Pioneer Norton racer, record breaker and tuning wizard, Dan O'Donovan at Brooklands, circa 1919.

In 1922 O'Donovan upped the 500cc kilometre record to 89.22mph on his beloved Brooklands speed bowl. Then, in 1923, Bert Denly was 'signed up' by O'Donovan and repaid his mentor by first raising the hour record to 82.67mph that June, and then to 85.22mph later that autumn. Not satisfied with this, Denly then returned to Brooklands in 1924 and averaged 87.07 mph for the one hour.

Nineteen twenty-seven saw the first of many visits to the Montlhéry circuit near Paris, later the scene of much Norton success, where Denly became the first man on two wheels to exceed the ton for an hour, setting a new world record at 100.57mph! But 1927 was also the year in which Walter Moore unveiled his new camshaft engine. All records to that date, including Denly's 100mph-plus effort, had been achieved with either side- or overhead-valve power units.

With the advent of the superior overhead camshaft engine, made even more superior with Carroll's re-design in 1930, Norton was once again in a position to challenge for honours, not only on the race circuit but also in terms of outright speed.

Bill Lacey, later to win fame as a top tuner, took a Carroll-engined machine to Montlhéry (by now Brooklands was almost at its limit for speed attempts) and after earlier suffering a mix-up with trackside signals, he set a new record for the hour, averaging 110.8mph. Then in 1935 works racer Jimmie Guthrie, using a specially tuned Joe Craig engine running on alcohol, raised the record to 114.09mph. An earlier attempt in 1934 had to be abandoned after both special engines blew up. This was after setting a couple of shorter-distance records and realising that Guthrie was in a position to comfortably beat Lacey's earlier one-hour figure.

Artie Bell, Eric Oliver and Geoff Duke seen at Montlhéry in October 1949; they broke 21 world records.

In 1937 the Italian Gilera company raised the figure to over 127mph, where it was destined to stay until 1953, when Norton were once again to take up this particular challenge. Before this, in the very week that the 1949 London Show took place, Joe Craig led a new Norton team back to Montlhéry, where over the period 25th to 28th October the marque smashed 21 world records, which included both two- and three-wheel records. The riders were Artie Bell, Geoff Duke and Eric Oliver. Besides Joe Craig the back-up team consisted of mechanics Charlie Edwards and Frank Sharratt. For about a week this small group had waited at Montlhéry for favourable weather conditions. Then on Tuesday, 25th October Eric Oliver wheeled his 596cc sidecar outfit on to the French circuit. He thundered off, intent on putting the one-hour sidecar record up to 100mph. (It stood at 92mph, set by the Frenchman Amort on a 574cc Gnome-et-Rhone at Montlhéry in 1934.) Expectations mounted as the laps rolled past. For 46 minutes Oliver roared round the roughly oval circuit, playing a three-wheel wall-of-death act on the high, steep banking at each end. Then misfortune intervened: his rear tyre had worn through. Nothing daunted, Oliver soon had another fitted and tried again. This time the rear tyre lasted for 50 minutes, and that was that. During the two attempts Oliver had been averaging about 101mph. Joe Craig then advised Oliver to try again later, but not to attempt breaking this particular record by such a wide margin! Although the old one-hour sidecar record stood intact at 92mph, the day's work had not been entirely in vain. Oliver had shattered, during his attack on the hour, three other sidecar records! He had taken the 50-mile at 101.09mph; the 50-kilometre at 100.97mph, and the 100 kilometre at 101.04mph. And not only this: it was the first time these distances had been covered at over 100mph with a sidecar outfit.

One of the 1949 team streaking round the Montlhéry banking.

More was to come, but not on the following day, Wednesday, which was too windy for any attempt. Therefore, instead of making onslaughts against records in the solo 350cc class, Bell, Duke and Oliver (who was also the third solo rider) were to be found with Joe Craig and the mechanics in one of the workshop garages housed beneath the high banking of the track. There, although some work could be carried out, the majority of the time was spent waiting for the foul weather outside to subside. The wind was so strong that it even set a van in motion on a slope by the track, with the result that the driver was forced to run and jump aboard the moving vehicle and apply the brakes. But at least this had the effect of making everyone laugh, and the atmosphere inside the Norton workshop became more cheerful.

Conditions were just the opposite on Thursday, with the day dawning bright and dry. The result was just what the team needed, with the same three riders between them breaking six world records in the solo 350cc class for Norton. These new records were as follows: two-hour, 101.05mph; three-hour, 101.10mph; four-hour, 100.19mph; five-hour, 100.09mph; 500-kilometre, 101.4mph; 500-mile, 100.106mph. You could not get much more consistent than that!

Friday was again a day of notable success. The 500cc Norton was taken out, and the solo 500cc two-hour record raised to 111.85mph. Further attempts in this class were then abandoned when a footrest came loose. However, Oliver took out the 596cc Norton outfit and proceeded to shatter three more world sidecar records. He bagged the one-hour record at 95.89mph; the 100-mile at 95.88mph, and the two-hour at 92.39mph. Asked for his comments afterwards, Joe Craig said: 'All the records we have just put up were world records; the engines have been measured and checked. Officials here have been very co-operative. A thing that struck us all is how useful it would be if we had such a track as Montlhéry at home.' The 500cc solo record applied also to the 750cc and 1,000cc classes, and the sidecar records established new figures in the 1,000cc as well as the 600cc class.

There were also a couple of other important developments that came out of the Montlhéry record spree: Oliver's flat and worn tyres from his attempt to beat the 100mph for the hour proved that considerable tyre development was needed, and Geoff Duke noticed that Artie Bell's better-fitting leathers gave him added speed, which led to Duke commissioning a new one-piece set for the following racing season, a trend that has lasted until today.

Ray Amm on the 'Kneeler' at Montlhéry in 1953.

A year later Oliver returned to the French circuit to raise the sidecar hour record to 97.04mph. In 1953 the Norton team returned to Montlhéry yet again, this time with the revolutionary Kneeler, nicknamed the 'Silver Fish', which had been ridden by works rider Ray Amm in the North West 200 and TT practice earlier that year and is described in Chapter 3. Like 1949, the visit coincided with the London Show, providing a valuable fillip to Norton's prestige at home and abroad.

Ray Amm, together with that veteran of earlier record attempts Eric Oliver, took part in a two-day attack that resulted in the establishment of no fewer than 61 new records. Of these, 43 were gained on the first day, Sunday, 8th November, when Amm and Oliver jointly claimed them with a 350cc engine fitted in the frame. This included the hour record at 124.30mph. Then the 350cc engine was removed and the larger unit fitted overnight, ready for business on Monday.

With a maximum speed of well over 140mph, the 500 was helped, no doubt, by its extensive streamlining, although the full shell as used by Amm in road race events was not employed. As in the majority of the attempts, no tail-piece was fitted over the rear wheel.

When Amm took the prestigious hour at 133.71mph it was a superb achievement, for the 'Silver Fish' was hardly one of the easiest machines to pilot at sustained high speeds. In taking the hour Amm secured for Britain the important record that had been held since pre-war days by Piero Taruffi on his supercharged four-cylinder Gilera at 127.7mph, and remember, Amm's Norton was not only unblown but was also a mere single. The fastest record obtained by the Norton team at Montlhéry that November was the 10-mile, at 137.6mph. This, like the majority of the other records, was for more than one class (in this case 500cc, 750cc and 1,000cc), and explains why so many new standards were set in only a couple of days.

Graham Smith is pushed off by Reg Dearden (right) and a mechanic during the unsuccessful 24 hours attempt in April 1961. The venue was, once again, the French Montlhéry speedbowl.

Almost eight years were to pass before the final single-cylinder Norton record attempt, again at Montlhéry, took place. Hot on the heels of successful 12-hour record missions by Velocette and BMW, the timekeepers were recalled yet again on Saturday, 22nd April, 1961, by the private Reg Dearden Norton team, who planned to snatch the recently set records. As one would expect, it was chilly at 5.40 in the morning, when 1959 Senior Manx Grand Prix winner Eddie Crooks eased home the clutch to set the wheels of the Dearden attempt in motion. The machine was not the intended 'yellow special' that Reg Dearden had constructed, with its factory-vetted engine and oversize frame holding seven pints of oil; this had given trouble in practice and had been replaced by a virtually standard production 1959 500 Manx model that had stood idle, since it was to have been ridden in that year's Manx Grand Prix by Colin Broughton. It even had a conventional dolphin roadrace fairing and no specialist streamlining.

Right away Crooks got into his stride with laps at 121mph. As the oil warmed the speed crept higher, and his fastest lap, in 46 seconds for the 1.58 miles, approached 124mph. Crooks thought a 500cc Norton should have lapped faster. Indeed, on the selected gearing and a maximum of 6,800rpm on the brief straights, almost 130mph was achieved. But at Montlhéry barely ten seconds of the 46 second lap was spent with the machine upright. For the rest the Dearden Manx was doing a wall-of-death act round the vast bankings, where centrifugal loading cut rpm by 400. With 76 laps to his credit Crooks came in. Forty-three seconds later, with a full tank, Keith Terretta was on his way at a similar speed. Signalled to slow by Dearden after ten laps, he seemed to find it impossible to pare the pace even fractionally, and after a few 114mph laps was back on full bore. A quick check on tyres, chains and tanks following Terretta's hour showed that only petrol was needed, and after 57 seconds it was the burly Frenchman Jacques Insermini who was peering through the screen. With his shoulder still strapped for a very recent collarbone fracture, the French 350cc and 500cc road-race Champion completed his stint with never a murmur and only the ashen shade of his face recording the pain he had suffered whilst out on the Montlhéry bowl.

Taking 5 minutes 25 seconds, the third pit stop was the longest because the primary chain was changed. Then it was the turn of Peter Bettison, whose consistency at 121mph was uncanny in its total reliability. As a last-minute replacement for Mike Brookes, Rhodesian Graham Smith matched Bettison's consistency for 35 minutes. Then, disaster - flat out on one of the banked sections there was a sudden 'piercing screech that interrupted the five-hundred's bellowing exhaust', as *The Motor Cycle* reported. With an ultra-rapid move Smith's left hand grabbed the clutch lever. Instantly his two mile-a-minute impetus carried him at ever decreasing speed round the remaining mile of Montlhéry's steeply banked bowl before at last coming to a halt. So, after 4 hours 38 minutes 10 seconds at an average speed of 115.44mph, including routine stops totalling 8 minutes 19 seconds, Manchester dealer Reg Dearden's Norton had failed in its bid for the world 12-hour records of 104.66mph, set up the previous month on a Velocette Venom Vee-line, and 109.34mph established in the 750cc and 1,000cc classes a week later by MLG's 600 BMW R69S. With so much speed in hand it was a galling failure - a broken hairpin valve spring was the culprit.

And so ended half a century of record breaking by single-cylinder-engined Norton machinery.

Opposite: Bonneville Salt Flats, Utah, USA. Don Vesco's 499cc Manx achieved 126.93mph with no tuning in the early 1960s.

6 Three Wheels

Any story of Norton on three wheels is closely related to the four-times sidecar World Champion Eric Oliver. Oliver was a pioneer of unorthodox ideas and techniques, 'the Geoff Duke of the sidecar sphere', as *The Motor Cycle* once put it.

Oliver's name first reached the headlines in 1947 when he became known as the uncrowned king of Cadwell Park, because of his hellfire driving of a Norton-engined outfit. Although his methods appeared crude, verging on an accident waiting to happen, he none the less got results. Many observers forecast a serious pile-up unless his tactics changed, but Eric Oliver quickly acquired a finesse and skill which he displayed to the full against the cream of continental talent during his first foray into Europe during 1948. He was successful across the English Channel from the first, winning races and building a reputation without equal across Europe. The following year saw the start of the official World Championships. The sidecar series was run over three rounds, in Switzerland, Belgium and Italy but, unlike the solos, the capacity limit was 600cc.

Early days: the future World Champion Eric Oliver and his 596cc Norton outfit, Cadwell Park, 22nd September, 1946.

Like the majority of other Norton sidecar entries, the engine capacity of the single had been raised to 596cc and Oliver's used dohc. The 1949 championship was decided in Belgium, where, although slowed by a leaking petrol pipe, Oliver made it two wins in the first two rounds. His two main rivals, Haldemann (Norton) and Frigerio (Gilera) both retired, so even before the third and final event counting towards the championship, which took place at Monza, Eric Oliver and his passenger Denis Jenkinson became the first Sidecar World Champions.

Denis Jenkinson with Eric Oliver's World Championship winning outfit, Belgian Grand Prix 1949. Together they were the first three-wheeler world title holders.

Piloting a four-cylinder Gilera outfit on home ground in Italy, Frigerio scored his first classic win of the new series, even though Oliver had set fastest lap at 86.74mph. Perhaps the British crew would have won had not the need to change a plug become necessary, but Oliver and Jenkinson finished fifth. Incidentally 'Jenks' went on to win fame as a journalist and as the navigator to Stirling Moss in the famous Mille Miglia of 1955, which they won with a Mercedes-Benz W196. As recorded in Chapter 5, Oliver was a member of the official Norton factory effort that successfully set up a number of new speed records at Montlhéry later that year. The record-breaking sidecar chassis formed the basis for the following year's racing outfit.

A pair of Norton outfits duelling at the Dutch Zandvoort circuit in May 1953.

1950 saw the World Championship series staged at the same three venues as the previous year. Using several passengers, including Peter Glover and the Italian Lorenzo Dobelli, Oliver won all three rounds, each at record speed. No one could touch him, not even Frigerio and his works four-cylinder Gilera. In all Oliver scored a total of 16 wins during the course of the season. The makers of the sidecar, Watsonian, provided Eric Oliver with more support than Norton. Jenkinson alleged in a letter published in *Motorcycle Sport* a few years ago that Oliver never really received the financial reward that was his due, preferring to ride for a pittance rather than ask for money!

For 1951 a new FIM ruling meant that all sidecar contenders in the World Championship series were of 500cc capacity instead of 600cc as in the past. Oliver's Norton now used a 1950 works-type 499cc double knocker engine with a Featherbed frame (previously he had an unsprung chassis) and telescopic front forks, but the latter employed a leading axle, unlike that fitted to the solos, which was of the central axle type. Any doubts about how the new outfit would handle were dispelled as soon as the first corner was reached at the season opener, the Spanish Grand Prix held in Montjuich Park, Barcelona. Oliver led the screaming pack from the starting grid and swept into the corner noticeably faster than the remainder of the field. After three laps he held a 40-second lead over his nearest challenger, Frigerio on the four-cylinder Gilera. At the end of the 17-lap, 63-mile long race the order remained unchanged, with Albino Milani on a Gilera single third.

Next came the Swiss Grand Prix at Bremgarten. When well in the lead, Oliver had the misfortune to suffer a broken primary chain just before the start of the last lap. All he could do now was wait until the crew who were second (Frigerio) had received the chequered flag and then push the outfit across the line to take fifth place. Before this misfortune *The Motor Cycle* had summed up his performance thus: 'Oliver was at his best. His superb, determined style seemed unaffected by the discomfort of the rain or the slides and snakes of the Norton outfit on the slippery surface. World Champion sidecar exponent in 1949 and 1950, no roadracing man is more clearly the master of his opponents and more likely, it appeared, to gain the honours (and the hat-trick) this year.' And to confirm this came wins at the following two rounds in Belgium and France. With the title assured the team of Oliver and Dobelli journeyed to Monza for the final Grand Prix of the year.

Cadwell Park, summer 1959. An unfaired Manx with a third wheel and passenger, in an age where the specialised kneeler outfits and full streamlining had virtually taken over.

Production-type Watsonian racing
sidecar, fitted to a Manx Norton
Featherbed frame; as used by Eric Oliver
before the advent of the Kneeler outfit.

Left; overplan of the Watsonian chassis
showing alternatives for a solid frame
machine.

Far left; down-tubes of the standard
Manx Norton frame were modified to
take the upper-front sidecar connection.

Prior to the start the Swiss rider Hans Haldemann had become involved in an argument with one of the paddock officials. The result was a fine, which Haldemann refused to pay. This meant that he would be unable to start. The reason he had refused to pay was that the payment of the fine would have been an admission of guilt, and he firmly maintained his innocence. The result was that fellow competitor Oliver paid the fine for him! Haldemann was to finish the race in fourth place. How many World Champions today would have responded in similar fashion?

The race had begun with Gilera's number one, Frigerio, who had been level on points with the British Norton star, retiring almost as the race started. However, Gilera had given a second four to Albino Milani (brother of solo star Alfredo), and he proceeded to engage in what was described in *The Motor Cycle* as 'one of the most famous duels with which Eric Oliver has ever had to contend'. Their battle was one of the highlights of the whole meeting. The lead changed hands repeatedly, even several times a lap. The Gilera was faster, but Oliver's cornering simply defied description. At the finish there was really nothing in it. But the official gave it to the Italian by a fraction of a second. Even so, Oliver and Norton were World Champions for the third year running.

Technically the most interesting sidecar outfit of 1951 was the one used by Hans Haldemann. This employed either a 499cc or 596cc (for non-championship events) Manx engine with Norton gearbox and brakes. But the remaining components were far from standard. Light alloy tubes welded at the joints formed the low, duplex cradle frame of the machine and sidecar chassis; construction was integral, with the frame and chassis permanently attached. A shortened BMW telescopic front fork was fitted, and ground clearance was reduced to a minimum. A tendency over preceding years had been for larger fuel tanks to eliminate replenishment stops in

The German Norton/Steib outfit of
Bohm and Fuchs seen at Hockenheim in
April 1952. Hermann Bohm had broken
the world sidecar speed record
the previous year piloting a
supercharged NSU twin.

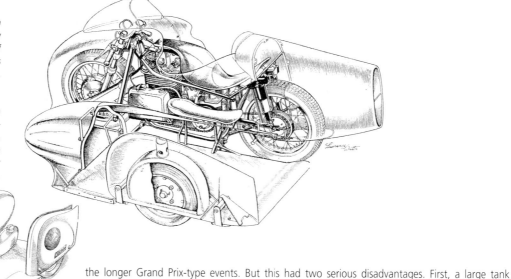

The 1954 Oliver Watsonian/Norton Kneeler, the Mark 2. This cutaway drawing shows the unusual position of the fuel tank and the leg rests for the driver.

Oliver's outfit had evolved into a kneeling riding stance by mid 1953 – and thus the Mark 1 Kneeler. Also of interest was the comprehensive front and rear aluminium-streamlined fairings.

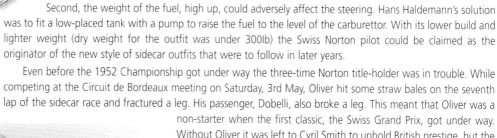

Although not a Manx, this 1956 photograph taken at Brough Airfield, East Yorkshire, is none the less one of a classic cammy Norton – a sohc 490cc International outfit.

the longer Grand Prix-type events. But this had two serious disadvantages. First, a large tank usually meant that the machine and rider were higher and this created more wind resistance. Second, the weight of the fuel, high up, could adversely affect the steering. Hans Haldemann's solution was to fit a low-placed tank with a pump to raise the fuel to the level of the carburettor. With its lower build and lighter weight (dry weight for the outfit was under 300lb) the Swiss Norton pilot could be claimed as the originator of the new style of sidecar outfits that were to follow in later years.

Even before the 1952 Championship got under way the three-time Norton title-holder was in trouble. While competing at the Circuit de Bordeaux meeting on Saturday, 3rd May, Oliver hit some straw bales on the seventh lap of the sidecar race and fractured a leg. His passenger, Dobelli, also broke a leg. This meant that Oliver was a non-starter when the first classic, the Swiss Grand Prix, got under way. Without Oliver it was left to Cyril Smith to uphold British prestige, but the dice were loaded against a British win. A crash at Mettet, Belgium, only three weeks before had resulted in head and shoulder injuries, so, although passed by the circuit doctor, Smith was not absolutely fit. More than that, his Norton was powered by a standard Manx engine, an exasperating situation, since Oliver's works prepared engine lay idle at the factory in Birmingham. Smith surprised everyone by finishing a superb second after a race-long duel with the Italian Gilera fours piloted by race winner Albino Milano and Ercole Frigerio. Sadly, the latter rider crashed on his last lap and died from his injuries.

The next round, at Spa-Francorchamps, Belgium, was in early July. Although not fully recovered, Eric Oliver insisted on competing and amazed everyone by winning! Milani was second and Cyril Smith, who had been loaned a spare factory engine, third. Rebuilt from the Bordeaux crash, the Watsonian sidecar was now using lighter experimental square tubing, the wheel diameter was reduced from 18 to 16 inches, and the sidecar had been much lightened, including the sidecar wheel spindle support. Unfortunately the weight saving had gone too far and the result was that in the German Grand Prix the sidecar wheel spindle support fractured, forcing Oliver's retirement while holding a commanding lead. This effectively eliminated all chances of his retaining the world title.

With Oliver out, victory at Solitude went to Smith, who followed this up with a second at Monza and a third at the final in Barcelona to take the title and retain it for the Norton marque. His passenger in 1952 was Bob Clements. The nearest Smith ever came to repeating his 1952 success was the following year when he finished second in the title chase. From then on it was downhill all the way: third in 1954 and finally fifth in 1955.

For 1953 Lorenzo Dobelli, the passenger who had shared so many ups and downs with Eric Oliver, was not available, so the three-times World Champion, now fully recovered, had been joined by Stan Dibben, an enthusiast employed on the Norton testing staff. But the most noteworthy item on the Oliver/Norton front that year was an all-new outfit. This looked very different from its predecessor. There were now extensive front and rear streamlined fairings, with the front section blending into the sidecar nose cowl. Since this streamlining had been evolved round a kneeling position for the rider, the previously used Featherbed-type frame was unsuitable and a new frame had to be built. This was on similar lines to the one used on the experimental Norton solo streamliner built that year and used by Ray Amm a few times (see Chapters 3 and 5). The aluminium fairing completely enclosed the front wheel, forks, steering head and handlebar. When tucked in, the driver was shielded most effectively by the streamlining.

Pip Harris and Ray Campbell with their Eric Oliver-prepared Norton outfit in the 1958 Sidecar TT.

The 1952 Sidecar World Champion, Cyril Smith (Norton) during the 1958 TT; he was destined to retire. Smith raced until 1959 and died in 1962.

Bernie Mack, Australia's leading sidecar ace in the early 1950s, seen in winning form at Fisherman's Bend, an airfield circuit three miles from Melbourne, on 20th March, 1954.

A Manx-powered outfit at a Continental Grand Prix in the mid-1950s, with a Watsonian chair.

Opposite page; Pip Harris with his Manx-powered Watsonian outfit at Aintree in 1958. He later switched to German BMW power.

Ernie Walker's prototype 499cc Norton Kneeler, a particularly well-finished and neat piece of engineering seen in 1957.

Although he finished second, as the first British competitor home, Jackie Beeton won the British Championship title at Thruxton in August 1958.

Experiments also took place with a brake for the third wheel. Even so, Oliver chose to rely on his 'old' Featherbed-framed outfit with its conventional solo-type 'sit up' driving position for all the World Championship rounds that year. He regained the title once more, winning four of the five rounds. In the other, after a fierce duel with Cyril Smith, he had his engine seize right at the end of the race, allowing Smith to take an easy victory.

For 1954 Oliver finally used the streamlined 'kneeler', now considerably modified, with a new passenger, Leslie Nutt. Stan Dibben had joined Cyril Smith (whose only daughter he later married). The classic season on three wheels started in the Isle of Man - only the fourth time in history that a sidecar TT had been run (the three predecessors having been staged 30 years before, in 1923, 1924 and 1925). But unlike the earlier races, the 1954 event was held not over the famous Mountain Circuit but over the much shorter 10.79 mile Clypse course. Oliver's time for the ten-lap race was 1 hour 34 minutes 0.2 seconds, an average speed of 68.87mph. He also set the fastest lap, in 9 minutes 9 seconds, a speed of 70.85mph. Leading from the start, Oliver was never overtaken. His chief rival, Cyril Smith, chased hard for three laps before dropping out when the collets came adrift from the valves. The Manufacturers' Team Prize went to the Watsonian 11 team, comprising F. Taylor, L.W. Taylor and J. Drion, all of whose outfits were Norton-powered. But a warning for the future came in the form of three BMW outfits, which secured second, third and fourth places. The next two rounds were the Ulster and Belgian Grands Prix, and Oliver won both. But a mere week prior to the German Grand Prix at Solitude, both Oliver and his passenger, Leslie Nutt, were injured when their outfit skidded off a wet track at a non-championship meeting near Frankfurt on Sunday, 18th July. Oliver broke his arm while Nutt injured a shoulder. Without the four-times World Champion the German Grand Prix was quite simply a walkover for the factory BMW twins, which now featured Bosch fuel injection.

Peter Russell at the start of the Sidecar TT on 10th June, 1963.

Eckington (near Sheffield) motorcycle dealer Charlie Freeman was a well known sidecar racer in the 1950s and 1960s. He is seen here in action at Cadwell Park, summer 1959.

The Swiss Grand Prix took place a month later. Somehow, although far from fit, Oliver had struggled to make an appearance. But with four works BMWs in the race and his best practice lap some ten seconds slower than the BMW team leader Noll, the Norton driver looked up against it. And so it proved. At the end of the first lap Noll was in the lead, with Oliver down in sixth, obviously not his usual self. By the end Noll had won comfortably, with Oliver and passenger Nutt down in fifth spot.

A notable absentee from the Italian Grand Prix in mid-September was the Oliver/Nutt pairing. The British champion's fractured arm was still proving a problem and was not strong enough to allow him to take part - in retrospect he had tried to come back too early in Switzerland. Noll took victory for the third time that year. This left both drivers with three wins apiece. But the Championship went to the German because of his superior placings in the other three events. And as far as the Sidecar World Championship series went it was the end of Norton's years at the top, with BMW going on to win a record total of 19 titles over the next 21 years (the others went to Helmut Fath-designed fours in 1968 and 1971).

After a poor start to the 1955 season, Eric Oliver announced his retirement. Then 44 years old, the maestro had finally called it a day. Besides his four World titles, Oliver had pioneered several important innovations on three wheels, including rear springing (1951) and the streamlining kneeling position (1953). He then 'retired' to his motorcycle business in Staines, Middlesex, which specialised in Nortons, of course! Cyril Smith finally retired from racing in 1959 (still on Nortons), after a succession of expensive engine blow-ups. He was found dead in a hotel in Keswick, Cumbria, in November 1962.

Back in Britain, 1954 had seen a futuristic outfit appear from the workshops of Birmingham based Ernie Earles (of Earles fork fame). Its design represented an attempt to achieve the ideal of a sidecar outfit built as one clean, integral unit. The basis was a rectangular-shaped, cross-braced chassis

ERIC OLIVER

Englishman Eric Oliver was the world's first sidecar superstar - even though, when he won his four world titles (all on Norton-powered machinery) the phrase had yet to be coined.

Born in 1918, Oliver rode solo bikes before concentrating his efforts on three wheels following the Second World War. He is remembered for his never-give-in approach to racing and his great sportsmanship. He also ran a Norton dealership.

A tough, independent character, he paid great attention to every detail of his racing; studying other teams, practising his starts and racing techniques and not forgetting the mechanical preparation of his highly successful Norton machinery, on which he won countless races and no less than a quartet of World Championship crowns.

His first racing experiences came in pre-war days and in 1937 he competed in the Isle of Man TT, as he did the following year in both the Senior and Junior events. His best solo performance in the Isle of Man came in 1948, on a Mark VIII KTT Velocette, when he finished eighth in the Junior race at an average speed of 76.94mph. (He also rode the same machine to come home in tenth position in the Senior TT that same year).

Already a member of the 'Continental Circus' by the time the first World Championship series was staged in 1949, Oliver and his passenger Denis (Jenks) Jenkinson won two of the three rounds on their dohc Manx Norton with Watsonian sidecar. The pairing of Oliver and Jenkinson won two of the three rounds (Switzerland and Belgium) and came fifth in the final round in Italy.

In 1950, this time with Italian Lorenzo Dobelli as ballast, Oliver thwarted a serious challenge from Gilera (who had won the final round in 1949). Dobelli was again the passenger when Oliver gained his third consecutive title in 1951 and might have done so again the following year, but an accident in France, combined with a retirement through a sidecar wheel problem, cost him dearly.

In 1953, with new partner Stan Dibben, Oliver became champion for the fourth and final time. Although he won the first Sidecar TT in the 1920s, in 1954 he finally had to give way to the additional power output of the factory-entered BMW twins. He retired the following year - although making a famous comeback with a road-going Dominator outfit in 1958 (passengered by Pat Wise) before retiring again, this time for good, to concentrate on his bike business. Eric Oliver died in 1981 after suffering heart problems.

Eric Oliver's 500 Norton sidecar outfit, 1951. A new FIM ruling that year meant that all machines were of 500cc capacity instead of 600cc as in the past. Oliver's Norton had a works type dohc engine in a Featherbed frame with leading axle telescopic forks.

Billown Circuit, Isle of Man; Charlie Freeman (1) on his way to victory in the 1963 Southern 100 race narrowly leads Nigel Mead's Triumph.

Interesting Manx-powered Earles three-wheeler, BMCRC Trophy Day, Silverstone 7th July 1956. And below, showing the former BSA off-road star Bill Nicholson (left) working on the machine

of all-welded construction in Reynolds 531 tubing. The massive 2¼-inch diameter steering head tube was supported by hoop-shaped members and carried a specially strengthened Earles pivoted front fork. Power came from a 1948 Manx engine with Norton gearbox and hubs. Constructed from magnesium alloy sheet, the streamlined body was divided into two portions, one front and one rear. The front section, though made up from several parts, formed a one-piece dual nose, which gave it the appearance of a sports car from the front. The edges of the cowling were wrapped around the chassis tubes and welded where necessary. It was also envisaged that a road-going version (powered by a different engine) would be able to accommodate the driver and two passengers sitting three abreast. But neither the racing nor the road version ever entered production.

Later in 1956 there appeared another Earles three-wheeler. This time the appearance was even more car-like, with a one-piece alloy body. But like the earlier example it never achieved success. The press reported it would be used in that year's TT. However, the intended driver, Bill Boddice, used his conventional Norton/Watsonian outfit to score a well-earned third place in spite of being troubled by a faltering fuel supply in the closing stages. Second place went to Pip Harris, also Norton-powered. The previous year had seen a reverse of these positions, with Boddice taking second and Harris (using a Matchless G45 engine) third. On the continent the leading Norton partnership was that of Frenchman Jacques Drion and the German lass Inge Stoll - they finished fourth in the 1955 World Championship, while Pip Harris added second places to his Isle of Man runner-up spot in Belgium, Ulster and Italy to score an excellent third place in the 1956 series. 1957 was Jackie Beeton's year, with a fourth in the TT and second in Holland to finish fourth overall in the Championship, a feat he repeated the following year by scoring a superb third in the Island and a fifth in Belgium. After that no Norton was to finish in the top five positions of the World Championship table again. Although drivers such as Boddice, Charlie Freeman (third in the 1960 TT) and Len Wells (fourth in the 1960 TT) continued to wave the Norton flag, as the 1960s progressed, anyone without a BMW was in a different league and increasingly the role of the Manx Norton-engined three-wheeler was relegated to appearances at British short-circuit events. And so it remained, until with the 500cc class being largely replaced at national level by the 750cc twins, the sight and sound of a single-cylinder double-knocker Norton-powered sidecar outfit passed into history.

Bill Boddice (left) with passenger Bill Storr finished a superb second in the 1955 TT. The youngster is Bill Boddice's son Mick, later to become a sidecar star in his own right.

Silverstone, June 1961, and a pair of Norton outfits round Abbey Curve at high speed. Number 69 is veteran Jackie Beeton.

Birmingham's Bill Boddice; in action at Mallory Park during 1961, just one of the famous sidecar names who campaigned Norton singles.

7 **Four Wheels**

Castle Combe, Wiltshire. Formula 3 cars at the start, circa mid 1950s. Besides the Manx engine the other favourite power unit was the ohv JAP single.

Five hundred cc car racing was born in the immediate postwar era, a direct descendant of the earlier cyclecar movement, which used machines such as the GN and Morgan three-wheelers. Motorcycle engines had been a source of attraction, in view of their simplicity and lower cost compared to the expensive purpose-built multi-cylinder power units employed in conventional four-wheel racing cars. The formation of the 500 Club came directly from a meeting organised by the Bristol Aeroplane Company's Motor Sports Club in December 1945, the original idea being that, in the words of *The Autocar* Sports Editor Sammy Davis, 'real sport and racing could be had with 500cc engined cars, probably costing less than £100 to build, and capable of speeds up to 90mph!'

The first of the new breed of car was powered by JAP, HRD-Vincent, Rudge, Triumph and push-rod Norton engines. Builders included Colin Strang, Frank Bacon, Wing Commander Frank Aitkins, Charles and John Cooper and Adrian Butler. One of the earliest race meetings for the new club was held on Lord Hesketh's Towcester estate after the 'official' meeting at the nearby Silverstone circuit had to be abandoned because the owners decided not to allow the 500cc drivers to race there!

The following year, 1948, saw the 500 Club's place in motor racing considerably strengthened by the appearance of a large number of new drivers and cars. The most famous combination was that of Stirling Moss and Cooper. That year also saw the formation of the 500 Club of Ireland, and record-breaking performances at Shelsley Walsh and Prescott hill climb venues.

Although Moss's Cooper was JAP-powered, the Cooper company later offered a Norton version. The problem here was that, unlike JAP, the Bracebridge Street factory refused to sell separate engine assemblies. This meant that any driver who wished to use one of the overhead camshaft Norton singles either had to purchase a second-hand unit or buy a complete new motorcycle and dispose of the frame. But as the class progressed it soon became evident that although it was a much more costly option, if one wished to win races, the double-knocker Norton was most definitely essential. Only on short, twisty circuits could the push-rod units such as the JAP score on superior low-down

Jim Russell with the winner's trophy, Stirling Moss was second. The Daily Telegraph International Trophy, Brands Hatch, 2nd August 1954. Over a hundred thousand spectators attended this blue riband of Formula 3 racing.

performance. From 1948 onwards the National Formula for 500cc cars was: Engines - un-supercharged up to 500cc; Fuel - any type; Fuel tanks - any capacity; Gearbox - with or without reverse; Bodywork - optional, but desirable; Minimum weight - 500lb unladen wet weight.

In 1949 the class became even more popular, with events at Goodwood, Lulsgate (Bristol), Brough, Blandford and Silverstone. British drivers also competed on the continent, at Brussels and Zandvoort. BMW offered a tuned version of its push-rod flat twin engine for sale to 500cc car owners, but compared to the Norton this was easily outclassed, as were a number of other continental units, including the Belgian FN single.

At a meeting of the 500 Club Committee in London during January 1950, the category became known as Formula Three, a reduction in weight to 440lb was permitted and that year 500cc racing became recognised as an International Formula. The year 1950 also witnessed the first races for 500cc cars at Brands Hatch, quickly destined to become the main venue for the class in Britain. November of that year saw a Norton-powered Kieft car driven by Moss, Gregory and Neil establish a number of new speed records at the French Montlhéry track. Both 350cc and 500cc double-knocker Norton engines were used, tuned by Steve Lancefield. The records ranged from 50 to 200 kilometres, and in the 350cc class the speeds were between 77 and 80mph. In the 500cc class the Bridgend-built Kieft averaged 91.34mph for the 200 miles. Strangely, the car turned in lower speeds over the shorter distances, including the 50 miles at 90.63mph.

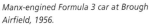

Manx-engined Formula 3 car at Brough Airfield, 1956.

Formula 3 car action at Brands Hatch, April 1955. Note selection of cars in the background.

In 1951 the very first Grand Prix for 500cc cars was staged, the Grand Prix of the Duchy of Luxembourg. Attracting a class entry from all over Europe, the race was dominated by British drivers and won by Alan Brown driving a Francis Beart-tuned Cooper-Norton. Brown was also British 500 Club Champion that year. The Autosport British National 500cc Driver's Championship went to Eric Brandon with a Lancefield-tuned Cooper-Norton.

In International Formula Three events in 1951, the new Kieft-Norton of Stirling Moss took the Daily Telegraph International Trophy race at record speed at Goodwood. Not only this, Moss also proved unbeatable at Silverstone in the event preceding the British Grand Prix. He also put up outstanding performances at Zandvoort and in the ultra-difficult German Freiburg hill climb.

To meet the Kieft challenge for 1952, Cooper introduced a new car, the Mark VI. This was much lighter than before and employed a tubular chassis. That year Kieft fielded a team of five works drivers, including Moss. Other British 500 cars of the era included Arnott, Revis, Emeryson (with front wheel drive), Arengo, Marwyn, Bond (of three-wheeler fame, whose 500 lacked any suspension), Trimax, CFS, JBS and JP (Joe Potts, see Chapter 12).

1952 also saw the first race of the man who was subsequently to become synonymous with the class, Jim Russell. A former RAF Flight Sergeant during the war, Russell began racing with a Cooper-JAP Mark VI. In his first race, at Snetterton, on 26th June, he finished next to last. Even so, the 32-year-old had gained valuable experience and picked up a number of useful tips from the man who was to become 1952 and 1953 Formula Three Champion, Don Parker, driving a Lancefield-tuned Kieft-Norton.

Future champion Jim Russell (third from left) unloads his brand-new Norton-powered Cooper Mark VIII at his Downham Market, Norfolk, base in late 1953.

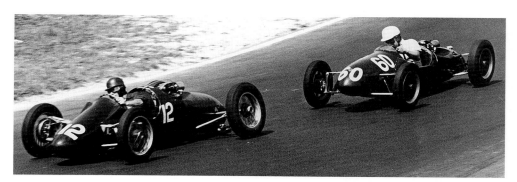

1953 saw Jim Russell start the season with a JAP engine. But in July the Downham Market, Norfolk, garage proprietor journeyed down to the South Norwood workshop of London tuner Steve Lancefield and purchased a new Norton engine 'for £350 - the carb was extra'. His first victory with the new engine came the following month, when he took the chequered flag at his local Snetterton circuit on August Bank Holiday Monday. Then, at the end of 1953, Jim Russell bought a new Cooper Mark VIII, to which was fitted the Lancefield Norton double-knocker, 30M, 499cc Manx engine.

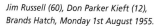

Elsewhere in 1953, the latest brainchild of the Ulsterman Rex McCandless's had been born. This was a 500cc racing car, but, as might be expected of the man who had conceived the Featherbed Norton frame, it was a car of unusual conception. Total height was little more than that of the wheels, which had light-alloy rims and were recessed within the aerodynamic light-alloy body. This material was chosen for its low weight. The wheels had no brakes, but instead two disc brakes operated on the transmission. Four-wheel drive was employed. But most unorthodox of all was the control layout, which closely resembled that of a motorcycle. A handlebar controlled the front wheels. A twistgrip throttle was on the right and a hand-operated clutch on the left. Gearchange and brakes were foot-operated. Power was provided by a suitably tuned Manx engine. But although fast, the car proved temperamental and following McCandless's split with the Norton factory later that year, the concept was

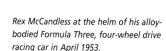

Rex McCandless at the helm of his alloy-bodied Formula Three, four-wheel drive racing car in April 1953.

never developed to its full potential. Without doubt had McCandless pushed ahead with its development, it would probably have been a serious challenge to the established four-wheel brigade.

Back to the Formula Three Championship. At the beginning of 1954 a dispute erupted over an oil contract between Steve Lancefield and his top driver Don Parker. Jim Russell decided to make another visit to the Lancefield emporium, this time to ask if he could replace works driver Parker. But Lancefield's reply was short and to the point: 'No!' However, undaunted, Jim Russell set about proving that he deserved serious consideration. Making his first ever appearance at Silverstone for the Daily Express International Trophy meeting, he distinguished himself by finishing a notable third behind Stirling Moss and Les Leston, both in faster cars, as Russell was still using his original standard Norton engine purchased from Lancefield the year before.

ECURIE RICHMOND

For one season, 1951, a single team dominated the 500cc international car racing scene, Ecurie Richmond. This was the joint venture of three men; Jimmy Richmond, a 22 stone civil engineering contractor from near Retford, Nottinghamshire; and the two team drivers Eric Brandon and Alan Brown.

Eric Brandon was already something of an old-hand in 500cc racing, having helped constructor John Cooper (the two being boyhood friends) to create the original Cooper 500, back in 1946. Since then he had driven Coopers consistently in all sorts of competition. Brandon was then (1951) 31 years of age, living in Surbiton, Surrey and was a director of an electrical company.

Alan Brown working on his car (chassis No.7) in an unknown Paddock in 1951. A good shot of the engine which looks like an early long-stroke. Probably England, note uniform in background.

Alan Brown's greying hairs belied the fact that he was the same age as his teammate. He had first come to the public's attention in 1949, when having spectated at 500cc events, he announced that he could do as well as most drivers, and acquired a Cooper to prove it.

Both Brandon and Brown (together with team manager Richmond) believed in a professional, colourful presentation, so not only were the Ecurie Richmond cars always immaculate, but each marked with an individual coloured nose-band and leather seat – the colour coding also extended to the drivers overalls! Brandon having red, whilst

Steve Lancefield (in specs) and Alfred Moss (Stirling's Dad) in duffle coat. The big chap with back to camera is team boss Jimmy Richmond. Eric's wife Sheila is cleaning the nose of the car.

Brown had blue. The Richmond Cooper MkV's were otherwise left unpainted (to save weight!) and their aluminium bodies shone like the sun.

The preparation of the Team Ecurie Cooper-Nortons was taken care of by Michael (Ginger) Devlin (still alive in Brixham, Devon) and Freddy Sirkett. Eric Brandon's wife, Sheila was the team's secretary. The basis of the Richmond team was an agreed three-way partnership, having at its disposal for the 1951 season, three Cooper MkV cars, five dohc Manx engines, and a dozen gearbox and clutch assemblies. If all this was not enough, the organisation also carried a large stock of consumable spare parts – such as piston rings, bearings, gaskets, spark plugs and tyres in their Bedford van. By standards of the time, this was a very well organised outfit.

Engine tuning was left to the specialists; Brown using Francis Beart and Brandon Steve Lancefield. Both of these notable Norton engine tuners (see chapter 12) being able to provide Ecurie Richmond with both speed and reliability. In other words championship

material, but of course you still had to drive the cars.

A piece of Ecurie Richmond survives to the present day, thanks to enthusiastic 500 Owners Association member, Pete Wright.

Pete, a 54 year-old retired civil engineer now living near Minehead, Somerset began his own racing career with a 1,071cc Mini Cooper-engined Terrapin single-seater in July 1981.

Then in February 1982, he purchased an engine-less Cooper, which upon checking surviving Cooper Car records revealed that this was Alan Brown's 1951 Mark V car; albeit with the Manx engine missing.

After competing in a number of hillclimbs and sprints the car was badly damaged whilst competing in Scotland during 1984, using a JAP engine. A long-winded rebuild ensued, after which yet more hillclimbs (having moved from Northampton to his present home), saw another restoration in the mid 1990s. In 1998 Pete Wright was invited to the first Goodwood Festival meeting, where high interest in his and other 500cc cars ensued. This led in 2000 to the car being driven by Nick Leston (son of Les) to a 5th at the same meeting.

Ginger Devlin (kneeling) and Freddy Sirkett working on Alan Brown's car in the paddock prior to the Luxembourg Grand Prix, May 3rd 1951, Ecurie Richmond's transporter alongside, Brandon's car with it's tail up in foreground.

The ex Alan Brown's Team Ecurie Richmond Cooper Mk V now owned by 500 Owners Association member, Pete Wright.

ECURIE RICHMOND SUCCESSES IN 1951

26th March **Goodwood International**
Brandon 2nd and fastest lap

8th April **Brands Hatch**
Race 1: Brandon 2nd (1st in heat); Brown 2nd (3rd in heat)
Championship race: Brandon 1st (lap record); Brown 3rd

21st April **Brands Hatch**
Race 1: Brown 2nd (1st in heat); Brandon 3rd (1st in heat)
Championship race: Brandon 1st; Brown 3rd. Both drivers broke lap record.

3rd May **Luxembourg Grand Prix**
Brown 1st (3rd in heat)

5th May **Silverstone International**
Brandon 1st (fastest lap); Brown 2nd

12th May **Brands Hatch International**
Race 1: Brandon 1st; Brown 2nd
Championship race: Brown 2nd

14th May **Goodwood International**
Brown 2nd (1st in heat); Brandon 5th (1st in heat).

26th May **Boreham**
Brandon 1st (1st in heat)
Lap record

24th June **Draguignan International**
Brown 1st (1st in heat); Brandon 2nd (1st in heat)
Lap record (Brandon)

29th June **Boreham**
Brandon 1st (4th in heat); Brown 2nd (1st in heat)

14th July **Silverstone**
Brandon 5th; Brown 6th

29th July **Nürburgring**
Brandon 1st; Brown 2nd
Lap record (Brandon)

9th September **Grenzlandrennen**
Brown 1st; Brandon 2nd

21st October **Madrid**
Brandon 1st

Goodwood International May 14th 1951. Alan Brown coming back into the paddock with Curly Dryden hitching a lift. Brown finished second to Stirling Moss (in his new Kieft).

As if to prove that his Silverstone performance was no flash in the pan, Russell and his Cooper Norton were up amongst the leaders yet again during a meeting held on the new Aintree circuit a week later. Although Moss won the race, at 70.92mph, the Norfolk driver was all set to take second after a race-long duel with rivals Reg Bicknell and Don Parker, until an unlucky spin on the last corner but one, of the 30-mile race, put Parker in front. Russell made a determined bid to recover the lead, and the two cars crossed the line side by side, with the Kieft's nose inches in front.

Stirling Moss, Jim Russell and the editor of the Daily Telegraph, Brands Hatch, 2nd August 1954.

After the Aintree performance Steve Lancefield finally agreed to provide some 'official' support. This was in time for a specially tuned Lancefield engine to be in his car for the Daily Telegraph Trophy at Brands Hatch on 2nd August, 1954. It was Bank Holiday Monday and the Blue Riband event of the 500cc racing calendar. Everyone of the top stars was there, including the likes of Moss, Leston and Parker. Right from the start the 100,000 crowd witnessed a tremendous duel between Moss and Russell. For lap after lap the pair pulled farther and farther away from the rest of the field. It was a battle of wills between the two leaders, with Russell leading Moss throughout to take the chequered flag, proving his right to be ranked with the very top drivers not only in his class but also in motor racing as a whole. A superb performance from someone who had only started racing a mere two years before!

From that day onwards Jim Russell was never to look back. Amongst his successes in the Formula Three class were winning the Daily Telegraph Trophy four years running, 1954, 1955, 1956 and 1957 (no trophy after 1956, as he had won it outright after his third win), the Autosport National Formula Three Championship in 1955, 1956 and 1957 and numerous other wins and lap records throughout Britain and Europe, to make him the uncrowned king of 500cc racing.

From 1955 onwards he was an official works driver for Cooper, who, besides Formula Three, provided the Downham Market driver with various other racing and sports cars. But as regards the Norton engine that he used exclusively in his Formula Three car from mid-1953 onwards, he is the first to acknowledge the work of tuner Steve Lancefield. Jim Russell commented recently: 'His (Lancefield's) workshop was like going into a doctor's surgery - spotless.' Unlike some stars, this man appreciates the work of others. Russell's team-mate in the Cooper team was the late Ivor Bueb, with whom he enjoyed a number of close-fought races over the years. Besides those already mentioned, other legendary Formula Three drivers included Bob Gerard, Stuart Lewis-Evans and George Wicken.

In all his five-year-long association with Lancefield, Jim Russell only had one serious engine problem, a defective oil pump while racing at Ingleston in Scotland. His Scottish hosts were eager for the Formula Three Champion to race, so in an attempt to cure the oil problem the engine was partly stripped. However, when Russell returned south and mentioned this to Lancefield he received a severe reprimand, Lancefield saying: 'You idiot, never, never let anyone see inside my engines again!' Even so, the two remained together, each respecting each other's abilities to such an extent that until 1990, when Lancefield died, they still kept in touch.

Opposite: Jim Russell, Brands Hatch, Daily Telegraph International Trophy, 2nd August 1954.

The start of the 500cc Formula Three race at the British Grand Prix, Aintree, on Saturday, 16th July 1955.

During May 1957, realising that many potentially good racing prospects could not make the grade because of the high costs involved, Jim Russell founded the world-famous Driver's School, which at its peak had branches all around the world. Several future World Champions were among its pupils. Towards the end of that year he came to the sad conclusion that interest in Formula Three racing was dwindling. 1958 saw him concentrate his efforts on Formula Two and the new Cooper Monaco 2-litre sports car.

His feelings about Formula Three were proved right in 1959 when the class was abandoned in favour of the new Formula Junior. But unlike its predecessor the new cars were powered by specially prepared 1,100cc units, usually Ford or BMC. The day of the Manx Norton on four wheels had come to an end. But for over a decade the double-knocker single had reigned supreme, quite simply no other 500cc engine could touch it in this form of racing. Of the earlier long-stroke design (later short-stroke versions not being suitable) and running on alcohol ('dope') they could reach 7,800rpm. A properly prepared engine could complete a season's racing with next to no spares required, despite the fact that their output on 'dope' was higher than the original petrol figure. And so one of the interesting periods of post-war automobile racing came to an end. But what of Jim Russell, the man who had dominated his branch of the sport in an equally commanding way to multi-sidecar world champion Eric Oliver? His racing career came to an abrupt end on 20th June, 1959, while holding ninth place (and leading his class) in the Le Mans 24 Hours race, when his 2-litre Cooper was involved in a serious accident which left him on crutches for two years, after breaking several bones and suffering severe burns. Determination not only saw him make a complete recovery, allowing him to race (and win at a few meetings in 1961), but also settle back into a successful business career after his racing days were over. He celebrated his 80th birthday in 2000.

Opposite: eventual winner Jim Russell (60) follows Les Leston during the Daily Telegraph International Trophy race at Brands Hatch on Monday 1st August 1955.

"THAT NORTON ENGINE"

Interview with Steve Lancefield by Oliver Sear, circa 1955.

Even top tuner Steve Lancefield could be a practical joker at times... with the world's biggest megaphone at Mallory Park, 1956.

Steve Lancefield, ace tuner and scientist of Motor Racing, is acknowledged by experts, to be in the forefront of the world's most brilliant engine tuners and designers. Quiet and unassuming in manner, his corduroy jacket and ready smile are to be seen in the motor racing paddocks at any circuit where motor cycles are ridden and Formula III cars raced.

We are fortunate to be able to publish an interview with this famous motor racing personality, so without much ado, let us start firing questions at you Steve and see if we can extract some of your secrets as to why your engines seem to give a little more steam than anyone else's.

Steve - Well Oliver. I don't suppose you will extract many secrets from me, I will, however, try to answer your questions fairly.

Q - Can you start by giving me a brief history of the famous Norton engine. When was it first designed and by whom? When was the twin cam head and short stroke first introduced?

A - The first 500cc overhead camshaft/rocker engine raced by Nortons in 1927 was designed by Walter

A Cooper Norton, Daily Telegraph International Trophy, Brands Hatch.

Moore. He left Nortons to go to NSU's and in 1930 the Bracebridge Street concern brought out a new design of overhead camshaft engine which was basically the fore-runner of probably the most outstanding and successful single-cylinder engine series of all time. This was designed by Arthur Carroll, a young and brilliant designer, whom I knew well and greatly admired - sad to relate he met an untimely death as a result of a road accident. The famous "International" and "Manx" engines were offsprings of this design up to 1949, using a bore and stroke of 79mm x 100mm later altered to 79.62mm x 100mm on the "Manx" engines with the introduction of the "square" type cylinder head.

In 1935/36 the Works raced an ohc Rockerbox using short tappets to operate the valves - 1938 saw the first of the "narrow" crankcase engines with double camshaft cambox and a bore and stroke of 52mm x 94.3mm the latest of which used in 1954 an over-square bore and stroke of 94mm x 78.4mm. Similar "Featherbed" engines now in ''Manx'' machines having a slightly over-square bore and stroke, ie, 86mm x 85.62mm.

Incidentally and for the record Joe Craig, who had a garage business in Ballymena, Northern Ireland, joined Nortons as development engineer in 1929.

Q - You are, I believe, brother-in-law to the famous TT rider, Harold Daniell. Have you yourself ever been associated with the Norton Works Team?

A - Yes, HLD is my brother-in-law and naturally I know him very well - he rode my 500 Norton both before and after the war with conspicuous success. I consider that as a rider he was in a class of his own and his 91mph lap in the Island in the 1938 TT on the Works' Norton was an achievement few could have equalled. Clare, his sister, and I were married during the "Bomb and Blitz" days and are now in our 15th year.

After the 1948 racing season I was invited by Gilbert Smith, Managing Director of Norton Motors, to take over the Works Team during 1949 with Johnny Lockett, Harold Daniell and Artie Bell as riders. Successes were not easy

At Snetterton in April 1954, Les Leston leads Jim Russell over the line to win by a few yards. Both are at the wheel of Cooper-Nortons.

Steve Lancefield and Jim Russell.

Jim Russell, with his Lancefield-tuned
Norton-Cooper, on the start line at the
International British Automobile Racing
Club meeting, Crystal Palace, Saturday,
30th July 1955. He won this event.

to come by, but we did kick-off by winning both classes in the NW 200, also the Senior TT, and were generally "about the place" in the rest of the Classic road races.

Q - In your view, do the Continental multies present a better tuning "base" than the short-stroke Norton engine?

A - As things are the multi has the edge on the single, but comparison between multies and singles always needs qualifying because their potentialities alter somewhat with the fuel permitted. Using hydrocarbons such as 80 octane petrol or petrol/Benzole the multi-cylinder engine has a distinct advantage over a single-cylinder of the same capacity, but if higher octane or alcohol fuels were permitted, I think the single would respond more favourably, particularly if the stroke/bore ratio is not overdone - a case of MEP (Mean Effective Pressure) versus RPM.

Q - Can you get as good a "Torque curve" from a single as a multi?

A - Whilst present short stroke engines are now very good at the lower as well as the top of the torque curve there is no doubt that the curve of a good multi-cylinder engine is more constant and useful longer.

Q - Are the automatic "rev restrictions" on a large single a drawback in obtaining maximum power? or do you think a short-stroke and large cylinder head compensate by offering "better breathing" and gas flow thus obtaining in a "usable" engine speed range, of say between 4,000 and 8,000rpm better BMEP?

A - I would not say that the rpm limitation of the larger masses of the single are "automatic" in restricting a potential increase in performance. It is as well to bear in mind the considerable increase in rpm and power of present engines as compared with those used pre-war and it would be fair to assume that with continued single-cylinder research and development this increase will continue, but whether it will approach, equal or better the performance of the multi is open to question. The use of a shortened stroke in conjunction with an appropriate cylinder head design, porting and valve lay-out does undoubtedly help to improve the power output but how far this will yield to still higher power also remains to be seen. There are of course many racing singles of today that give a useful torque curve ranging from 4-8,000rpm plus.

Q - In balancing the "top" and "bottom" end of the engine, would you say that the extra centrifugal forces placed on the bottom end, calling for stronger and heavier design with more friction and weight, outweighs the advantages of more r.p.m. at over say, 8,000rpm?

A - This is one of the major difficulties that designers have to face in both singles and multies, more particularly however in the case of a single in so much that with higher rpm and power output often an increase in strength is required - this may be a change in material, design or increase in section - the latter expedient bringing in its train once again the problem of inertias and loadings, factors inseparable from ever increasing rpm.

Q - I would like to take this imaginary engine which we have designed from your previous remarks and have a more detailed chat.

Valve gear. Do you hold the view that desmodromic valve operation is a "must" in future engine design, and the spring operation finished? It would seem to me that this is a logical development.

A - While in the academic sense the spring is looked upon as a most unmechanical device, much credit is due to valve spring manufacturers and engine designers that they have been able to achieve almost trouble free operation at the high rpm's used in some engines today. In view of the degree of reliability the Germans have obtained with desmodromic valve operation on the Mercedes it would appear that they have succeeded in achieving a satisfactory application and I believe that positive valve operation will be the "modus operandi" of future high output poppet valve engines.

Q - Would you have more than two valves per cylinder ? What are your views on the "rotary valve"?

The Hon. Mrs. Gerald Laselles presents the winning trophy to Jim Russell, Lancefield-tuned Norton-Cooper, Ibsley, Hampshire, 30th April, 1955.

Typical action in Formula Three (500cc) car racing; the venue is Snetterton in the early 1950s.

A - I would prefer two valves per cylinder where the bore size does not exceed 90mm - above this multi-valves would be considered.

There is no design of rotary or sleeve valve that I would entertain were I designing a new engine - as crude as the poppet valve operation is, it is still a very efficient and formidable competitor to any other form of valve in existence today.

Q - Do you on your engines alter the normal "cam-profile"? I imagine you have carried out innumerable experiments with valve timings.

A - Over many years of experimenting I have naturally modified the cams on my engines and of course tried every conceivable position of cam settings, all with the main object of improving "breathing" and volumetric efficiency, and all-in-all have found it necessary to compromise operationally and mechanically to obtain the best trouble free performance.

Q - Do you alter your degree of overlap for different fuels according to the "mass" of the mixture in the inlet pipe?

A - I have found no worth while gain in performance when varying the valve overlap one way or another whilst using different fuels.

Q - Do you use a "Sodium filled" exhaust valve in your Norton engines? If so, why?

A - Yes, most of the Norton engines I prepare are fitted with "Sodium" exhaust valves - it is open to question whether these are really necessary on such a well-cooled engine using alcohol, particularly as very good results have been obtained with engines using non-sodium valves. However, for what it is worth, the sodium valve is a shade lighter in weight than its solid counterpart and the use of this type of valve is on this score alone worthy of consideration.

When using hydrocarbon fuels, unhesitatingly - sodium-filled exhaust valves please!

Q - Do you favour the two-plug head? Do you think it gives more instantaneous burning?

A - The gain from using two plugs is very doubtful in a well ordered and designed cylinder head. It seems a queer thing to me to produce a cylinder head having reduced turbulence and swirl - two most important factors governing the rate of burning of the gas - and then try to off-set this deficiency by using more than one plug.

Some engines converted to two-plug operation are in direct contradiction to established internal combustion engine practice as evidenced by their "roughness" and tendency to detonate, conditions inherent with an incorrect and uncontrollable rate of pressure rise.

I am fully aware that the Italians and Germans have raced with success certain two-spark engines, but these engines were designed and developed with this type of ignition in view and not as a conversion or palliative.

Research has established that a single sparking plug in the centre of the cylinder head sphere is the most efficient position, and by necessary compromise the plug should be as near to this ideal as possible.

Q - Can we dwell for a moment or two on carburettors? You are the acknowledged master of the "Gas works."

Do you think the carburettor's racing days are numbered? I see Mercedes Benz use direct injection, on the surface this would appear ideal. How do you feel?

A - In spite of the fact that - at least on single cylinders - we are getting extremely good results with atmospheric carburettors I have been of the opinion for some considerable time that fuel injection will be the method of the future. It may take time to better the efficiency of present day carburettors; it is, however, encouraging that already a Norton D/C engine has been converted to fuel injection and tested with promising results.

A Cooper Norton 21st September, 1954, Dunholme, Lincolnshire. Number seven is Stirling Moss.

Russell winning the Daily Telegraph Trophy for the second time, Brands Hatch, Monday, 1st August, 1955.

Future development will determine whether direct injection into the combustion chamber is adopted, bearing in mind that Mercedes Benz are not yet completely "out of the wood" using this method.

Q - I suppose Bosch are years ahead of everyone else in the technique of direct injection. They were the pioneers after all. Apart from Diesel engines they pioneered its use in aircraft piston engines as well?

A - Yes, the Bosch concern unquestionably have a great deal of knowledge in the field of fuel injection and I doubt very much whether it can be matched by any other country or concern at present.

Q - Do you think the "injection piston" type carburettor; eg, Solex or Weber, has any great advantage over the Amal type?

A - I have always looked upon a design of carburettor using a piston to inject fuel at some phase or other as an admission that either the engine or the carburettor is not as good as it might be, and this method is used as a palliative - it certainly has no place in carburettors used in motor cycle racing.

Q - Do you reckon to get a similar natural action by the harmonic between choke and pipe length, setting up a pulsation action?

Jim Russell receiving the garlands of victory from the British Racing and Sports Car Club, Brands Hatch, Sunday 9th October 1955.

A - Depending upon a number of design factors irrespective of the type or make of carburettor there is a length/area of induction system that will give the best result - once again depending upon the rpm at which one requires the pressure wave to be of most benefit.

I have found some difficulty in matching up the theoretical requirement with those found most suitable by test on the road.

Q - Do you alter the shape of the inlet choke to give you a better "venturie" action on the jet?

A - Carburettor modifications I have made have always the same object in view; ie, to reduce losses to a minimum and ensure a stable fuel/air control. It is by no means necessary to have the smallest cross-sectional area over the main jet to obtain these.

Q - It was you, I think, on Don Parker's Kieft, who first sloped the engine backwards. Was this to assist the carburation, or another reason? If so, why and how? I see this is standard now on the new Coopers.

A - The Kieft of Don Parker was the first car to use the rearward inclined engine - three objects were in view - better carburation, improved cooling and oil scavenging from the sump. This system is the subject of a Patent and was fully printed up in "Motor Racing" and "The Motor Cycle." Briefly:

1. Carburation: When using a track-type carburettor it is possible to raise the fuel level substantially, thereby reducing the time lag and amount of work required to induce the fuel to flow from the jet.

2 Cooling: An increased "scrub" action takes place on fins lying at an angle to the air flow, which materially assist the cooling.

3. Oil scavenging on the Norton engine oil is collected and drawn from the sump in a small pocket at the rear of the crankcase. Leaning the engine backwards effectively lowers the sump pocket and suction pipe to the oil pump, thereby improving the dry sump design of the engine.

Q - Let us jump from one port to the other now and come back to fuels later.

A brief word on the "megaphone." What advantages do you derive?

A - A megaphone assists the action of the outgoing exhaust gases to create a useful pressure drop across the combustion chamber during valve overlap, thereby assisting the early part of the induction cycle - the rpm range depending upon the length and area of the exhaust pipe/megaphone.

Q - I suppose you cannot use a "trumpet" on a multi-cylinder "in line" motor where more than one exhaust leads into the same pipe?

A - Owing to the reverse pressure and sound waves in an exhaust pipe it is extremely doubtful whether a single megaphone fitted to a multi-pipe system would be of any practical value. Obviously all exhaust pipes should lead away from each cylinder independently and have the same volume and length whether fitted with a megaphone or not.

Q - Can you tell me briefly why the "harmonics" of pipe length and diameter are so important for extraction effect?

A - Briefly, the exhaust pipe length and diameter should be such that the reverse pressure/sound waves arrive at the exhaust valve after it has closed, hence the co-relation of rpm introducing a time element.

Opposite: Russell leading at Paddock Hill bend, Brands Hatch, 4th September 1955.

CYLINDER HEAD DESIGN

Q - Do you think the hemispherical head is the only one worth development? I liked the porting on Claude Hill's pre-war 2-litre Aston Martin single ohc engine very much. It gave you a big inlet valve over the piston, pushed the mixture into a pocket round the exhaust valve and exploded it there?

A - For high specific power output the hemispherical form of cylinder head is accepted as being the most efficient, a fact that has been well known and established in motor cycle racing engines for many, many years.

The cylinder head design and operation of the pre-war 2-litre Aston Martin engine you refer to would not be accepted today as good practice - the surface/volume ratio is excessive, the squish action of pushing the mixture into a pocket around the exhaust valve would be very inducive to detonation - it is a far better practice to keep the volume of gas at a minimum in the exhaust port/valve area and arrange for ignition to take place from as near the exhaust valve as possible so that the flame burns towards the cooler areas of the combustion chamber.

Q - You remarked to me a few days ago that you would have to write several pages on piston design to give us any real gen. However, can you tell me briefly what kind of piston you recommend for a "dope" or "petrol" motor, number of rings, clearances, etc?

A - It is, of course, not possible to disclose all the details on these piston modifications for obvious reasons. Briefly the ring layout follows standard practice of two compression and one oil control ring, a reduction in weight where possible with safety including a slight shortening of the piston skirt and relieving the sides of the thrust faces.

Apart from ensuring that the valve cut-aways avoid contact with the valves at maximum rpm the shape of the piston crown has, in addition to other factors, also a big bearing on two very important desirables:

1. Breathing.

2. Turbulence.

It is by compromising of these two requirements in conjunction with the compression ratio required that the ultimate shape of the piston crown is determined.

Although surface volume-ratio does enter into the shape of the piston flame area I feel that the emphasis usually laid on this aspect is very much overdone.

Q - Do you prefer steel or alloy rods?

A - Unhesitatingly steel rods - they are not so prone to premature fatigue and when well designed, have a low weight and can be used in a smaller compass.

It is of interest that I know of 250cc racing engines using alloy rods which are heavier than the steel ones fitted in the Norton 500 Manx engine!

Q - Now for the bearings. Roller or plain. I know there is a lot to be said for both, depending on the general design. On a racing "in line" multi would you like to see a main between each cylinder?

A - On an in-line multi, consideration would be given to a roller set up for the crankpin bearings, although I realise that such must necessarily be somewhat difficult to design but it has been done successfully and with very good results. I think a main bearing between each cylinder would be considered essential.

Q - We come now to what I believe is one of your pet hobby horses, oil. I believe you stick to vegetable base oils, you feel strongly about this I know, can you tell me why?

Jim Russell (28) and Ivor Bueb (27), Paddock Hill bend, Brands Hatch, Sunday, 9th October 1955. One point separated the two for the British Championship, Jim's victory ensured the title.

Opposite: Cooper Mark VIII Formula Three – the top cars (like this one) were all Norton powered.

Jim Russell (28), Ivor Bueb (27) and Cliff
Allison (34) all in Norton engined
Coopers, Crystal Palace, Saturday, 30th
July 1955.

Race winner Jim Russell first
international meeting at Snetterton,
Saturday, 13th August 1954.

A - Yes, I consider essential a vegetable oil of the castor base type for single-cylinder racing engines with their very high surface rubbing speeds and unit loadings - also its ability to resist sustained high temperature, and conduct unwanted heat away from the engine internals is an important asset. It is an established fact that such oils have a higher film strength and resist rupture of the boundary layer to a degree greater than the best mineral oils, particularly under adverse operating conditions. I consider the slight loss of power due to its viscous nature more than offset by the increased safety factor that this type of oil will sustain. In such engines in which I am concerned the new and rather expensive castor base compounded oils are undoubtedly the last word in modern racing engine lubrication.

For the record - Mercedes use a castor base oil in their F1 engines.

Q - What about Colloidal Graphite? I have always fancied its use and I cannot understand why it is never used. It has such excellent lubricating properties under heat and pressure.

A - In the past when the science of oil refining and lubrication was not so well understood as it is today undoubtedly Colloidal Graphite did a good job, but with modern methods of oil manufacture the benefit of Colloidal Graphite has been offset somewhat, although I believe it is still entitled to a place in some spheres of lubrication - such as in a new engine.

Q - Now another question and probably the most important from your angle. I have heard it said that you are the "Chemist of Motor Racing." Can you give me a word or two on fuels? I see oxygen-bearing fuels are banned in Formula III. Do you agree with this policy (for major meetings anyway). I appreciate the expense but for sheer power output I suppose it is essential. What sort of proportion of other fuels do you recommend?

A - In view of the very real fire danger and high cost of Nitro Methane I am in complete agreement with it being outlawed in Formula III racing, furthermore it contributed nothing whatsoever to improving the design of

Opposite: British Racing and Sports Car
Club, Brands Hatch, Sunday
9th October 1955. Steve Lancefield is to
the far right of the photograph.

Jim Russell, Brands Hatch 1954.

engines other than making it necessary to take steps to strengthen some components to cope with the increase of power which really came from the use of this unique oxygen-generating substance. I would like to add that I found it extremely interesting during the short period it was being used in my engine.

Regarding other types of fuels I prefer to prepare engines to use the best allowed by the regulations rather than modify a fuel to suit the engine.

Fuels used in Formula III - other than Nitro Methane - are in the main of the 94/6 Methanol-Acetone blend. It is of course possible to use other compounded fuels - some rather complex and expensive - but I have purposely avoided these, as in some instance, a different technique of engine build and tuning is required, also some are inclined to be unstable in use and need expert attention. All-in-all, for the little extra that can be obtained from such fuels I do not think their use in Formula III is justified.

My choice has been for fuels having a fairly wide latitude of operational vagaries - simplicity and freedom from trouble is very high on my list of MUSTS.

A WORD OF WARNING - It is not generally known that Methanols are toxic and classed as an Industrial Hazard - both by handling as a liquid or inhaling as vapour.

Q - Last Question. I do not suppose you can answer this one. Why is it that the vast experience acquired in designing and tuning un-supercharged "motor cycle-type" engines has not been utilised in the design of a Grand Prix engine (so it would seem). Presuming you are getting around 60bhp from your 500, not an unreasonable figure, yet over 250 from a 2¹/₂ litre GP engine is considered almost incredible, in this country anyway?

A - This question has often cropped up during the many talks I give from time to time. I feel that I would be very disappointed if I could not obtain something approaching 60bhp per half-litre irrespective of the engine size with an unrestricted fuel, although one must realise that fuel consumption is a very important factor in Grand Prix Racing and a compromise may have to be made. From current engines one would deduce that the approach of the GP engine designers to their problems is somewhat different from those of Motor Cycle technicians who can claim a higher specific output per litre unblown than any other sphere in the world of internal combustion engines.

Thank you very much Steve for answering all my questions, I would just like to remind readers that Jim Russell's engine is prepared by you, and that Jim attributes a great deal of his success to you, and your meticulous preparation, you both richly deserve the success you have had, best of luck for the future.

Eighth RAC British Grand Prix, Aintree, Saturday 16th July 1955.

8 Joe Craig - Wizard of Tune

Joe Craig was born in the town of Ballymena, near Belfast, Northern Ireland, on 11th January, 1898. This Ulsterman could never have imagined that upon his death some 59 years later he would be acclaimed by motorcycle enthusiasts everywhere as the 'Greatest Racing Team Manager the World Has Ever Known' (as *The Motor Cycle* called him in their 14th March, 1957 issue), after guiding the Norton racing team to a glittering array of successes for almost 30 years.

All this was very much in the future when he began his apprenticeship in a local garage, dealing almost exclusively with cars. Soon afterwards he bought his first motorcycle, a side-valve Model 16 Norton, with which he competed regularly in local hill climbs and on the Magilligan Strand. His interest in two wheels had developed almost overnight - resulting from the chance purchase of a copy of *The Motor Cycle* describing the Isle of Man TT races. Seeing photographs of the stars of the era, men such as Tommy de la Hay and Duggie Brown, provided the initial spark that fired his interest. Then came the first Ulster Grand Prix, staged in 1922. Joe Craig chose to spectate rather than compete, fearing that his lightened and tuned side-valve would not last the distance. But the following

Later to become Norton's race supremo, Joe Craig sits astride his Model 18, after taking victory in the over 500cc race at the 1926 Ulster Grand Prix.

year he entered the event on a borrowed overhead valve Model 18 Norton. The race was a handicap then, and the newcomer was given a handsome time allowance. Craig won the 600cc class, averaging 69.99mph, partly, it must be said, because of the retirement of the two leading riders, but the next year he won again to prove that his debut victory had not been a flash in the pan.

In 1924 he rode another Model 18 in the Senior TT, but a fuel leak on the last lap dropped him from sixth down to 12th place. In preparation for the Ulster Grand Prix that year he modified the Norton's exhaust valve timing to achieve better scavenging and cooler running. And he had the satisfaction of not only completing the distance but also winning his native Grand Prix for the second time. Results like this could not go unnoticed and he was rewarded by joining the official Norton team for the 1925 season. The Bracebridge Street squad included Alec Bennett and Jimmy Simpson - he was in famous company. But even though Craig scored a hat-trick by taking victory in the 1925 Ulster Grand Prix, won the over-500cc race in 1926, and had considerable success in continental events, it was after he stopped racing that his fame grew. Joe Craig's last race was the 1929 350cc Ulster Grand Prix, in which he set a record lap before retiring. Thereafter he became the high priest of tune at the Bracebridge Street works with responsibility for the Norton race effort.

It had been Craig's technical ability rather than his riding skill, as he freely admitted, that brought him his personal racing success. Right from the start of his racing career technical development of the machine meant a

With part of the 1951 works team, including Geoff Duke and Dickie Dale.

Norton record-breaking team at Montlhéry in 1949. Geoff Duke seated, behind him stands Artie Bell, winner of the 1947 Senior TT; in front is Joe Craig; second from right, Eric Oliver and wearing cap is Ron Watson, Watsonian's chief - Oliver used Watsonian sidecars.

great deal more to him than the mere pleasure of riding. One can but imagine, therefore, the thrill and excitement that Joe must have experienced when the first factory machine, for whose preparation he was responsible, won the Grand Prix of Europe at Barcelona at the end of 1929, ridden by Tim Hunt. From that time (except for the war years) the softly spoken Irishman with the prominent nose, jutting chin and stooped shoulders dominated European racing as no one else, not as a glamorous ace rider or even a brilliant designer, but as a tuner and development engineer and team boss. *The Motor Cycle* once described Craig's efforts thus: 'No other chief d'equipe has acquired a thousandth part of his renown. No other has been responsible for so many successes. No other has done more for British prestige in his own particular sphere.' The early fame achieved by the majority of the greats in racing during his reign, among them such names as Stanley Woods, Jimmie Guthrie, Harold Daniell, Freddie Frith and Geoff Duke, owed much to Joe Craig's engineering and team management skill.

Without any doubt road racing was Joe Craig's very life. He displayed a dedicated purpose that very, very few men could muster - and don't forget, this was over a time span of many years, not days, or even months! But it has to be said that this was also instrumental in seriously affecting the development of Norton's standard production models. The single-cylinder engine with which he had achieved the vast array of successes was often

At the TT in 1953, Joe Craig and Jack Brett discuss a technical point.

referred to by the great man in his lighter moments as 'the design of 1930 brought up to date'. This statement was in recognition of the major redesign carried out by Arthur Carroll during that period from the original overhead camshaft engine conceived by Walter Moore some three years earlier. Ironically Carroll died in a road accident in 1935, the very same way in which Craig was to ultimately pass on, albeit much later. The engine underwent a vast array of changes under Craig. Year after year, with the apparent magic of a conjurer producing rabbits out of a hat, Joe Craig found more power from a unit, which many had long since thought at its peak development years before. Such wizardry earned him the title of 'Professor' among the racing fraternity. It was a title that he modestly disclaimed, but none the less fully deserved.

The second Mrs Craig, Mrs Van Wijngaarden, formerly of Rotterdam, whom he married on 20th December, 1955.

If anything the advancement of years, his fame already built, only seemed to intensify his purpose. He became increasingly a mixture of things; a hard taskmaster, a martinet even, yet having a warm side to his character that he could never quite conceal. He firmly believed that to do a job correctly, that task had to receive top priority and all his personal concentration. In other words, he was not someone who found delegation easy.

It was no secret that while, by virtue of his position as Technical Director of Norton, he was duty bound to take an interest in the development of the production models, he did so reluctantly. This illustrates just where his real interest lay, his beloved racing machines. This also explains why for considerable periods the development of the roadster stagnated, while during the very same years racing successes were being scored all over Europe. Bert Hopwood, in his book *Whatever Happened to the British Motorcycle Industry?*, openly accuses Craig of taking 90 per cent of the engineering budget for racing development, leaving a meagre 10 per cent for standard production.

In spite of seemingly selfish ways, his undoubted displeasure of riders who failed to perform, his skill at extracting ever more power and engine revolutions from a given engine, he was not the cold, calculating machine that many considered him to be. He could, and often did, enjoy social gatherings, when many other lesser engineers were only happy in their work. Abroad during the classic racing season he displayed a shrewd knowledge and appreciation of good food and the local wine. Joe Craig was also someone who could inspire others and, perhaps most important of all, possessed an ability to carry through any theory until it either triumphed or was proved a failure, very important in a development engineer. And no doubt another reason why his association with the serious production side at the factory was difficult, to say the least.

When interviewed in the 30th December, 1937 issue of *The Motor Cycle* by 'Torrens' (Arthur Bourne), Craig was at pains to point out that the Norton race effort was very much a team effort and not the work of one man. And that 'whereas a dozen years ago Norton started to think about the races a couple of months beforehand, today no sooner is one racing season over than they are busy on the next'. 'Torrens' agreed with his statement, saying: 'There are many contrasts between these days and when I first visited the Norton factory nearly 14 years

ago. For instance, today that shop with the notice on the door about it being private and you are to keep out - in other words, the experimental department - has a floor area of well over 3,000 sq ft. Indeed, it is larger than certain motorcycle factories I have visited, and that is not including the smaller shop where engines are tested on the bench.' He also noted that, 'Today racing not only is research, but involves continuous research. At the Norton factory information on research is collected from anywhere - the Continent, the United States and at home.' So it is possible to appreciate that Joe Craig was in reality an outward thinking person, someone ready to take on board any worthwhile innovations, from whatever source, although it must be said that many would not agree with this statement.

All manner of technical sources were tapped. A steel manufacturer, for instance, developed a new alloy, and he wanted data arising from working conditions. Norton were prepared to try it out if it offered them possibilities - for their benefit and his. Joe Craig, therefore, was well used to co-operation. Again, not everyone who came into contact with him would agree. In fact, Joe Craig said during that interview, 'ideas come more from failures than successes'. He then proceeded to give an example of this. In 1934 there was no big-end trouble - no races had been lost owing to a faulty big-end or anything of that sort - but when the engines were stripped it was found that the big-end eye of the con-rod had become very slightly oval and no longer absolutely concentric with the outer race, or, if you prefer it, liner. This was rectified and in 1935, 1936 and 1937 the new-type big-end assembly had remained perfect. What was presumably causing a fractional loss of power had been detected and the necessary remedy applied.

The 1937 Senior TT had been won by Norton rider Freddie Frith, who had also raised the lap record to 90mph. The factory that year was using the new twin overhead camshaft cylinder head design that had first appeared in March 1936. In its original experimental form it not only had a couple of mechanical gremlins, which were rectified whilst it was still being bench tested, but the power output was precisely the same as the single overhead cam type. Thus, Joe Craig knew that without any development work the new design was equal to the old one. One of the first things for 1937 was, therefore, to develop this. So with the racing season (1936) over, there was time to try various cams. As a result of this work there was now offered more power and therefore a superior track performance, witnessed by the Isle of Man lap record. The 1938 racing season was to be Joe Craig's final one until the post-war years. As the storm clouds of war gathered, he moved first to BSA in 1939 and then to AMC, where he stayed until December 1946. It was during this period, in 1945, that the Institution of Automobile Engineers awarded him the Crompton Medal for his paper entitled Progress in Motor Cycle Engines With Some Notes On Combustion.

Joe Craig's return to Norton was greeted by the motorcycle press of the day with genuine enthusiasm - witness the following extract from 'On the Four Winds' in The Motor Cycle dated 26th December, 1946: 'Joe Craig, MSAE, MIAE, who was Norton team manager during the years in which Nortons had the most remarkable run of racing success in the history of the game, is going back to Bracebridge Street. Nortons announce that he is rejoining them on January 1st. His post? He has been appointed Technical Director to the company. In the past, when at Norton, Mr Craig concentrated almost entirely upon the racing side and his success as a development engineer was reflected in the way that year after year Nortons won nearly all the classic road races in which they competed, the unblown singles on many occasions beating blown twins. The future should be interesting...'

The period after Craig first rejoined Norton is related elsewhere in this book, but suffice it to say that the level of success gained at least equalled those glamorous pre-war days. But not all was joy. In the same year (1949) as the official World Championship road racing series came into being, his wife and he were involved in a road accident that August near Margate, Kent, in which Mrs Craig suffered fatal injuries. In fact, 1949 was none too happy a year for Norton, either, with only the sidecar crew of Eric Oliver and Denis Jenkinson winning a world title. In the solo classes Norton's only classic victory was in the Senior TT, where works rider Harold Daniell took his 'Garden Gate' Norton to victory.

1950 was to see the launch of the famous Featherbed models - and Geoff Duke - but still no world titles, except Oliver retaining his sidecar crown, and the Manufacturers' 500cc title. But if the first two years of the World Championships had been something of a disappointment, 1951 was just the reverse, with Geoff Duke becoming the first rider to score a double in the World Championships that same year on his 350cc and 500cc Norton singles. With Oliver once again taking the three-wheel crown, the Norton team had scored a fantastic treble. These were heady days indeed for Bracebridge Street and Joe Craig.

The following year, 1952, Duke easily retained the 350cc title, while Cyril Smith (still Norton mounted) replaced Oliver in the sidecar chase after the three-times champion suffered an accident in France. Although Norton teamster Reg Armstrong won the TT and German Grand Prix in the 500cc category, it was the Italian pairing of Umberto Masetti and the four-cylinder Gilera that took the title.

Realising that the Norton single was becoming outpaced by the Italian multies of Gilera and MV Agusta, Duke opted to ride the Arcore factory's four-cylinder models for 1953. And even though new Norton star Ray Amm rode like a demon, he could not stop either Guzzi (350cc) or Gilera (500cc) from taking the titles. Norton's only World Champions that year were the sidecar pairing of Eric Oliver and Stan Dibben. No one realised it at the time, but this was to prove Norton's last world title in any class, even though they took second in the 1954 350cc and 500cc classes (Amm). When Ray Amm finally left the British company at the end of 1954, Norton were all but out of racing, with only specially prepared production racers taking part in certain events thereafter.

Although various other projects were rumoured, nothing except a horizontal single and drawings of a four-cylinder bike ever appeared, and certainly none took the place of the factory's double-knocker singles.

At this time Craig was openly criticized as being too conservative for his loyalty to the single-cylinder four-stroke engine. But the truth is that following the AMC-Norton merger in 1953 there simply was not the finance to develop new designs.

The last real moment of glory for the Ulsterman came when three of his beloved singles, ridden by Hartle, Surtees and Brett, scored a one, two, three result in the non-Championship 1955 Swedish Grand Prix. Shortly after this Joe Craig announced his resignation with effect from the end of the year, and that he would be marrying Mrs Van Wijngaarden of Rotterdam on 20th December in Birmingham. Further, that he intended to settle abroad in the Netherlands and 'enjoy a rest'. However, he did add that he would not be retiring completely, but intended offering his services in a consultative capacity.

With the announcement of Joe Craig stepping down, Guzzi star Fergus Anderson, who was also a respected journalist, wrote the following in *The Motor Cycle*: 'An uncrowned king has abdicated. He was not king of a very great empire; in fact he governed a realm of only a few square yards in the middle of Birmingham. But if the territory over which he ruled was small he raised in it a healthy, efficient fighting machine and over a period of three decades he sallied forth to conquer a continent. On rare occasions he was repulsed. But when beaten he was never dishonoured, and the exploits of his armies will remain engraved in history.' Anderson's article concluded: 'Perhaps without this great witch-doctor the single will now be allowed to die a natural death. He kept it alive a very long time.'

The final chapter in the Joe Craig story came in early March 1957, when the car Mr and Mrs Craig were travelling in skidded and was in collision with another vehicle whilst on holiday near Landeck, Western Austria. Joe Craig died at the scene of the accident. At first it was reported that the fatal accident was caused by a heart attack. However, when the post-mortem was carried out it was found that while travelling over ice-bound roads the Craig car had hit the other vehicle, with the result that Joe Craig was thrown against the steering column, sustaining a broken rib, which pierced his heart. Mrs Craig suffered chest injuries from which she fully recovered.

In bright, sunny weather on Wednesday, 13th March, 1957, the funeral of Joe Craig took place at the Nieuw Eykendwyen cemetery, The Hague. A service in the chapel of the cemetery was conducted by an English clergyman. One of Joe's two sons (Desmond and Reg from his former marriage) spoke briefly at the graveside. Floral tributes from a vast number of British and European sources, private and industrial, flowed in, giving striking evidence of the esteem with which this great man was regarded. Among those in attendance, as well as his two sons, and one of his two daughters (the other was in Canada), were former Norton stars Geoff Duke, Harold Daniell, Jimmy Simpson and many other personalities. Mrs Craig, however, was still recovering from her injuries in an Austrian hospital. Besides the floral tributes there were many words of tribute. Here's just a sample; Graham Walker (former rider and then Editor of *Motor Cycling*): 'His like will not be seen again, for he was the last of a generation of rider-tuners and perhaps the only one who adapted himself successfully to modern conditions. Hail and farewell to a man who deserved well of his country, for by his unremitting labours he kept the Union Jack flying long after others would have seen it furled.'

Harold Daniell (winner of the 1938, 1947 and 1949 Senior TTs on Nortons): 'When Joe Craig retired from Norton the racing world lost a great figure. He had spent most of his life on engine development and those who knew him believed that after a short break he would return to the racing sphere. When I served under him as a factory rider, it was obvious that his remarkable results were achieved by steady and methodical development. Nothing was taken for granted and every improvement thoroughly tested before being accepted. He was quiet and unassuming and was never prepared to rest on his laurels. In defeat he was the first to congratulate the winner.'

And finally Geoff Duke: 'It was tragic to hear about the loss of a great friend just as I returned from South Africa. In 1948 Joe Craig was responsible for my start at Norton, which led ultimately to my life's ambition - a career in racing. Joe was a man with great knowledge of his chosen career. He possessed in full measure that great attribute which is so rare and yet so essential a characteristic of the successful development engineer - he had an open mind.'

If one man was responsible for the Norton racing legend, that man is, without doubt, Joe Craig, master development engineer and tuner.

Opposite: Norton race supremo Joe Craig studying one of the works engines on the Bracebridge Street factory's dynamometer.

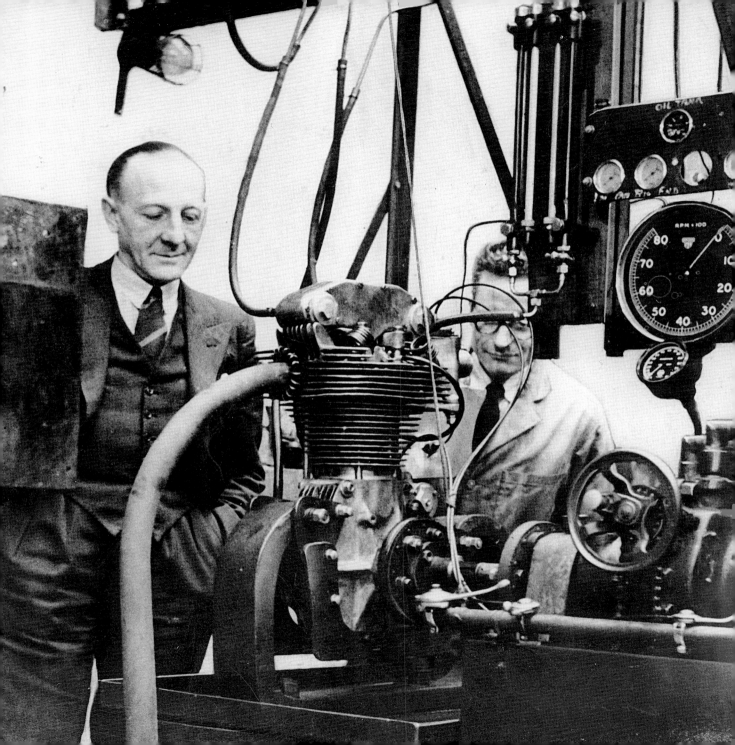

9 Off-Road

The Archer Norton, with modified frame, seen in April 1963.

Les Archer, from Aldershot, Hampshire, with one of his famous Manx-engined moto-crossers during the late 1950s.

If one discounts the various one-day trials exploits, which were gained with push-rod engines, or the ISDT-type events in which the International overhead camshaft model took part early in its career, hence its name, one is left with the saga of the Manx Scramblers and one man, Les Archer. The story began in 1952, when the factory built four scramblers using a combination of racing and trials components. The chassis used was from the 500T ohv trials bike of the era, but modified to swinging arm rear suspension with units of similar design to those fitted to the racers, but longer. Either the 350 or 500 ohc engines, based on the long-stroke Manx, could be fitted. These used a racing bottom-end and barrel, with an International cylinder head.

In November 1952, Norton announced that it would be officially supporting Les Archer and Eric Cheney, both of whom were associated with the Aldershot Archer family dealership. Apart from the usual scrambles at home, the pair would also compete in international moto-cross events on the Continent. Les Archer got off to a flying start when he won the important Moto-Cross de Marseilles in February 1953, his first event abroad that year.

Before riding the Norton dirt racers, Archer had competed in both scrambling and road racing in the immediate post-war period. But it was with the cammy Norton dirt iron that he was to make his name, stretching well over a decade from the early 1950s to the mid-1960s and including becoming European Champion in 1956. Meanwhile, team-mate Cheney soon went over to BSA, and thereafter set up as a frame builder and entrant of considerable repute.

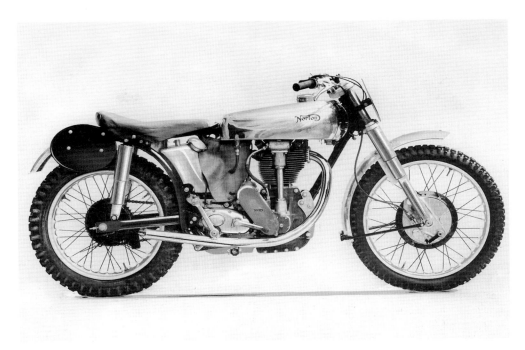

The works 500 Norton as used during the 1953 season by Archer and Eric Cheney.

A Manx engine of the type used by Archer in the early 1960s.

Les Archer's off-road debut had come as a 16-year-old in the early spring of 1946. The event was the North Hants Scramble at Elvertham and his mount was a far from perfect ex-War Department 350 Matchless. He ended the day by collecting the award for the best performance by a rider under 20 years of age. In 1947 the young Aldershot rider made his mark in the road-racing world by finishing third on a Velocette in the Lightweight Clubmans TT, and with a win on an EMC (350cc) at Dunholme in the BMCRC Mellano Trophy Handicap event. Archer was later to reveal that he attributed much of his success on the rough to high-speed skills acquired in road races. He considered that racing speeds demanded, above all, a cool head and the ability to weigh up a situation in a flash and act instantly.

After giving up road racing, his first Norton scrambler was a home-built effort at the end of 1951, and he stated that much of his off-road success was due to one man, Aldershot craftsman Ron Hankins. In the early and mid-1950s the power units used by Archer were of the long-stroke overhead cam type housed in special frames. And as 1956 was to prove, the battle-scarred Archer Norton combination was good enough to shower mud over riders on even the very latest and finest of the modern dirt racers. By then his works-based bikes were some four years old and as Archer freely admitted 'needed the spanners to be used fairly often'.

In the 1956 European Championships (the forerunner of today's Moto-Cross World Championships) Archer hardly got off to the best of starts, suffering three retirements in a row (front brake trouble in Switzerland on 16th May, a cooked spark plug in Holland on 23rd May and a crash in Italy on 3rd June). So a third of the series had slipped away without the British Norton rider gaining a single finish, let alone any Championship points.

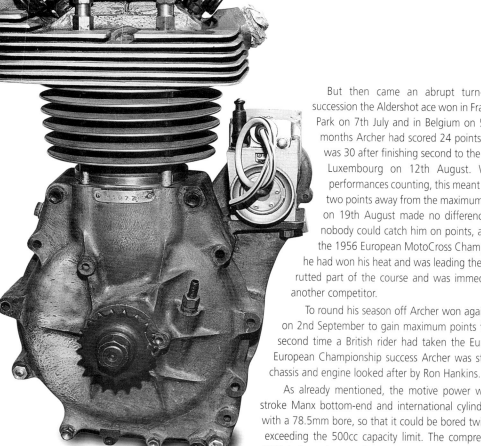

Two views of the Archer Norton engine showing details such as bevel gears, hairpin valve springs, timing chain and Lucas magneto.

But then came an abrupt turn-around in fortunes. In quick succession the Aldershot ace won in France on 10th June, at Hawkstone Park on 7th July and in Belgium on 5th August. So in less than two months Archer had scored 24 points (eight per victory), and his total was 30 after finishing second to the 1955 title-holder John Draper in Luxembourg on 12th August. With only a rider's best four performances counting, this meant that the Norton man was a mere two points away from the maximum possible! So a fourth in Sweden on 19th August made no difference to his total. After this round nobody could catch him on points, and this gave Archer and Norton the 1956 European MotoCross Championship. Incidentally, in Sweden he had won his heat and was leading the final when he spilled on a badly rutted part of the course and was immediately rammed from behind by another competitor.

To round his season off Archer won again in the final round in Denmark on 2nd September to gain maximum points for the series. This was only the second time a British rider had taken the European title. By the time of his European Championship success Archer was strictly a privateer with both the chassis and engine looked after by Ron Hankins.

As already mentioned, the motive power was essentially a standard long-stroke Manx bottom-end and international cylinder head. The barrel started life with a 78.5mm bore, so that it could be bored twice to 79 and 79.62mm without exceeding the 500cc capacity limit. The compression ratio was normally set at 8.75:1, but when a plate was removed this could be raised as high as 9.2:1, depending on the octane rating of the local petrol. The cylinder head had been modified to accept Manx valves, and the cams were reground to provide more mid-range power. The carburettor was an Amal TT, with particular attention paid to the design of an effective air filtration system. The transmission consisted of a standard Manx dry clutch, but the gearbox was a one-off, with special ratios and a kick-starter incorporated. With a dry weight of around 340lb, modified Roadholder forks were used, together with Avon knobbly tyres, a 3.00 x 21in front and 4.00 x 19in rear. Both the fuel and oil tanks were in steel.

Almost a decade later, and following a highly successful continental moto-cross career, Les Archer was still campaigning a camshaft Norton in 1965 at the 'old age' of 36. By now the engine was prepared by Ray Petty, had a double-knocker head, short-stroke, needle race vertical shaft and a host of other changes. For example, the cylinder barrel was a German Mahle assembly, with hard chromed bore and greatly reduced finning area. The compression ratio had been bumped up to a high 11:1 and there was twin spark ignition. In place of the normal hairpin valve springs, coils were used so that these could be enclosed and so cut out the rapid wear experienced in the dirt-filled atmosphere of off-road competition. The carburettor was now a GP, rather than the earlier TT instrument, and most of the crankcase finning had been machined away. A sturdy sump 'bash-plate' had also been fitted.

Les Archer in action with the definitive version of his legendary Manx moto-crosser. He finally retired in January 1967.

The frame, although similar to the original duplex affair, now carried the engine oil, while the front forks were up-to-the-minute Italian Cerianis. Retained were the Manx-type conical brake hubs, high-tensile steel rims and Girling rear shocks. With revitalised machinery the Aldershot 'flyer' continued to pile up his victory tally over the next couple of seasons.

But even with his vast experience, Les Archer was finding the going ever more difficult against the likes of the Greeves and CZ 'strokers', even though the old Norton single was still a match for almost any four-stroke.

So, sadly, at the end of 1966, the 1956 European MotoCrosser, then aged 38, decided to sell his Norton equipe to an American buyer, and ordered a new 360 Greeves 'stroker' for the 1967 season. At the same time he said he 'would never race a big bike on the continent (meaning mainland Europe) again'. Less than a month later, in his first race of 1967, on a borrowed 500 Metisse, Les Archer crashed on Sunday, 25th January in a start-line melee during the 750cc Experts race at Tweseldown, Hampshire. The crash resulted in a broken collarbone and finger, and Archer there and then decided to quit after 21 years in motorcycle sport. With this decision came the end of a career in which the combination of a 'cammy' Norton and its rider had together blazed a glorious trail across the motocross circuits of Europe, amassing a host of trophies and admirers along the way as almost no one has succeeded in the world of dirt-bike racing before or since.

Opposite: Les Archer aviates his Norton scrambler at the Point-to-Point, 5th April, 1952.

10 Over-the-Counter

Brough Airfield, East Yorkshire 1954. A Garden Gate Manx – in standard, 'as built' specification.

Alec Bennett's Senior TT victory in 1927 on the very first Walter Moore-designed CS1 ohc racer to be built set the stage for the production of 'replicas' for sale to the public. This first machine featured an all-iron 79 x 100mm long-stroke single-cylinder engine and a Sturmey-Archer non-positive-stop foot-change gearbox. For the 1931 season, a redesign was carried out by Arthur Carroll (who had replaced Moore, the latter having left by that time to work for NSU in Germany). Although the engine retained the same basic dimensions, it was considerably different and could be easily distinguished from its predecessor by having a bolted-on bottom bevel housing instead of the internally placed drive devised by Walter Moore. The CS1 was continued in 1932, but was supplemented by a semi-stripped machine with a close ratio gearbox. Valves, as before, were controlled by coil springs, but the exhaust port was now directed to the offside of the front down-tube, instead of its former nearside position. For the rider who wanted to go racing this bike, christened the 'International' after the factory's use of prototypes in the ISDT (International Six Days Trial), was later to win equal fame as a sporting roadster par excellence.

Some of Norton's heroes of the pre-war era. Left to right: Walter Rusk, J. Duncan, Joe Craig, Jimmie Guthrie and "Crasher" White; Isle of Man TT, 1935.

Two optional extras were listed for the 1934 season. These were a light-alloy cylinder head with a 14mm spark plug and a positive-stop foot-change. A pukka racing version of the International was prepared for the following year. This featured a full racing gearbox (with no kick-starter) of Norton's own manufacture. By this time Norton were acknowledged as the premier racing concern in the world, thanks to the works bikes ridden by stars such as Tim Hunt and Jimmie Guthrie. Even though the factory team controlled by Joe Craig did not have anything directly to do with the production racers, the TT and Grand Prix successes certainly helped sales. It also ensured that there was a constant stream of improvements - besides the pukka racing gearbox. 1935 also saw the introduction of positive oil-feed to the cams and the use of the familiar works-pattern wraparound oil tank and, of course, the tasteful black and silver decor. That year, sadly, also saw the brilliant Arthur Carroll killed in a car accident.

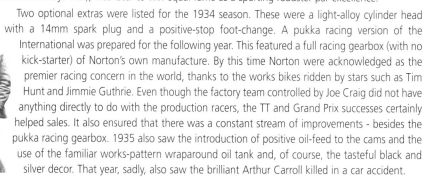

For 1936, a light-alloy cylinder barrel was offered as an extra. Although the Inter still sported girder forks and rigid frame for 1937, it did receive hairpin valve springs, which had been used for a number of years on the factory racers. The major changes that arrived for 1938 centred around the chassis. Plunger rear suspension appeared (two years after it had made its debut on the works bikes), while rider comfort was looked after by the sporting saddle and sponge-rubber pad of the era. The production racing engines were built with a 7.5:1 compression ratio and employed Norton's proven constant-diameter straight-through exhaust pipe.

Over-the-counter racers for 1939 were known as the Manx Grand Prix model and differed from the previous specially adapted Internationals by being intended purely for racing and employing some subtle improvements, the most notable being the use of a megaphone exhaust system and a steel conical front hub. It was also a Norton policy to ensure that the most fancied runner got priority in the queue. Although the war stopped the 1940 catalogue from being issued, it had none the less been prepared, and listed telescopic forks in place of the racing girders for the first time on a production Norton. These forks were undamped, except by corrector springs, and were designed by the man who was to take charge of the Manx shop in the early post-war period, Edgar Franks. Indeed, it was Franks and not Craig (who has often been given the credit in the past) who was responsible for much of the production racers' development and production for well over two decades.

The first post-war, over-the-counter racers were made available for the 1947 season. Announced in September 1946, these models were now referred to for the first time simply as the 'Manx'. They came fully equipped for the fray, even to the provision of racing number plates with built-in fixings. There were two capacities, the 499cc (79.62 x 100mm) and the 348cc (71 x 88mm), both at the same price of £235 (purchase tax £63. 9s. 0d.). Pre-war, the larger engine had had a capacity of 490cc. Magnesium crankcases and aluminium-alloy cylinder barrels and cylinder heads were standardised. The latter had now taken on a square appearance. The larger engine had a compression ratio of 7.23:1 and was provided with three compression plates, two of them 1.5mm thick, the other 0.5mm. Thus a ratio up to around 9:1 was possible (provided, of course, that one could find a high enough octane fuel in those days of 'pool' petrol!). Plates of the same thickness were also specified in the case of the 348cc engine; this had a ratio of 7.33:1, which could be upped to approximately 9.5:1.

Among the features of these first Manx models (prefaced by the pre-war 40 and 30 for the 350 and 500 respectively) were a 4½-gallon fuel tank 'floating in rubber' as *The Motor Cycle* described it, the supporting bolts running right through the tank with rubber mountings top and bottom; a conical front hub (still in steel) with an aluminium-alloy brake plate; long pressed clutch and front brake levers (the latter were 7³/₈in from fulcrum to end); Dunlop racing tyres (3.00 x 21 front and 3.50 x 20 and 3.25 x 20 rear on the 499 and 348cc models respectively); racing three-

Rudi Allison with the garlands of victory; Natal 100 road races. Machine is an early production Featherbed Manx.

The Manx over-the-counter racer first went on sale in late 1946, it was built in the form shown here, with plunger "Garden Gate" frame until the end of 1950.

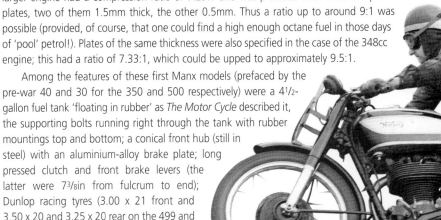

Norton, Gilera, MV, Moto Guzzi, BMW and Benelli works rider Dickie Dale at the beginning of his racing career with his Garden Gate Manx, circa late 1940's.

Denis Parkinson was born in the West Yorkshire town of Wakefield in June 1915 and in many ways can be described as the ultimate privateer.

He first rode in the Manx Grand Prix in September 1932. The regulations stated then, that 'every entrant driver shall be a male person over the age of 18 years'.

What is certain is that Denis Parkinson was not yet of the prescribed age. None the less he finished in both Junior and Senior races riding the same 350cc machine - an excellent result for one so young.

In 1933 he again finished in both races. He also rode in 1934 and 1935 without achieving any notable success, and then decided his 'apprentice' days were over. At that time there was in the Junior event a race within a race - as there was a special category for Lightweight (250cc) machines. Denis proceeded to make this class his own private property, and he won the Lightweight three times in succession - 1936, 1937 and 1938. He also rode the Senior race of 1937, finishing 13th and got another

DENIS PARKINSON

Replica to add to his fast growing collection. This Replica was the third in the same year - a feat no one had ever done before - or for that matter, has done since in the Manx Grand Prix series.

There was no race in 1939 and after the war in 1946 Denis Parkinson returned and finished third in the Junior and fourth in Senior. He won the Junior in 1948 and in the next three years was respectively 4th, 3rd and 8th in the Senior Manx Grand Prix. In 1953 he won the Senior at record speed on his Featherbed Manx and in the process became the first man to lap at over 90mph in the Manx Grand Prix.

In practicing and racing he lapped the TT course 388 times - a distance of 14,647 miles. In addition Denis set record laps on four occasions and was twice a member of a winning team and won a total of 15 replicas.

Denis Parkinson also won the Clubman's TT and had innumerable successes on short circuits (notably at venues such as Scarborough and Brough) and in all, won over 600 awards.

When he retired from racing he devoted himself to, as he once described, 'helping out'. He was a travelling marshal in the Manx Grand Prix for many years and was even an ACU official.

Yorkshireman Denis Parkinson won a record number of Manx Grand Prix races. He is seen here at Brough Airfield on his way to victory in a 350cc race event during 1954.

Rod Coleman taking his Norton to a popular victory in the New Zealand Hamilton 100, 1952.

plate dry clutch with Ferodo bonded asbestos linings; racing four-speed gearbox and Smiths rev-counter and megaphone exhaust. The Dunlop mudguard-mounted 'pads' were now almost deserving of the term seat, as they were considerably larger than the pre-war type. Quick-action, larger-diameter filler caps were fitted to both the fuel and oil tanks. The brakes were of 8-inch diameter, with 1½-inch-wide linings. The gear ratios on the two models were different; 499cc: 4.42, 5.36, 5.86 and 7.82:1; 348cc: 5.16, 5.67, 6.85 and 9.14:1. But the only real change over the pre-war models were the new front forks. Tested by Ken Bills on his 1946 Junior Manx Grand Prix winner (he also finished second in the Senior on a similarly equipped mount), these were the hydraulically controlled Norton Roadholders and offered a vast improvement over the earlier pre-war undamped type, which they superseded.

The hydraulic damping was effected simply and efficiently. Extending up from the base of each slider was a double-acting restriction plunger. This had a parallel portion that occupied the restrictor plug when the forks were in their normal, static-load position. It was parallel over a distance of 2 inches. Hence, over the initial travel of the forks there was substantially free movement so far as the hydraulic side was concerned - merely the action of the fork springs. A greater deflection and, on upward travel, a long, gentle, tapered portion of the plunger entered the restrictor plug and provided a gradually increasing damping effect. At extreme deflection (say, an unusually severe road shock) a parallel portion entered the restrictor plug and there was a complete cut-off, with oil trapped to form a buffer. The reverse travel was achieved in much the same way, providing a highly efficient method of damping. Finally, an Amal RN carburettor was fitted in place of the pre-war 10TT9 instrument.

For 1948 the specification remained unchanged. But in April 1949 it was announced that in future all production Manx Nortons would have dohc cylinder heads. The double-knocker type was to be based on the type used since 1937 on the works bikes, except that valve clearance adjustment on the production machines would be by means of shims, whereas on the factory bikes a grinding operation was involved. The other changes were improved brakes with conical light-alloy hubs and alloy tanks. These changes were confirmed when the 1950 Norton model range was announced in October 1949. Prior to this some 25 of the new models had made their debut in the TT during June. Arriving late in practice, they had none the less given an excellent account of themselves. The 1950 price was £346. 14s. 2d. for both the 30 and 40 Manx models.

Hot on the heels of the double-knocker engines came the news, when the 1951 model range was announced during October 1950, that the Manx models would employ the 1950 works-type pivoting fork spring frame. When production got under way at the end of the following March it was seen that the new frame and deep crankcase of the works machines were both specified. *The Motor Cycle* had this to say of the 1951 model Manx: 'A magnificent-looking job and probably as near an approach to a pukka works racer as anything that has been available "over the counter" since the days of "specialisation" in racing began.'

The Sif-bronze welded frame was almost a replica of the 1950 model works Featherbed design. The swinging arm was controlled by a pair of spring-loaded hydraulic shocks similar to those employed on the previous year's

American Nick Nicholson made a successful visit to the Isle of Man to finish eighth in the 1953 Senior TT. This was the last year of the old long-stroke 79.62 x 100mm engine and single leading shoe front brake.

*Rudi Allison winner of the 500cc Scratch
Race of the South African Natal 100
passing Barracks Bend on his victory lap;
Easter 1952.*

works machine, but cleaner externally since the damping oil was now contained within the spring boxes. Another change was no streamlined tail section as used on the 1950 works bikes. Both engines featured the works-type 'tall' crankcase, and this had its cylinder joint face so high that the 348cc cylinder was spigoted into it, to a depth of 2³/₈ inches. The depth of the spigot on the 499cc cylinder was 2 inches (the smaller engine's spigot being deeper because of the engine's shorter stroke). On both engines the bore and stroke measurements remained as for 1950. Initially the cylinder head remained unchanged, but in August 1951 a sodium-cooled exhaust valve was fitted. A slight difference from the previous year's works practice was apparent in that the top bevel box on the Manx model was separate, whereas the 1950 works machines had the bevel box cast integrally with the head. However, as in the case of the works mounts, there was a large-capacity oil-filter housed in the BTH magneto chaincase and interposed between the delivery side of the pump and the mainshaft. The new fuel and oil tanks were still of light alloy construction, with capacities of 5¹/₂ gallons and one gallon respectively. The former sat on the top frame tubes, insulated from them by rubber and held in position by means of a single hinged metal strap with a bolt and yoke fastener at the front, an improvement, it was claimed, over the camtype arrangement employed on the 1950 works machines. The oil tank was secured by long bolts passing vertically down through it into a rubber-mounted platform. Access to the oil filler cap, mounted centrally on top of the tank, was gained by a cutaway provided in the front of the racing seat.

*The 20-lap, 50-mile Senior class of the
International races held at Zandvoort,
Holland on the 10th May 1953 was
won by the Australian privateer
Tony MacAlpine.*

1946: Manx over-the-counter racer announced, 30M 499cc (79.62 x 100mm) and 40M 348cc (71 x 88mm). Alloy engine, sohc, square cylinder head, hairpin valve springs, four-speed close-ratio gearbox, Amal RN carb, plunger rear suspension, telescopic front forks, megaphone, quick-action filler caps for fuel and oil tanks, 21in front and 20in rear alloy wheel rims, conical steel brake hubs.

1947: No change

1948: No change.

1949: Dohc cylinder head and alloy tanks, alloy conical brake hubs.

1950: No change.

1951: Featherbed frame based on previous year's works racers. Updated engine, gauze filter in lower bevel chamber, cambox-driven rev counterdrive, laid down gearbox, 19in rims and tyres, internal front fork springs.

1952: Amal GP carburettors, and 40M modified inlet cam.

1953: No change.

1954: Major engine redesign; short-stroke engine dimensions, 30M 499cc (86 x 85.62mm), 40M 348cc (76 x 76.85mm), integral top bevel housing, barrel fins encompassing vertical drive tube, diagonal fins between valves, cambox not bolted directly to cylinder head, steeper inlet tract, welded rear sub-frame, 8in 2LS front brake, works-type oil tank.

MANX PRODUCTION RACER
CHANGES YEAR BY YEAR

1955: No change.

1956: Improvements carried from 1955 works development racers, including hollow exhaust valve, flanged double-row ball race timing side main bearing, rotating-magnet magneto and full ring clutch plates.

1957: Modified connecting rod and crankpin, sleeved big-end bearing, sodium cooled inlet valve, larger carb, coarser pitch bevels, higher lift camshaft for 350cc engine.

1958: AMC gearbox.

1959: Redesigned vertical drive-shaft, with needle roller and splined drive (no longer traditional Oldhams coupling), new camshaft bearings, sodium valves deleted, now Nimonic exhaust valve, clutch inserts bonded to driven plates, with one plate less.

1960: Higher 11:1 compression ratio, piston with chrome top ring, non-rotating piston circlips, wider big-end eye, eccentric big-end thrust washers, tappets with stellite tips, deeper top housing spigot, damped weir float for carb, magnetic oil drain plug, reinforced clutch centre, revised gear pedal linkage, fluted megaphone flat, stronger rear sprocket dowls, serrated wheel rims, oil tank strap, glass fibre seat base and front number plate, perspex fly screen, 9,000rpm Smiths rev counter.

1961: New lighter piston with single Dykes ring, Amal GP2 carb, modified valve gear, strengthened clip for rear of megaphone, rubber mounted oil tank held by rubber bands, tubular rear fork pivot.

1962: Dual 7in front brakes, larger capacity oil pump, with increased diameter for oil feed through crankshaft, cylinder barrels machined at both ends to avoid thinning top fin, 40M fitted with a larger bore carb, 30M carburettor spacer with taper bore also with modified tank to allow for clearance at rear for carburettor bellmouth.

A form of semi-unit construction was used to house the latest type of Norton racing gearbox, which had the new narrow end cover and linkage-type gearchange mechanism employed on the works machinery. Duralumin plates almost surrounded the gearbox, connecting it at the front with the crankcase, whilst at the rear it was attached to welded lugs on the frame. Standard gear ratios were now 499cc: 4.4, 4.86, 5.9 and 7.8:1; 348cc: 5.4, 5.93, 7.2 and 9.55:1. The forks were the latest-pattern Roadholders, while the 8-inch conical hubs were laced to WM1 front and WM2 rear alloy rims. Both tyres were 19-inch, 3.00 section at the front, 3.50 at the rear. It is worth noting that the 1951 Manx models had Avon tyres, not Dunlop as specified previously. This was in answer to the problems experienced by the works machines during some of the continental events the previous year and

By winning the 1953 Senior Manx Grand Prix 38-year-old Wakefield garage owner Denis Parkinson became the first man to win all three classes of the event. His Manx was a pre-production 1954 model.

referred to in Chapter 2. Completing the 1951 specification were the swan-neck clip-ons, comprehensive duralumin mudguards and racing flyscreen and number plates. Both machines weighed in at just under 300lb.

So successful were the new Featherbed Manx racers that very little change was seen for some time. In fact the only change of any note until 1954 was in 1952, when the 40M (348cc) received a modified inlet camshaft (stamped 392), giving increased lift but retaining the same timing. The price for the 1953 season had increased to £429. 6s. 8d., including tax.

If the previous year had not seen much change, when the 1954 range was announced in September 1953 this certainly made up for it. The biggest news was that both motors now had shorter strokes and larger bores. The Manx development shop (which, incidentally, was completely separate from Joe Craig's works racing department), under the experienced guidance of Edgar Franks, had chosen to adopt almost square dimensions, which for the 348cc model were 76mm bore and 76.85mm stroke and for the 499cc, 86 x 85.62mm. That change automatically demanded the use of shorter conrods. These 'square' Manx engines had the finning profile that embraced the vertical shaft cover tube, and the top housing was integral with the cylinder head. The head, in addition to being spigoted to the cylinder bore, was also located radially in the vertical shaft hole. Diagonal finning ran across the cylinder head between the valve guide bosses, and the cambox was mounted, and dowelled, on two large seatings immediately behind the valve springs. The size of the new cambox was slightly different, due to the altered valve angles demanded by a new head designed to cope with the differences in bore and stroke measurements. This also meant that the squish bands were altered.

Geoff Tanner looks happy as he pushes his 350 Manx away from the scrutineering area at the 1958 TT.

Geoff Tanner winner of the 1955 Junior Manx Grand Prix.

The Lucas rotating-magnet magneto, first introduced for the 1956 season.

Opposite: Denis Parkinson, Manx Grand Prix winner (on more than one occasion), short circuit specialist (including Brough and Scarborough) and motorcycle dealer. Invariably Norton mounted. This lovely period shot was taken circa 1954.

With changes also to the big-end eyes and such items as valve springs, few parts affecting performance were interchangeable with those of the earlier long-stroke units. Another major difference was the works-type two leading shoe brake, which had been adapted to fit into the existing Manx conical front hub. The brake assembly was mounted on a magnesium brake plate, each shoe being carried on a separate pivot pin. Adjacent to each pin was the cam for the opposite shoe, the unsupported ends of the adjacent pins and cams being braced by a pair of connecting plates. The plates were secured to the pivot pins by circlips. These acted as a steadier and provided a bush, or outrigger bearing, for the cams. The two external operating levers were connected by an adjustable tie-rod and the larger ventilating cowl used on the works model was retained. Strangely, the prices for both 1954 Manx models had dropped to £418. 16s. 0d.

For 1955, a flanged timing side main bearing was introduced and used in conjunction with a thinner mainshaft bevel. The price had risen to £465. 12s. 0d.

Another series of changes was inaugurated for the 1956 season. This was claimed to vindicate the factory policy during the 1955 season of using its works bikes as a stepping stone towards yet better production racers, rather than attempting to meet the challenge of the Italian manufacturers such as Gilera, Moto Guzzi and MV Agusta. The factory also claimed that buyers of the 1956 Manx models, therefore, would get 'equivalent machinery to that used, for instance, by the Surtees, Hartle, Brett threesome at meetings where they had been factory entered'. The engine's exhaust valve size was reduced, cooling improved, and a new and unorthodox, though more satisfactory valve timing system introduced, used in conjunction with new cams. Compression ratios were 9.72:1 for the 40M (350) and 9.53:1 for the 30M (500). Also for 1956 the normal GP float chamber was superseded by a Weir version, and for the first time on the production Manx model there was a rotating-magnet magneto. It is also interesting to note that the 1956 engines were not released until their power output in the test-house reached 35bhp at 7,200rpm for the 40M and 47bhp at 6,500rpm for the larger unit. Each customer received a performance data sheet for his particular engine.

Changes to the frame were few, but noteworthy was the provision of a reservoir carrying oil for the primary chain lubrication formed in the nearside top frame member. From this reservoir there was a feed to a modified chain oiler designed to ensure a double supply to each side plate. At the same time the primary-chain guard was lightly modified to provide increased protection. For the final drive there was now a side buffer to prevent undue lateral chain movement. The rear mudguard had been shortened, as had the front, and its bottom stay deleted, while the ground clearance was increased by mounting the exhaust pipe and megaphone higher. Not only this, but the two were now welded to form a single unit and a reverse cone megaphone fitted. Another change was the modification of the swinging arm pivot assembly, where phosphor bronze bushes on a solid steel pin replaced the previous metallistic components.

Before being signed by NSU, the 1954 125cc World Champion Austrian Ruppert Hollous campaigned a 348cc Manx, seen here after winning at Opatija in 1953.

On the transmission side the clutch received the full ring type friction discs, offering an increased level of reliability, while retaining a similar spring pressure to that previously encountered. The gearchange mechanism was provided with a more substantial lever and the spindle was now carried in a bush instead of bearing directly in the end plate casing. Minor items that received attention were a new-style of flyscreen; quick-release petrol tank straps; a lower seat, of different (stiffer), construction; improved seat mounting, avoiding all metal-to-metal contact; and rubbers for the rider's footrests. The price, including purchase tax, was £481. 2s. 5d.

More changes followed in 1957, with a new crankpin and sleeved con-rod eye, coarser-pitch bevel teeth, sodium cooled inlet *and* exhaust valves, a new inlet cam (on the 350 only) and larger bore carburettors - the running gear remained unchanged, as did the price. The only real change for 1958 was the fitment of the new AMC four-speed racing gearbox (also used on the AJS 7R). Although based on the unit then being used on the Norton and over-250cc AMC roadsters, the box differed in a number of respects, including the materials used and the clutch (which was of the type already used by Manx models) and its method of operation. Mainshaft and layshaft were supported at both ends in ball bearings, and were of En.355, an 85-ton steel containing nickel, chromium, manganese and molybdenum. The same material was also used for the gears.

The layout of the gear cluster followed normal practice: peg-type dogs were employed for the engagement of bottom gear, but otherwise normal block dogs were utilised. The floating gears (second on the mainshaft, bottom and third on the layshaft) ran on fully floating bronze bushes. Internal ratios were 1.78, 1.332, 1.1 and 1:1.

The positive-stop mechanism was of the type employing a spring-controlled, double-ended pawl. Coaxial with the pedal shaft, the ratchet quadrant carried a peg that engaged with a knuckle joint at the offside end of a traverse rocker; the rocker pivot was mounted inside the front wall of the gearbox shell. On the other end of the rocker was a toothed quadrant that engaged with a pinion on the cam plate.

Old and new: left, Rudi Allison with the new Featherbed, while J.H. Fhrees relied on the older 'Garden Gate' model. The setting is a typical South African race meeting in the early 1950s.

Identical to that fitted to earlier Manx models, the clutch was notable for having friction inserts in the sprocket, protruding on each side, and three-tongued Ferodo RZL driving plates alternating with four steel drive plates. Each steel plate had eight radial keyhole slots to prevent any tendency for the plate to become conical when hot. The cast-aluminium pressure plate carried three springs of square-section wire and a centrally mounted threaded adjuster. The internal clutch thrust mechanism was by a ball and camlever very similar in operation to the type used on the then current AMC two-strokes.

With Doug Hele now in charge of the Manx development programme, a fresh look was taken at the venerable double overhead cam singles. The result was that a considerable number of changes were introduced to the production racers for the 1959 season. This followed a season of testing with the works development machines the year before. As Hele was responsible for both factory machines and production racers, there were no separate empires as in the days of Craig and Franks.

Rudi Allison (92) leading the field around the first hairpin following the start of the South African Natal 100 on the 31st May 1952 on his five-hundred Manx. What about those track conditions?

This 1954 photograph shows the
primary chain oil feed.

The annual improvements to power output were by now beginning to be felt through the failure of certain components that had previously proved utterly reliable. These included big-end bearings and camshaft drive bevels. A respite for the camshaft bevels had come in 1957 by redesigning the drive with coarser-pitch bevel pinions which incorporated a hunting tooth, in other words, driving and driven bevels having an unequal number of teeth, so spreading wear more uniformly. During 1958 (see Chapter 13) Norton had built a desmodromic Manx engine for bench test purposes. This had unusually fierce cam profiles to provide much quicker opening and closing of the valves. In turn this meant more stress on the vertical drive-shaft, which soon expired. The result was a redesigned drive that was extremely robust yet simpler than before, and its ability to withstand punishment on the desmo unit prompted Hele to adopt it for the 1959 over-the-counter Manx models. The design comprised a single-tube, light-alloy casting that carried pairs of needle-roller bearings at top and bottom. Within the casting was an internally splined coupling tube, into which the short shafts that carried the upper and lower bevels were a tap-in fit. Secured to the crankcase bevel housing and spigoted into place there, and through the cylinder head casting, the drive formed a complete unit. There was also the added advantage of little chance of an error when the engine had to be stripped and rebuilt in something of a hurry, at a race meeting for example.

South African Paddy Driver with his
three-fifty Manx at the 1959 Ulster
Grand Prix.

The desmo valve gear experiments brought in another minor, although important, change that was also adopted for 1959. Previously a hardened-steel bearing housing, pressed into the cam-box cover, had a flange that also served to locate the valve tappet; however, the disadvantage of this method was that should the housing move inward, the tappet could become trapped. In the complete redesign carried out by Hele, the housing was not only of a larger diameter (to accommodate a standard journal bearing instead of itself serving as the bearing outer race) but the screwed plug on the outside of the cover now engaged with a thread at the rear of the bearing housing, thus preventing inward movement.

Another change was the use of solid Nimonic valves to replace the lighter, but more troublesome, sodium-filled type. Breathing of the 350 engine in the upper speed range was improved by increasing the inlet valve size by 1/16in, the port size by 1/32in and using a carburettor with a parallel bore instead of a venturi. On the 500, measures had been taken to ensure precise consistency of compression ratio, 10.7:1, in production. Power output for the larger engine was now a claimed 50.5bhp. A new-pattern Lucas magneto was also specified.

*A standard over-the-counter dohc
348cc 40M Manx at Brough Airfield
East Yorkshire, 1954.*

Alan Trow with one of his privately owned short-stroke Manx models, circa 1955. This is the five-hundred 30M.

The clutch was modified with the use of bonded-on rectangles of friction material instead of the previous inserts for the plates. This was in an attempt to improve heat dissipation and was successful enough to dispense with one clutch plate. Another transmission improvement was easier bottom-end engagement as a result of elongation of the slots for dogs.

When details of the 1960 Manx models were released that February, it was instantly seen that the racing department's development had not been lavished on the cycle parts so much as the mechanics. Externally the machines appeared little different from their 1959 counterparts. Instead, it was within the engine construction that most changes had taken place, none of which was a major departure from what had gone before. Collectively, however, they added up to quite an impressive total. One of the few external changes was in the design of the clip-on handlebar stubs. The grip extensions were now welded tangentially to the fork-leg laps, with the handlebar tube being shaped to fit. The result was a greater area of weld and, in consequence, a stronger handlebar. Also noticeable was a change in material for the front racing number plate, from pressed steel to moulded glass-fibre, and the substitution of a small Perspex screen in place of the familiar gauze flyscreen. Much less obvious was the further use of glass-fibre for the seat pan, a change that reduced the weight of this component by almost two-thirds, from 6¾lb to 2½lb. Security bolts were omitted from the light-alloy wheel rims and instead the tyres were prevented from turning by serrations on the rim inboard faces. Another small change was a stiffer bracket for the exhaust megaphone. The problem of oil-tank fracture had been minimised by the use of a thick rubber base pad and by a new upper mounting in which a strip of Duthane (a synthetic rubber of great durability and increased strength) linked the tank mounting bolts to the frame tube clamp. A prototype of this type of mounting had been used throughout the 1959 racing season with no sign of wear or chafing.

Norton practice was to locate the rear wheel sprocket on dowels that fitted into sockets in the hub. Previously these sockets were ¼in deep, but after considerable use wear in the sockets could allow the dowels to work loose. To provide longer life the sockets had been increased to ¾in.

In an attempt to provide a more comfortable gearchange with a greater degree of leverage, a shorter pedal was used in conjunction with a longer gearbox arm. Attention had also been paid to the clutch mounting. A steel washer, copper-brazed into the bore of the shock absorber centre unit, afforded a much greater area of metal in contact with the shoulder of the mainshaft, holding the centre unit more firmly. In addition, the securing nut was prevented from turning by an external tab washer seating on a D-shaped section of the shaft-end, while the washer was itself held by a circlip. The carburettor float chamber was now of the latest Amal top-feed type in place of the earlier bottom feed design. Incorporated in the weir-type chamber was a bypass to ensure that a small quantity of fuel trapped by the weir was not lost by a sudden opening of the throttle.

Alan Trow, 9th in the 1955 Junior Manx Grand Prix, 349cc Norton.

ALAN TROW AND PETER GOODWIN

Peter Goodwin was born on the 12th May 1931, in Horns Cross, a small village near Greenhithe, Kent. A close friend of the Australian Hinton racing family, he was for many years Alan Trow's mechanic, travelling companion and friend.

Peter, who was turned down for RAF service due to perforated eardrums, was a lifelong motorcycle enthusiast who not only rode a number of high performance roadsters, but also competed in trials, scrambling and even sidecar trials (as the driver). He first met Alan Trow (born 11th January 1933) at The Bull pub in Horns Cross in 1954. In July 1954, Alan had his first race at the local Brands Hatch circuit on a five-hundred BSA Gold Star. Both Peter and Alan shared not only a love of motorcycles, but as Vic Willoughby described once in *The Motor Cycle* 'the odd noggin' – hence their original meeting place! The Gold Star was soon replaced by an ex John Surtees long-stroke Manx, but from late April 1955 it too made way for a pair of new short-stroke Nortons – a three-fifty and a five-hundred.

Alan Trow first came to the general public's attention, when he, together with Peter travelled to the Isle of Man for the Manx Grand Prix that year, and won the Newcomers Award by finishing 4th in the Senior event (at an average speed of 88.28mph). This after coming home 9th in the Junior race two days earlier.

Even bigger things happened a few days after the team's return from the Island, Alan hit the headlines when he and John Surtees (both Norton mounted) finished ahead of world champion Geoff Duke and his works four-cylinder Gilera, at Brands Hatch on the 2nd October 1955. Hardly having had time for these events to sink in came a phone call out of the blue, from none other than Jock

Alan Trow, Silverstone 1958.

West at AMC (by then owners of Norton) to offer Alan a contract to race for the official Norton squad the following year. He accepted and joined Jack Brett and John Hartle aboard factory development Manx models for the 1956 season. Like the other two, Alan Trow's performances suffered as factory policy meant that streamlining was not allowed. This at a time when almost everyone else was using 'dustbins' to provide a substantial increase in lap speed.

For example at Floreffe in Belgium, Alan was passed by Fergus Anderson on a fully streamlined BMW Rennsport twin which *The Motor Cycle* reported as 'rocketing past and disappearing in the distance like a guided missile'. This was galling for the Trow team as before the season had started they in fact

carried out airfield tests of a Manx, equipped with low-slung pannier tanks and a streamlined snout. The lower distribution of weight gave improved handling and an increase in maximum speed (of around 10 per cent).

Norton quit racing at the end of 1956, and for 1957 the Trow squad picked up support from Manchester dealer, Reg Dearden.

Alan and Peter then travelled all over Europe for the next three years. During this time they visited many countries including Germany, Sweden, Austria, Italy and France, but due to the needs of his Dartford-based motorcycle business, Alan quit racing in 1960 (although he did have a few outings on four wheels) and sadly died after being taken ill, whilst visiting his daughter in Folkestone Hospital, on the 18th June 1962.

As for Peter Goodwin, he returned to his old job at Littlebrook Power Station (right next to the Dartford Tunnel), got married (in 1962) and thus took on the responsibilities of married life. However, he never lost his enthusiasm for motorcycles and when seriously ill with cancer in 1997, still went to the Festival of 1,000 Bikes at Brands Hatch that year. Peter died on the 14th November, 1997.

In August 1999, the author was booked into a guest house at Sutton-at-Hone, a few miles from Brands Hatch, by the Ducati Owners Club. Little did he realise that this was run by Peter Goodwin's daughter, Suzette. Since that time Suzette and her husband Brad have become close friends of Mick Walker. This piece is intended as a tribute to both Peter Goodwin and Alan Trow, also to the great work which Suzette does for terminally ill children – a charity set up in memory of her father's life.

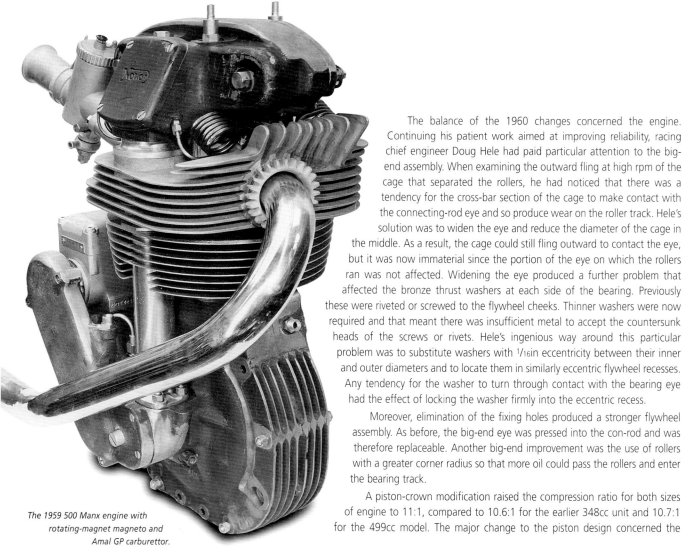

The balance of the 1960 changes concerned the engine. Continuing his patient work aimed at improving reliability, racing chief engineer Doug Hele had paid particular attention to the big-end assembly. When examining the outward fling at high rpm of the cage that separated the rollers, he had noticed that there was a tendency for the cross-bar section of the cage to make contact with the connecting-rod eye and so produce wear on the roller track. Hele's solution was to widen the eye and reduce the diameter of the cage in the middle. As a result, the cage could still fling outward to contact the eye, but it was now immaterial since the portion of the eye on which the rollers ran was not affected. Widening the eye produced a further problem that affected the bronze thrust washers at each side of the bearing. Previously these were riveted or screwed to the flywheel cheeks. Thinner washers were now required and that meant there was insufficient metal to accept the countersunk heads of the screws or rivets. Hele's ingenious way around this particular problem was to substitute washers with 1/16in eccentricity between their inner and outer diameters and to locate them in similarly eccentric flywheel recesses. Any tendency for the washer to turn through contact with the bearing eye had the effect of locking the washer firmly into the eccentric recess.

Moreover, elimination of the fixing holes produced a stronger flywheel assembly. As before, the big-end eye was pressed into the con-rod and was therefore replaceable. Another big-end improvement was the use of rollers with a greater corner radius so that more oil could pass the rollers and enter the bearing track.

A piston-crown modification raised the compression ratio for both sizes of engine to 11:1, compared to 10.6:1 for the earlier 348cc unit and 10.7:1 for the 499cc model. The major change to the piston design concerned the

The 1959 500 Manx engine with rotating-magnet magneto and Amal GP carburettor.

gudgeon pin bosses. At their outward ends they were extended downwards so that circlips with external tabs could be employed; recesses in the extended bosses ensured that the circlips did not turn when the engine was running. To enable it to have a longer working life, the gudgeon pin changed from being case-hardened to nitrided En.40c steel. The top compression ring on the piston was now chromium plated. Nitriding had also replaced case-hardening in the tappet blocks interposed between the cams and valve stems. The steel in this instance was an En.40b specification and the alteration was dictated by the adoption of exceptionally hard 1/16in thick Stellite tappet crowns. Proved under competition use in the 1959 Manx Grand Prix and adopted for the 1960 production Manx models were Terry hairpin valve springs of a type offering increased life.

The camshaft drive and housing introduced for the 1959 season had proved trouble-free, except that in a few cases wear at the point where the housing passed into the cam-box produced oil leaks and a degree of chattering. For 1960, therefore, the cambox casting had been thickened locally and the outer tube of the housing lengthened so that the depth of register between the two components was now 3/4in instead of the original 1/4in. Finally, a change that affected the 350 engine only was that the shape of the inlet port had been altered in the valve seat to increase gas velocity. The difference in price between the 1959 models, at £496. 10s.1d. and the 1960 figure of £496. 19s. 6d. was a mere 9s. 5d. So much for inflation during this period!

More punch was the priority when the annual list of changes came around for the 1961 Manx models. This centred around the need in Doug Hele's opinion to improve the power available in the early part of the output curve. Acceleration, especially speed out of corners, needed to be improved, but not at the expense of maximum velocity. Efforts were also directed at improving reliability.

Yorkshireman Rob Fitton rode a variety of Manxes all over Europe from the late 1950s until the 1970s. He is seen here at Scarborough in September 1962 on his 499cc model, purchased new that year.

John Cooper (before his 'Moon-eyes' era) with his unfaired 499cc Norton at Olivers Mount, Scarborough in 1962.

Dennis Pratt taking his Bracebridge Street single to fourth place in a very wet 1961 Junior Manx Grand Prix.

The first move had been to lighten the pistons, which were also modified to carry only one compression ring (of the L-shape Dykes variety). On the 350 the piston height above the ring was reduced by $1/16$in, thus lowering the squish crown level. The overall decrease made it possible to use a shorter ($3/16$in) cylinder barrel (and bevel coupling shaft) for both engine sizes. A section of the power increase at low torque for the smaller engine came from a new cam profile, which produced an earlier valve opening. To accommodate this the inlet seat was recessed by 0.20in. A similar arrangement, but with only a 0.15in recess, was used on the 500, and although the cam profile remained unaltered on the larger engine, the ignition was advanced. Improved filling for both engines was obtained by larger inlet ports, the new size for the 40M 350 being $1 1/4$in (previously $1 3/16$in), while the 30M 500cc was now $1 1/32$in (previously $1 5/16$in). To suit these increases in port sizes the induction tract lengths were extended considerably. For the 500 the length went up by $5/8$in and for the 350 by $1 17/32$in.

The new Amal Type 5 GP2 carburettor replaced the Type 5 (350) and Type 10 (500) GP instruments used up to then. The prototype of this new carb had been race tested by Alan Trow in the 1960 Junior TT. The main differences centred around the pilot system, which on the GP2 incorporated manual adjustment for the air supply rather than the fuel, as hitherto.

Efforts towards further lightening of the internal reciprocating parts resulted in the use of a stronger yet thinner inlet valve-head and a reduction by $1/32$in in valve-stem diameter. The separate spring-hook cup, which bore on the valve collar, was replaced by a integral cup and collar that prevented rotation of the valve while the engine was running. The practice of using Stellite as a hardener for the working faces of the tappets, was abandoned in favour of case hardening with a 0.21in layer of chromium plating on the cam track. Cam tracks were copper-plated and a more rigid valve mechanism assembly resulted from the use of lengthened tappet guides and bushes. Much of the running gear showed very little change. However, the frame was modified by the use of a tubular cross-pivot member instead of a bar for the swinging-arm pivot. This had the dual advantage of increased diameter (up from $9/16$in to $3/4$in) and a weight saving of $3/4$lb.

DEREK MINTER

Unlike his great rival Mike Hailwood, there was no silver spoon in Derek Minter's mouth. As racing journalist Charlie Rous once recalled; 'the result of hard-earned savings of £1 a week working as an electrician's mate, plus the £2 he could earn from evening and weekend farm labour, got him his first bike.'

That was 1954, Minter was 22 and the machine was a 499cc Gold Star BSA. 1955 brought him to the startline but he freely admits he was a 'complete novice'.

Even so he soon became a regular at his local Brands Hatch circuit and in 1956, his then employers, Wincheap Garages, bought him a 350 Manx, and the following year one of the larger Norton singles.

The real breakthrough came when Steve Lancefield took over the preparation of Minter's Manx engines. The Lancefield-Minter alliance brought a period of real achievement; victory over World Champion John Surtees (MV) at the final Brands Hatch meeting of 1958, and in 1960 the first 100mph of the TT circuit by a single-cylinder machine. This period also brought the first works rides, including MZ, Morini and Bianchi.

After 1961, Derek began his association with Ray Petty.

It was a much closer personal relationship than had been the case with Lancefield. On his Petty-tuned Manxes, Minter ruled much of the short circuit scene, collecting victories all over the British Isles and was regularly crowned 'King of Brands.'

In 1962 he rode a Honda four to win the 250cc TT - against team orders - which ensured he didn't ride for the Japanese giant again.

At the beginning of 1963 he signed for the Geoff Duke managed Scuderia Gilera team. At Silverstone in April 1963, Minter gave Gilera (after 6 years away from the sport) its first victory. However, his world class potential was never to be realised. Only a few short weeks after the Silverstone victory a fateful race curbed hopes of Grand Prix glory. The setting was Brands Hatch, with Minter on his Petty 500 Manx. A youngster named Dave Downer was aboard Paul Dunstall's 650 Domiracer twin, which challenged the 'Mint' with its superior acceleration. Charlie Rous again; 'It was the fiercest two-bike battle I ever saw and ended in a last lap collision in which Downer died.'

Minter ultimately recovered from spinal and other injuries and went on to many more victories - with a variety of bikes including, of course, Manx singles - but the sparkle had gone.

Right up to his retirement at the end of 1967 he was still winning around Britain - mostly on Petty-tuned Nortons. Recently, Derek Minter was still to be seen around the circuits riding the Summerfield Manx at classic racing events.

Derek Minter, 348cc 40M Manx, Silverstone, spring 1960.

Opposite: Finishers enclosure of the
1951 Senior Manx Grand Prix.
D.E Bennett (55) the winner,
D.G Crossley (76) second and
D. Parkinson (21) third;
all three on Nortons.

Local rider C. Horn caused a shock by
beating works Norton star Geoff Duke
at Brough Airfield, Easter Saturday,
1951. Horn was riding an ageing
Garden Gate Manx.

Brough airfield in East Yorkshire was
the setting for a little-recorded defeat of
Norton factory star Geoff Duke on Easter
Saturday, the 24th March 1951. The main
20-lap Festival of Britain Championship
race was won by local rider C. Horn,
aboard an ageing 490cc Garden Gate
Manx, whilst Duke who came home
runner-up was aboard one of the more
modern 499cc Featherbed machines.

BROUGH,
MARCH 1951

Horn's average speed was 58.7mph on
a day when after a snowstorm during the
morning, the weather brightened and there
was sunshine for the actual racing.

In the 350 event Horn (on a similar
engined Manx) finished 3rd, behind race
winner M. Featherstone (7R AJS) and Duke
2nd. A Norton won the Sidecar Scratch
race, with Jackie Beeton taking his big
engined Manx (596cc) to victory

Today Brough is all but forgotten in
racing circles, but in the immediate post-
Second World War years it was a popular
venue, which challenged Scarborough's
Olivers Mount, as Yorkshire's premier race
circuit.

Then and afterwards it doubled as an
airfield and in later years reverted
exclusively to its aviation role, first with
Blackburn Aircraft and subsequently when
Blackburn was absorbed into British
Aerospace, the latter organisation.

But certainly for that single day in
March 1951, Brough was the setting for a
major racing upset when that year's double
(350 and 500cc) World Champion was
beaten by an unknown rider piloting an
obsolete machine.

Jackie Beeton (596 Manx) on his way to victory on
the Sidecar Scratch Race at Brough.

Geoff Duke with his Featherbed models claimed
a pair of runner-up positions at the 1951 Brough
meeting.

499cc meggaphone.

Twin leading shoe front brake.

Nearside view of 2LS brake, showing conical hub.

1962-type double-sided front brake.

The oil tank came in for much alteration. Its design and appearance were totally different from the type that it replaced. Not only was it of an entirely fresh shape but it was also left unpainted, and was suspended from flanged rubber bushes and supported by a rubber band at each side against a rubber pad on the transverse frame bracket - simple but effective.

In an attempt to cure a spate of fractured megaphones, the mounting bracket was totally redesigned. This now consisted of a steel support that extended rearwards from the offside footrest bracket to secure the megaphone in a comprehensive clip near the end of the cone. The previous method had been a single nut and bolt fixing. The new method was claimed to hold the megaphone more securely, and at the same time allow some flexing to take place. The design of the clip allowed for a degree of megaphone expansion under heat and was also designed to prevent fracturing of the flattened portion and consequent breaking up of the exhaust system as the race proceeded. This was of particular importance in long races such as the TT.

1962 saw only two major changes. The first was the 7-inch-diameter twin leading shoe, dual drum front brake, the prototype of which was used by Roy Ingram during the 1961 Senior TT. The second was less obvious. On both the 350 and 500, hidden away from immediate notice, was a larger capacity oil pump with a correspondingly bigger feed through the crankshaft. On the smaller model there was once more a further increase in carburettor choke diameter, up from 1¼in to 1⁵/₁₆in. There was also an alteration to the cylinder barrel; the previous year this had been reduced in height by skimming metal from the top, leaving the uppermost fin rather thinner than the others, but for the 1962 season Norton restored the fin thickness, taking metal equally from top and bottom. The 1961 method had left the top fin prone to damage. For the 500 a bigger cutaway was provided at the rear of the fuel tank to allow increased air space around the carburettor mouth. In addition, the carburettor distance piece was given a taper instead of a parallel bore. Other than these changes the models remained as before. In any case the day of the Bracebridge Street Manx was almost over.

September 1962 brought the joint news that the Treasury had passed an order relieving road racing motorcycles from purchase tax (racing cars having been exempt from the tax since the Budget earlier that year), this having the effect of cutting the price of a new Manx (if in fact you could actually find one!) by £88, to £440, and that Doug Hele had finally left to join Triumph; Hele had resigned when it was announced that Norton were moving from Birmingham to London. The doors finally closed on the old Norton home in Bracebridge Street in early January 1963. By the end of 1962 much of the Norton production had already been transferred to Plumstead, and only a few loyal stalwarts remained. A very few new Manx models were constructed from spares by AMC for the 1963 season, but to all intents and purposes the famous silver and black over-the-counter racers died with Bracebridge Street. Post-1963, Colin Seeley purchased the remains of the Manx race shop when he acquired the rights to build and stock-in-trade from AMC of the AJS 7R and Matchless G50 in the mid-1960s. Seeley was never really interested in the Manx side and this was eventually sold in late 1969 to John Tickle, who ran a customising and accessory manufacturing business at St Neots, Cambridgeshire - Tickle had also raced a

Cylinder head details (350) including Smiths tacho drive gearbox and hairpin valve springs.

An unnamed Manx Norton competitor during a 500cc event at Cadwell Park, summer 1957.

Rear wheel including sprocket and rod-operated rear brake.

Manx-engined sidecar outfit with some success. For a time Tickle continued to produce much-needed spares for the hundreds of existing Manx racers around the world, plus a handful of his own T5 Manx-based racers, most of which, however, used a new frame, quite unlike the Norton Featherbed. In early 1974 Tickle moved to Peterborough, but by then his accessory business was going downhill rapidly. Soon afterwards the remains of the Manx operation was on the move once more, this time to Unity Equipe in Manchester. Unity continued to provide a spares service, but no more complete bikes were offered, so the Tickle T5 was truly the last of the line that could lay claim to the statement in the final 1962 Bracebridge Street-produced Manx brochure: 'The most successful standard production racing machine in the world.' If any proof was needed of this statement, a Manx Norton not only had the distinction of being the last British machine to win the Senior TT (Mike Hailwood in 1961) but also to gain the last British victory in a continental classic, the 1969 Yugoslav Grand Prix, when Godfrey Nash finished a glorious third in the 500cc World Championship.

Beautiful period shot of a pre-war production racer at the 1937 Manx Grand Prix.

MANX GRAND PRIX

Run as the Manx Amateur Road Race Championships from 1923 to 1929, the September race became the Manx Grand Prix from 1930. For some fifty years the races were seen very much as a breeding ground for the stars of the future. The Manx, like the TT declined from the mid-1970s onwards, becoming very much a social gathering first, a race meeting second.

From 1923 until 1927 there was a single race. This was mainly for 500cc machines, but with a 350cc class award. The inaugural 1923 event saw victory going to L. Randles who averaged 52.77mph for the 5-lap race. The fastest lap was set by R.O. Lowe at 56.42mph. Randles also won the 1924 race and set a new lap record of 63.96mph the following year.

The first year to see Senior and Junior races was 1928. Future Norton works rider Percy Hunt won both the 1927 and 1928 races (the latter being the first official Senior event).

A notable rostrum position for the 1930 series was a certain F.L. (Freddie) Frith, who finished 3rd in the Junior.

By now the Manx Grand Prix was fast becoming one of the premier dates on the road race calender - and the top one for the amateur riders.

Harold Daniell had finished runner up in the 1932 Senior, and won the race the following year, averaging 76.98mph (although the fastest lap was set by J.K. Swanston at 77.86mph. That same year, 1933, Austin Monks won the Junior, with Frith second.

By 1935 Freddie Frith was a star with victory in the Junior Manx Grand Prix and runner up spot in the Senior. Monks scored a Senior/Junior double in 1936, Maurice Cann repeated the act in 1937, as did Ken Bills in 1938.

In 1939 the races were cancelled due to the outbreak of war. The Manx resumed in 1946 and rapidly regained its pre-war popularity. 1949 was a notable year with Geoff Duke and Cromie McCandless

dominating the races. In the Senior, Duke won and set the fastest lap (87.482mph), whilst in the Junior McCandless, who had come home runner up behind Duke in the Senior, won with Duke second. This time McCandless set the fastest lap (at 83.503mph).

The stage was set for a truly superb set of Manx Grands Prix during the 1950s. It began with Peter Romaine winning the 1950 Senior and ended with Eddie Crooks winning the same race in 1959 (both on Manxes). Manx Grand Prix winners during the 1960s included Phil Read, Ellis Boyce, Joe Dunphy, Griff Jenkins, Malcolm Uphill and Jimmie Guthrie Junior.

As the 1970s dawned the British singles, including the Manx, were struggling, notably from the latest breed of Japanese two-strokes. As was the Manx Grand Prix itself. Plenty of entries, but the prospects of a works ride for a Manx Grand Prix winner had gone. The Manx remains today, as does the TT. Both have their army of fans and long may this state of affairs continue.

Pilots eye view of the 1962 Manx showing twin front brake cables, tachometer and flyscreen.

11 **Domiracer**

Tom Phillis piloting the works Domiracer to a sensational third place in the 1961 Senior TT.

The first use of the new twin-cylinder Bert Hopwood designed Dominator for road racing, was when a pair of these, suitably modified by their owners, took part in the 1951 Senior Manx Grand Prix. Using straight-through pipes rather than megaphones, these were ridden by Harry Bent and John Waite. The debut was hardly spectacular, as Bent came in 55th, while Waite brought up the field in 64th and last position. The only thing that could really be said was that both finished.

The factory's own attempt to build a racer out of the twin did not come until early the following year, when, in January 1953, a pair of specially adapted Dominator De-Luxe models, with Featherbed frames, were built at the Bracebridge Street works. Ken Kavanagh recalls that together with Leo Kusmicki (a former fighter pilot and lecturer in engineering) he did the actual bench testing, commenting in 1989: 'I worked the brake, he (Kusmicki) read the clocks...these were put together in the 'Manx Shop'...then I did the road testing and got the carburation right at MIRA.'

AMA, the sports governing body in North America, had not allowed the new Featherbed frame to be used since it had been introduced on the works racers in 1950. But with the advent of the Dominator De-Luxe and its sales in the States, the American officials were forced to accept the new twin. In the main 200-mile Daytona classic (run over the old beach course), Milt Lassiter managed to bring one of the twins home in a very creditable third spot. Both Norton twins were used at Laconia in June that year and in the 200-mile national 'Speedway' championship at Dodge City the following month. At the two-mile oval the twin once again showed up well by gaining another third place.

Although clearly built around the standard production roadster, to qualify for AMA's blessing, the Daytona specification 'Dominator Racers', as they were officially known at the time, were equipped with twin Amal racing carburettors with a single remote float chamber, an 8-inch front brake, lower 'bars' and rearset controls and short, dumpy megaphones. The racing specification was completed with a single bum-stop saddle, abbreviated mudguarding and racing number plates.

When two of the Daytona-type machines appeared at the Manx Grand Prix that September, ridden by travelling marshal Harry Craine and racer George Costain (the latter retired with a broken push-rod), many observers thought that it might be the prelude to a Norton-type Matchless G45. But for whatever reason, these pundits were to be proved wrong. It was not until some eight years later that the factory got around to building another Dominator-based racer. In the meantime it was left to private owners to convert their own machines. These were usually not competitive, because riders who wanted to win took the easy option and bought a Manx.

Then in 1960 a Dominator 88 Sports roadster won its class in the Thruxton 500-mile race ridden by Fred Swift and Dennis Greenfield. Although an excellent performance, it is doubtful if this result led to the next development, the appearance of a full-blown racing model, which the factory entered in the 1961 Senior TT (although it was originally built to compete at Daytona).

In *The Motor Cycle* dated 1st June, 1961, Norton development chief Doug Hele commented: 'Experiments during the past four years have indicated that the Dominator would readily respond to development so that it should not be difficult to extract as much speed as from the Manx, maybe even more. Even with the engine in its present semi-standard form we start with an advantage, for it is already 28lb lighter without having to resort to Elektron crankcase castings. Moreover, it is smoother, so we can get away with a much lighter frame. Finally it has a lower centre of gravity, which should ease

With Tom Phillis fully occupied riding works Honda's in the Grand Prix, Derek Minter was loaned the works Domiracers, which by now included a machine with a six-fifty engine. He made a winning debut at Brands Hatch on Easter Friday, 19th April 1962. He is seen here at Oulton Park four days later on the smaller Domiracer; he came home third, behind Bob McIntyre and Alan Shepherd (both Matchless mounted).

handling problems.' Tests at the MIRA proving track near Nuneaton had shown that the twin possessed both speed and reliability, but the track could not test the high speed handling; only the Isle of Man could do that and fully expose any shortcomings in that respect.

Both the Roadholder forks (shorter) and Featherbed style frame (lower) gave the new machine a 2½ inch height advantage over the production Manx model. Unlike the pukka racer the twin had a neatly styled glass-fibre rear mudguard, which also formed the seat pan, while between the frame loops there was a light-alloy oil tank, located at the top by a cross-bolt that passed through the tank with the base resting on a rubber-padded cross-member. The familiar Manx-type gear-change linkage was dispensed with and instead a simple pedal projected rearwards from the gearbox cover.

Tom Phillis with the works development five-hundred Domiracer at Mallory Park, Race of the Year, September 1961.

The factory then took the bold move of taking the machine to the Isle of Man TT. Initially the Manx Fairies looked with disfavour on the new 'Domiracer'. The first attempt to practise on the evening of Monday, 5th June was forestalled by carburation bother. On Tuesday morning the fairing had to be modified before the scrutineers would approve it, then, having made the sixth-fastest time on his own single-cylinder Norton, Phil Read heaved the experimental twin into life on a glistening wet road. Despite fog on the Mountain section of the course he had reached Craig-ny-Baa in, as *The Motor Cycle* put it, 'a commendably short time; but here the two parted company and finished up with a generous coating of mud and grass'. Tearing off the battered fairing Read completed the lap in 37 minutes 3 seconds. Tribulations apart, he was most impressed, reporting the handling as good as that of the Manx and the power equally impressive. Even so, later during the practice week, Australian works Honda star Tom Phillis took over the factory Dominator. A new engine had by then been fitted, which provided more power than the standard unit previously used. Observers noted that Phillis's standing-start lap, although not timed, was obviously rapid.

Then came the race, which everyone thought would be yet another MV walkover, with Gary Hocking riding the sole Italian 'Fire Engine' in the 1961 Senior TT. At the end of lap 1 it was Hocking in front, with Hailwood, McIntyre and Read on specially tuned single-cylinder Manx models leading the British charge. But then came the Domiracer, going very quickly with a first-lap speed of 98.93mph, giving Phillis fifth place, which, as *The Motor Cycle* said, 'he could be proud of if he blew up on the next lap. On the next circuit Hailwood was right on Hocking's tail after the MV rider had made a mistake at Ballacraine. The big news of lap 2

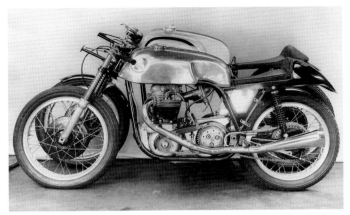

This photograph clearly illustrates just how much lower the Domiracer was compared to the production Manx of the era.

was a 100.36mph (22 minutes 33.4 seconds) blast by Phillis. This hoisted him into fourth, only 1.4 seconds away from Bob McIntyre, who had also moved up on Read. Prior to the race, Norton development chief Hele had predicted that his creation was a flyer with real potential, but few had taken this too seriously. Now everyone could see his statement was entirely accurate. Until the end of lap 4 the leading four places remained unchanged, then race leader Hocking made a dramatic and unscheduled pit stop, and Mike Hailwood took over at the front. Although Hocking restarted, he was destined to retire at his pit the next time around.

At the finish it was the amazing picture of three Nortons in lead positions in a Senior TT, the first time this had happened since the heady days of the early 1950s! Perhaps most surprising of all was the third place Domiracer. In its first ever competition event Phillis had completed the six laps of the gruelling 37¾mile Mountain circuit in 2 hours 17 minutes 31.2 seconds, an average speed of 98.78mph.

Later, at the presentation, Phillis was full of praise for the experimental Norton twin. Although there had been a slight falling off in power in the last half-lap, one piston crown having slightly nudged the cylinder head, there was no other obvious problem when the engine had been stripped for examination. Phillis's verdict was that steering and acceleration were superior to those of a standard Manx model, but maximum speed was perhaps fractionally slower. The lighter weight made the front more prone to lift on full-bore bumps.

There was no doubt that in many ways it had been Phillis's third place on the Norton twin in the Senior TT that was the major talking point in the period immediately after the races were over. *The Motor Cycle* commented: 'In the technical sense, this year's TT series did not come into focus until the very end. That was when Tom Phillis's great third place in the Senior race, with a best lap of 100.36mph, demonstrated the exciting potential of the experimental Norton push-rod twin, still in the infancy of development by engineer Doug Hele!'

Prior to the race the majority of informed observers had regarded the project as nothing more than an interesting 497cc Dominator variant, which, if it could eventually be made to match the performance of the 499cc dohc Manx single, might score on lower production costs. Many also doubted if it could be any more successful than the ill-fated Triumph Grand Prix and Matchless G45, both of which were also based on production push-rod twins. By the end of the Senior TT the newcomer was seen in a totally different light, as the prototype of a model with several clear advantages which had considerable possibilities in both development potential and marketing costs.

The Phillis family.

Taking the latter point first. Hele estimated that the twin could be marketed up to 20 per cent cheaper than the Manx model (on which items such as the cam-box, bevel gears, valves, crankshaft assembly and piston were particularly expensive to manufacture), while the twin offered not only cheaper costs but also easier maintenance.

Functionally, the twin's interest stemmed from its compromise between the two extreme engineering approaches to racing motorcycle design. Then, this was either the sheer power of a four (or six or eight as had been tried by MV and Moto Guzzi respectively), with its penalty of greater weight and bulk and higher centre of gravity, or the Moto Guzzi idea of putting the priority on ultra-light weight, extreme slimness and the lowest centre of gravity by utilising a horizontal single with its inevitable

Paul Dunstall, seen here working in the Brands Hatch paddock during 1967, eventually purchased the remains of the factory Domiracer stock, after it had been first sold to Norton dealer, Reg Dearden.

lower power output. Since for a given swept volume, multiplying cylinders multiplies breathing potential, a twin comes somewhere between a single and a four on power. But when installed vertically (as with the Domiracer), the twin is (or should be) much less cumbersome than a four; and if kept slim enough it should enjoy a considerable advantage in penetration over the wider multi.

As it was lighter than the Manx, the Domiracer also had the advantages in acceleration, braking and handling. If Norton had chosen to follow Manx practice and employed a light-alloy barrel and Elektron crankcases, the difference would have been even greater. Constructed from thinner tubing than the single-cylinder Manx, the frame, as already mentioned, was also lower, thus again helping penetration. So the lower centre of gravity, combined with a shorter wheelbase, offered improved cornering abilities.

Two experimental engines were tried in the Isle of Man, both of which used valves of standard size; so once again breathing could have been improved. Both these power units used the roadster model's 66 x 72mm bore and stroke. One differed from the Dominator 88SS only in so far as the camshaft, inlet ports and valve gear were concerned. The other engine, the one used by Phillis in the race, was more extensively modified and, it was claimed, not only offered a 5 per cent power advantage, but also smoother running. The latter also had the advantage that it was not subject to the same level of vibration as the standard unit. Crankshaft strength had been increased by an increase in dimensions and using larger main bearings, roller on the nearside, ballrace on the offside. The plain white metal big-ends (and small ends) were also upped in diameter and the length of the light-alloy connecting rods decreased. With a compression ratio of 11:1, the full-skirt pistons were both shorter and lighter than the standard components, but also used only one compression ring, and this was of the Dykes L-section type A cylinder head from the 650 Manxman (later known as the 650SS) was employed because it featured a steeper inlet port downdraught and wider splaying of the exhaust ports for increased cooling. The

Opposite: Dave Downer on the Dunstall Domiracer at Snetterton, 14th April, 1963. A few days later he was to meet his death at Brands Hatch in an accident involving Derek Minter.

Rudi Thalhammer (5) leads the field on his Domiracer at the start of the 1963 500cc Austrian Grand Prix.

centres of the inlet ports were further apart so that a pair of Amal GP2 1³/₁₆ inch carbs could be fitted. The relatively narrow angle of 58 degrees between the valve stems (the exhaust stems were inclined at 30 degrees, the inlets only 28 degrees) ensured compact combustion chambers with a low surface-to-volume ratio for good thermal efficiency and a respectably short flame trail. There was no squish band. The valves were of nimonic steel, and the clearances were adjusted by turning the eccentric rocker spindles. This design not only cut reciprocating weight by a small amount, but it also meant that the rocker ends could be ground to give line contact with the valve tips instead of employing the conventional ball-end type adjusters. The alloy push-rods had been lengthened to reach down into the flatbase tappets, and were hollowed to reduce their weight by half. In place of the normal bronze bushes for the camshaft more effficient rollers were used, while the rocker gear was lubricated by a pressure bleed from the timing cover in place of the standard model's scavenge bleed. As used in the TT, output was limited by valve float coming in at 7,400rpm, and so Hele employed the 4.1:1 top gear ratio of the standard 500 Manx for the Phillis bike. An important step in the Domiracer's development would have been to make suitable changes to exploit the engine's breathing potential at higher rpm. Hele was sure that 8,000rpm, was easily within the development team's reach. Power output of the 1961 Senior TT third-place bike was around 50bhp, so it should have been possible to comfortably exceed the output of the 500 Manx, which was by then pumping out some 52bhp. And of course the Domiracer had other advantages, which have already been catalogued.

Following the TT (in which the Domiracer had made history by becoming the first twin or a push-rod engine to lap at over 100 mph), Norton were to receive much encouragement to build the Domiracer. In August all they would say was: 'We will not be marketing the Domiracer next year (1962). The established Manx singles in three-fifty and five-hundred sizes are to be continued with, probably, a few modifications, and the production schedules have already been settled.'

For the rest of 1961 very little was seen (except for a few local shows) of the Domiracer. But in January 1962 Doug Hele was reported by *The Motor Cycle* to have said: 'Watch out for quite a number of factory Norton twins, and in several forms.' But even though the 650SS went on sale that year, and gained much success in production machine racing, the Domiracer project stagnated. Except, that was, for Derek Minter doing the occasional short circuit meeting and practising on the ex-Phillis machine for the 1962 Senior TT. For the race, however, he decided to stick with his own single. Minter did, however, race a larger 650 version, winning in the process his first ever event on the machine at Brands Hatch in the unlimited class. But with Norton moving to Woolwich and a general decline in the factory's financial fortunes, the whole factory Domiracer project was shelved and the existing bikes and spares sold off to Reg Dearden and Paul Dunstall later that year.

For 1963 Dunstall entered the up-and-coming Dave Downer on both the 500 and 650 Domiracers, and it was on one of these latter machines that Downer duelled wheel-to-wheel with Minter (Manx) in a never-to-be-forgotten race at Brands Hatch that April. However, as the pair came towards the end of what had been a magnificent, closely fought race they both crashed, Downer fatally and Minter suffering serious injuries. Dunstall then employed other riders, including Syd Mizen, and the Dunstall name was thrust into the limelight. The Dunstall Domiracer created success not only on the track, but helped to establish Dunstall as the premier customising business of the 1960s, based around Domiracer tuning and accessory components. Meanwhile, Dearden did very little with his Domiracer haul, concentrating instead on Manx business.

Austrian Rudi Thalhammer, at work on his home-tuned Domiracer in 1963.

Then, of course, later in the decade came the Commando, and later still the 'new' works racing twins, raced by men such as Phil Read, Peter Williams and Dave Croxford. But with its isolastic frame the Commando, as such, is outside the scope of this book. The Domiracer could and should have brought a new era in Norton racing at factory level, instead, with its fortunes controlled by the crumbling AMC empire, the once famous marque was destined to slip into a downward spiral.

In the final analysis, the Domiracer was the ideal replacement for the long-running Manx, but it was a chance passed by, a truly sad fate for a concept that had promised so much during its 1961 Senior TT debut. Even so, a number of privateers did build their own Domiracers, including Austrian star Rudi Thalhammer, who used his quite successfully, even at Grand Prix level, during the early 1960s. But finally, instead of being developed to its full potential, it just simply slipped quietly from the racing scene.

12 **The Tuners**

Cutaway view showing mechanical details of the final version of Norton's Manx engine. Note slipper piston, straight cut bevel gears, double-webbed con-rod and hairpin valve springs.

During the period immediately after World War II and through until the late 1960s, a small group of men emerged who won fame not because of their efforts on the track but in the workshop. These highly respected individuals, who used spanners rather than throttles, were high priests at the altar of Norton's speed achievements - they were the tuners. *The Motor Cycle* once commented: 'Engine tuners are the most versatile breed on earth. They are at once theoreticians and dab hands with anything from a hammer to a micrometer. Mostly they can use machine tools. They can all turn, screw-cut, fit. I don't know of one who cannot weld and braze. They become tuners because they have all these skills and many more.' The following are pen portraits of nine of the leading exponents of the Manx Norton tuning art.

PHIL KETTLE

Phil Kettle with Manx rider Ron Grant, at the Manx Grand Prix, early 1960s

Phil Kettle was born in Weybridge, Surrey on the 30th May 1919. His first motorcycle was a Levis 250, whilst his first experience of motorcycle racing, as a spectator, came at his local Brooklands circuit.

During the Second World War, Phil saw service with the British Army in India and Burma. Returning to a post-war England his first contact with the Manx Norton came when he joined the famous tuner Francis Beart. His enthusiasm for the cammy Norton extended to his owning an International model, which as he said recently; 'I rode as my transport on the road for 20 years'.

The list of riders Phil Kettle prepared engines for, during his time with Beart, and after he set up in business on his own account is impressive, and includes: Mike Hailwood, Joe Dunphy, Peter Darvill, Ernie Washer, Griff Jenkins, Jimmie Guthrie Jnr, Billy McCosh, Rex Butcher, Ed Minihan, Ellis Boyce, Peter Middleton, Ken Huggett, Brian Penfold, Dave Pither, Brian Hussey and Tony Dunnell.

Asked in September 2000 'When did you retire'. The answer came back 'I've not retired as yet'. Which says a lot about the man.

ALLEN DUDLEY-WARD

Allen Dudley-Ward with his first DW Special, a 500cc JAP V-twin; this is at Cadwell Park, 5th August,1946.

Dudley-Ward's training and background was of the type that instilled craftsman perfection. He was apprenticed as a tool and gauge maker and worked at the trade during World War II. Born in 1916 he started racing with a KSS Velocette in 1938, the same machine which he used as ride-to-work transport. His racing career was rudely halted by the outbreak of hostilities the following year. Later, towards the end of the war, he started building the first DW Special, a superbly finished, distinctive and functional piece of raceware powered by a 500cc JAP v-twin.

Dudley-Ward's special-building by no means ended there for, as he later explained, at that time he never seemed to have enough money to buy a 'pukka' racing job. Other DW Specials included ones powered by 350 BSA Gold Star and Triumph T100 engines. Together with his friend and business partner, Geoff Monty, he was also a member of the SPORT Equipe, a private racing team formed in the early 1950s. Then came a period of continental racing, including several months in Finland, where he met and married a Swedish girl.

Allen Dudley-Ward at work in his Kingston upon Thames workshop during the early 1960s.

The Monty and Ward partnership had started at West Molesey, Surrey, during 1946. One of their first products was a design, by Dudley-Ward, of a rear suspension conversion for rigid frames. Then came a move to Kingston upon Thames and finally to the Monty and Ward showrooms in Twickenham, although Dudley-Ward himself remained at the establishment in Kingston, where he was head of the tuning and repair side of the business. One of his most interesting developments was a one-piece crankshaft and plain bearing big-end for Manx Nortons. Riders who used the Allen Dudley-Ward tuning services included Bob Anderson, Paddy Driver and Chris Conn.

RAY PETTY

*A young Ray Petty, with his 250
New Imperial at Brooklands,
15th July 1939.*

The Petty 'Back-to-Front'
Manx 350cc in 1965.

Ray Petty was a man of many talents. Besides being a first-class engineer, he was also a racing man, sprinter and trials rider of considerable note - he was even a builder of some interesting specials. It was, however, as a tuner of Manx Nortons that he is most famous.

He started racing at Brooklands in 1939 on a 250cc New Imperial, but had only appeared at three meetings before war was declared. By then Petty's apprenticeship as a fitter in a local Farnborough garage had finished. He was then sent to an engineering company, where he was employed as a detail fitter making small parts to drawings. Promotion brought a clerical job, which he detested, so he moved on to the tank design department of Vivien Lloyd. From there he moved on to the Vickers Armstrong experimental shop at Fox Warren, not far from his home, where he stayed from 1942 to 1946, working on aircraft engine installation. It was here that he met the legendary Francis Beart, at that time employed by Bristol as the technical representative whose job it was to check that engines, some of them installed by Petty, were behaving correctly.

Ray Petty in his workshop.

So it was that in 1946, released from Government work, Petty joined Beart in preparing Manx Nortons for racing. This was a full-time job, involving many long hours at the bench. But even so Ray Petty managed to squeeze in a considerable amount of racing on his own account with various machines, including a 7R AJS and, later, a couple of Manx Nortons. He still managed to compete in another branch of the sport, one-day trials. Many thought he could have gone to the very top as a mud plugger and he even won a gold medal in the ISDT!

Dan Shorey on bike, Ray Petty and young David May behind.

Derek Minter (11) on the Petty Norton leads Dave Croxford (3), John Cooper (4) and Ron Chandler (1) at Snetterton in 1967.

From 1955 Petty entered the tuning business on his own account, operating in a workshop behind his parents' house in Farnborough, helped by his first wife Peggy. As is evident from the information contained in Chapter 13, Ray was involved with his beloved double-knocker Nortons until the very last, in more ways than one. For a Petty-tuned Norton took the final British Championship won by a single, in 1971, and he was still preparing them for classic racing enthusiasts almost until the very end, when he died in 1987. In the final analysis Petty even eclipsed his former employer, Beart, with more wins and race records to his credit than anyone, except the factory and Joe Craig. A list of his customers reads like a Who's Who of Norton racing: Derek Minter, John Cooper, Dan Shorey, Bob Keeler, Geoff Tanner, Jack Ahearn, Billie Nelson and the Austrian star Bertie Schneider.

Ray Petty at Trent Park Speed Trials 1948.

Summerfield Engineering eventually purchased the Petty Manx business from Ray's second wife Jane (see box in chapter 14). Tina, Ray's daughter commented recently 'Selling the business to them (the Summerfield brothers) gave us great peace of mind as it was such a troubled time for us. They have become great friends of ours and I know Dad would have liked them very much.'

REG DEARDEN

This famous Manchester tuner and dealer had a quite remarkable Isle of Man record, for by the end of 1961 his bikes had won 186 TT and Manx Grand Prix awards! Dearden once said: 'I must be the Island's best customer.'

Although eventually one of the Norton factory's biggest supporters (also customer!), Reg Dearden was also well known for a super-quick 1949 Velocette Mark VIII KTT. This had dohc, as on the works bikes. Ridden by Les Graham, it proved fantastically fast. One secret of its success was the special Dearden cylinder head with an inlet port 1⁹/₃₂in in diameter, a far bigger size than the Velocette factory's development engineers at the time had ever dared to try on their own machines.

Dearden and Domiracer in 1961. Note the model Manx he is displaying.

Another bike on which Dearden lavished his tuning skill was a Vincent 998cc v-twin with which he had hoped to go for the world speed record in the early 1950s. But it was the Manx Norton with which he gained most of his successes. One of the first came when George Catlin won the 1954 Senior Manx Grand Prix using a virtually untested motor that had been put together behind the Castle Mona Hotel, Douglas, just before the practice started. In fact, Dearden believed that many of his best results had come as 'the result of mistakes and often they had never been bench tested before they were taken out on the track'. Typical of this was at *Motor Cycling's* 'Silverstone Saturday' meeting in 1958. Dearden had Geoff Duke mounted on one of his 350 Manx models. During the final practice session on the day prior to the race, Duke bent one of the special inlet valves Dearden had fitted. It was a one off design and no spares were available, so Dearden grabbed a hammer and sat in his van tapping at the valve all night until it was straight. He got the engine running, but it sounded very flat when Duke took it to the line. Then, to cap it all, the former World Champion had a terrible start and was almost last away. As recorded elsewhere in this book, flat-sounding or not, that Manx engine went like a bomb once off the mark, with the result that Duke overtook rider after rider to score one of the most popular wins ever witnessed on the famous Northamptonshire circuit.

Geoff Duke racing a borrowed Manx in the Les Graham Trophy Race at Oulton Park, Cheshire in May 1959. Geoff had borrowed the machine from Manchester dealer/entrant Reg Dearden the previous evening, when mechanic Charlie Edwards had discovered the big-end of Duke's special Norton was ready to disintegrate.

Dearden also believed that riders should have been allowed to run their Norton singles at British short-circuit events on dope. He claimed: 'They won't need to wear their boot-soles out trying to keep up with the works men.' Speaking of the benefits that dope brought, Dearden revealed that he got almost 57bhp out of an otherwise standard Manx short-stroke motor.

Perhaps the most famous incident of the Dearden policy of sponsoring up-and-coming riders, rather than established stars, was Gary Hocking. In fact, if it had not been for Reg Dearden it is unlikely that the world would have seen the combination of Hocking and MV. The young Rhodesian wandered into Dearden's shop one day and, while wistfully viewing a line-up of Manx Nortons, asked Dearden if he would sponsor him. There was the usual discussion and then Hocking pulled out a return ticket to Rhodesia. 'If you don't sponsor me, Mr Dearden,' he said, 'this is all I've got left and I'm going to use it.' Dearden recalled later, 'He looked so keen that I couldn't let him go, so I called him back and told him to take a Norton with him.' That started an association that lasted until Hocking was signed up by Count Domenico Agusta. Besides Duke and Hocking, other riders who straddled Dearden Nortons included Dave Chadwick, Ralph Rensen, John Hartle, Fred Fisher, Terry Shepherd and Keith Terretta.

Opposite: Reg Dearden and son outside his Manchester showrooms in January 1960.

FRANCIS BEART

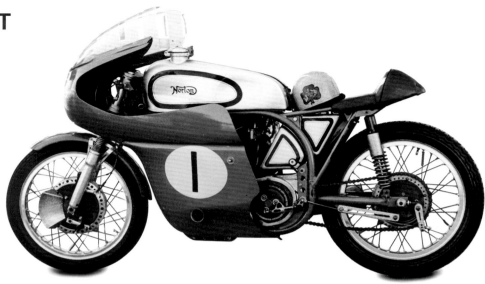

Joe Dunphy's Beart-tuned Norton, which he brought home in second place to Mike Hailwood in the 1965 Senior TT.

Francis Beart (with hat) and Australian Continental Circus star Jack Findlay in the Isle of Man, circa early 1970s. By then Beart was tuning Italian Aermacchis rather than Nortons.

If Reg Dearden openly admitted that his best tuning was often by chance, Francis Beart was just the opposite, never allowing anything to be, in his opinion, 'less than 101 per cent'. I remember being fortunate enough to share a garage next to him during the Manx Grand Prix many years ago. I will never forget his statement 'that if anything goes wrong over here I wouldn't bother attempting a repair, but just load the bike straight into the van'. This summed Francis Beart up perfectly.

The name F.L. Beart first found its way into the pages of the motorcycling press during the 1930s, when the Brooklands track was the Mecca for speedmen the world over. He was a regular competitor for a number of years, until, in 1937, he moved into a small workshop (*The Motor Cycle* described it as a 'shack') on the circuit and set about making other people's engines go faster instead of riding his own bikes. Building up a business, any business, from scratch calls for dedication and hard work. But Beart went even further, for he almost lived at his tuning establishment and worked hours longer than any man should be expected to. However, in terms of results if not financial return, he could claim complete success. Before Brooklands' gates were finally closed in 1939 his efforts had paid off in a big way: 12 track and three world records had fallen to Beart-inspired machinery.

Immediately post-war, Beart was even busier, tuning for many of the greats of the road racing game, including Johnny Lockett, who graduated to the Norton factory team, Ken Bills, who subsequently rode works Velocettes, Cromie McCandless, Manliff Barrington, Denis Parkinson, Don Crossley, Peter Romaine and many, many more. As detailed in Chapter 4, the Beart touch was also felt in the USA, where Nortons tuned by him swept Daytona for three years: 1949, 1950 and 1951.

Then Beart temporarily quit motorcycles. At that time 500cc car racing (see Chapter 7) was the thing, and demands for his services from the four-wheel brigade were overwhelming. But in 1958 the old interest in bikes was revived and Beart returned to his first love. He was approached to breathe on the Nortons to be raced by Ernie Washer in the Manx Grand Prix. The result of Beart's workshop skill and Washer's track-craft resulted in a

win in the Senior at record speed, hoisting the lap record in the process. Washer might well have won the Junior, too, had a missed gear change not let the valves kiss. As it was, the Beart runner finished third. Then came a whole host of Manx Grand Prix successes, including Peter Middleton's victory in the 1959 Junior and Ellis Boyce's over 90mph average to win the same event the following year. Other riders who benefited from the magic of Francis Beart during the late 1950s and early 1960s included Mike Hailwood, Joe Dunphy, Terry Shepherd and Bob Anderson.

In September 1962 it was announced that Beart intended to offer a limited number of rebuilt post-1960, 350 and 500 Manx Nortons to fill the void that would be left by AMC, who were then just building the last production racers. Assisted by Phil Kettle, the Guildford tuner continued to tune and rebuild Nortons for several years afterwards. He eventually turned his main attention to Italian Aermacchis towards the end of the 1960s, following a brief flirtation with Greeves two-strokes. Like the famous Beart Nortons, all these bikes were finished in a distinctive light green livery.

Cromie McCandless about to 'sign on' with his Beart-Norton at the 1950 Senior TT, in which he finished eighth. Francis Beart can be seen here in sunglasses second from the right.

BILL STUART

At the Silverstone sprint practice on 15th March, 1961, are Charlie Luck (left) and Bill Stuart. The giant single-lunger had a capacity of 715cc and a Stuart coil valve spring conversion.

Stuart is seen here modifying a Manx piston, with a trio of Manx engines awaiting attention, at his Warwickshire workshop in the early 1960s.

The Motor Cycle described Bill Stuart as 'Fugitive from the Craig-Gang'. This was because this tuner extraordinary had spent time with the famous factory race chief. Bill Stuart's life was full of the unexpected. He had been born in Russia, back in Czarist days. Stuart's father managed a cotton mill near Moscow, so his birth certificate caused more than a few raised eyebrows among the security boys when Bill was employed by the Armstrong Siddeley company on aircraft research work during the war.

A great enthusiast for the Isle of Man TT, he was also a sponsor during the inter-war period and, for example, in 1937 Stuart fielded no fewer than seven riders in the Lightweight TT. At that time he ran a motorcycle business in Blackpool. But after a period of 16 years in the trade the Second World War was unleashed. When it ended he headed for a new life in Birmingham, then the centre of the motorcycling world. Eventually he ended up working for Joe Craig in the racing department at Bracebridge Street. After four years of long hours, however, a bout of pneumonia caused him to give up the job at Norton and move out into the Warwickshire countryside. Bill Stuart once commented, 'I'm the only Norton race-shop man to escape from captivity.' His move to being a private tuner

Bill Stuart, working on Len Taylor's Norton-powered outfit, Silverstone, March 1954.

coincided with the growth of Norton-powered 500cc car racing. So with that, and a growing influx of work from the two-wheel boys, he had plenty to keep him occupied. Besides Norton, Bill Stuart was also involved in two-stroke work, including doing much of the bench work on Herman Meier's Ariel Arrow. Stuart was also the man behind the largest ever Manx engine. This was the 715cc (90 x 113mm) monster single that Charlie Luck used for sprinting and hill-climbing in the early 1960s. Power output was estimated to have been between 60 and 65bhp at 6,800rpm. Another innovation pioneered by Stuart was the use of coil valve springs in the Manx engine.

Riders who used his services included Geoff Duke, Dan Shorey and sidecar racer Len Taylor, plus hundreds of lesser known men. Bill Stuart was at his happiest working alone in his workshop with, as often as not, a beret on his head and a pipe in his mouth.

JOE POTTS

Alastair King on his Potts-tuned 348cc Manx at Silverstone, 1959.

Scotland's high priest of tune Joe Potts.

Opposite: Bob McIntyre leading the 500cc race of the North West 200, May 1960. He was robbed of almost certain victory when his Potts-Norton developed an oil leakage which smothered the rear of the machine with lubricant, forcing his retirement.

Joe Potts's motto was 'Have the right man handling the twist grip'. When one realises that he was the man behind riders such as Bob McIntyre and Alastair King it is easy to appreciate how true this saying was.

Like several other leading tuners, Potts had been a racer himself, from 1930 to 1934. He competed in grass and sand races in his native Scotland on Sunbeam machines. Then, after a lay-off of 13 years, which of course included the war period, Potts decided on a comeback. But this time, in 1949, it was on four wheels, starting with a Cooper car. He later constructed and raced his own rear engined JP racer. This car was variously powered by Vincent singles and twins. His dealings with the Stevenage concern brought Potts into contact with the legendary George Brown, and the common interests and mutual enthusiasm of the pair led to Joe Potts purchasing a Manx Norton. Tuned and modified in typical Potts fashion, this machine carried George Brown to a highly acclaimed seventh place in the 1952 Senior TT.

It was with Bob McIntyre that the Potts reputation was truly born. The first time that Bob Mac rode for Potts was at a Charterhall meeting towards the end of the 1953 season. McIntyre won the 500cc race, putting one across several better-known riders on the very latest short-stroke models. 1954 saw McIntyre signed up by AMC, but he was back with Potts for 1955 and 1956. Even with a Gilera contract for 1957, McIntyre still continued to ride Potts's Nortons, a combination that was to continue right up to the fateful accident in which Bob McIntyre was killed at Oulton Park in August 1962.

In many ways the career of Alastair King was overshadowed by his famous travelling partner, but in truth he was a brilliant rider in his own right. Jimmy Buchan was another who benefited from Potts' sponsorship. But for Joe Potts, racing was never more than a hobby, the rest of the time was spent carrying on the family business in Bellshill, Glasgow, of car hire, sales and repairs and a 24-hour garage service, plus funeral directing!

Potts always protested that he was no technician. Even so, he displayed a shrewd appreciation of mechanical fundamentals. His approach to a task was logical and his methods meticulous, and this combination, with the results he achieved, makes him more than worthy of being a suitable candidate for inclusion here.

BILL LACEY

Bill Lacey standing by his legendary Grindlay-Peerless JAP in the 1920s.

Lacey the tuner in April 1960. He is examining a Manx cylinder barrel.

Born at the turn of the 20th century, C.W.G. (Bill) Lacey was perhaps most famous for the preparation of Mike Hailwood's machines during the early part of the multi-World Champion's career. But Lacey's authority went back much further, for some 30 years previously, in August 1928, he had covered 103 miles in an hour at Brooklands on a Grindlay-Peerless JAP, to win *The Motor Cycle* Trophy for the first rider to record the magic hour at an average speed in excess of 100mph on a British track. Three years later, Lacey pushed the same record up to around 110mph on a Norton at Montlhéry; and ten months earlier, sharing the riding with Wal Phillips, he had helped put 306 miles into three consecutive hours with the same model at the same venue. Perhaps most important of all, Lacey had tuned all the bikes himself. Priority number one in Bill Lacey's opinion was reliability.

Years later, when talking about the Norton engine, he said: 'What you have to remember is that the Manx Norton is a production engine. I can get flash power, but too much boosting can lead to trouble.' He reckoned that bottom-end trouble was unlikely, but that the Achilles' heel was the highly stressed drive-side main bearing. This Lacey modified 'as a matter of course'. The crankcase was bored out to take a flanged bearing housing of his own design. The case was heated to above the working temperature and the housing inserted by hand, so that the 4-inch-diameter flange fitted hard up to the inner crankcase wall and was retained by four flush-fitting socket-head screws. Outside, the housing was screwed left-hand and fitted with a locking ring. Not that Lacey underrated the advantages an expert could gain from experimenting. Indeed, he tried coil ignition, twin plugs, larger valves and chromium cylinder bores on Hailwood's Nortons. Even so, he was a great believer in first

obtaining the very best performance from a standard specification by meticulous attention to detail. This, he considered, was the most important aspect of tuning. He also admitted that he did not always get on too well with Hailwood Senior. In fact at one stage Bill Lacey had had enough of Stan Hailwood and simply walked out on the Hailwood Equipé, only returning later because of Mike. His daughter Ann was also an integral part of the Lacey tuning team in the early 1960s. She was more than capable of stripping and rebuilding a Manx engine to a higher standard than the vast majority of men. Besides Hailwood, the Lacey touch was also responsible for providing the extra steam that helped riders such as John Hartle, Phil Read, Bruce Daniels, John Lewis and Brian Setchell to stardom.

Stan Hailwood employed Bill Lacey to fettle his son's machine during the Ercurie Sportive era (1958-61). Mike is seen here on the 499cc Lacey Manx at Mallory Park Race of the Year in September 1961. He won his heat and then finished 2nd to World Champion Gary Hocking's MV four in the final.

STEVE LANCEFIELD

Steve Lancefield works on Tom Dickie's 500 Manx.

A Londoner, born on 4th November, 1903, S.S. (Steven Silvester) Lancefield never liked the word 'tuner', preferring instead to be known simply as an engineer.

Lancefield began motorcycling with a borrowed Triumph two-stroke in the 1920s, thereafter owning an ABC flat-twin and then a Model 18 TT Replica Norton. In 1929 he did 28 laps of Brooklands in the MCC (Motor Cycle Club) High Speed Trials on the Norton, averaging 80.13mph on petrol, his first Brooklands victory coming the following year. Soon Lancefield made the decision that he was better at working on motorcycles than riding them. A trip to Donington Park with Harold Daniell in the early 1930s proved that a Lancefield-prepared Norton was quicker than a Daniell one, with the result that he joined Daniell in his motorcycle business at Forest Hill. So a hobby was turned into a profession. He also found time to marry Harold's sister Clare.

The coming of the Second World War in 1939 caused a break in racing activities, but Lancefield's engineering skills were put to good use, first with Rolls-Royce and later the Bristol Aircraft Company. Lancefield and Daniell restarted in business after the cessation of hostilities and continued together right up until 1949, when Lancefield was invited to join the Norton works team (Daniell was already a works rider for them). Team boss Joe Craig had noticed his skills, which had included a couple of seconds for Lancefield prepared bikes (both Nortons) at Daytona the previous year and with Billy Mathews losing the all-important 200-miler by only 18 seconds following a lengthy pit stop. Earlier in 1947, for the first time ever, one rider had won three Isle of Man races in one year. Lancefield Nortons carried Eric Briggs to victories in the Senior Clubman's in June, and the Junior and Senior Manx Grands Prix that September. The two Manx winners were completely standard, just 'carefully assembled', while the Clubman's was a borrowed roadster.

For most of the 1950s Steve Lancefield was involved with Formula Three (500cc) car racing, in which the top drivers, including Moss, Russell and Parker, used Lancefield tuned Norton engines (see Chapter 7). By the end of the decade, with the death of Formula Three, Lancefield was back with his original love, two-wheelers. The year 1960 saw him have the honour of preparing the first 500cc single-engined machine to lap the Isle of Man at over 100mph, ridden by Derek Minter. And when Phil Read gave the works four-cylinder Gileras of Scuderia Duke such a fright at Silverstone in April 1963 it was with a Lancefield Norton.

Steve Spencer at Signpost Corner on the Lancefield Norton during the 1966 Senior Manx Grand Prix; he finished third in 2 hours, 26 minutes, 58 seconds, an average speed of 92.43mph.

Never one for publicity, Steve Lancefield continued working on Manx engines until the early 1970s, when he assisted Tom Dickie, but he says that Steve Spencer's 100mph lap in his first TT, the 1967 Senior, was the outstanding performance of the latter-day Lancefield-Norton era. Spencer eventually finished third behind Mike Hailwood (Honda) and Peter Williams (Arter Matchless).

Without a doubt Lancefield was completely dedicated to the art of making Norton singles fast and reliable. He once summed things up like this: 'Some people say I take racing too seriously; to me it's a religion and science and nothing is too good to ensure success. In this respect often I express my considered opinion and it is not liked.' I see this as a sensible approach. Racing at the top is a serious business and requires 100 percent commitment and expertise. S.S. Lancefield had both in abundance.

Of course there are several others who can lay claim to being considered among the top tuners of single-cylinder Nortons; men like Australian Harry Hinton Senior, Allen Dudley-Ward's partner Geoff Monty, and Syd Mularney to name but a few. Steve Lancefield died in January 1990.

Lancefield watches rider
Derek Minter during tyre
testing at Brands Hatch on
6th January, 1960.

Harry Hinton Junior's 500 Manx
twin-plug cylinder head with twin
6-volt coils; March 1959.

Geoff Monty built this interesting
350 Norton during early 1960. The
frame modification was originally
aimed at accommodating an
outside-flywheel 90mm 499cc
engine.

13 Keeping the Flag Flying

John Hartle at Union Mills with his streamlined Manx during the 1957 Junior TT. He lay an incredible second until brought off on oil left by another competitor on lap 4.

By the end of 1954, the Norton single, at least as a serious World Championship contender, had all but been beaten into the ground by the continental opposition. As related in Chapter 3, this had come about by a combination of sticking to the bevel-driven dohc single and a lack of financial muscle.

When the 1955 Norton racing plans were announced that February, it was seen that the famous Bracebridge Street factory would not be entering a works team in the World Championship Series, an exception being made in the case of the Isle of Man TT, where Norton had won on 32 occasions since 1907. Two 21-year-old riders were nominated as members of the team: Londoner John Surtees and John Hartle from Chapel-en-le-Frith, Derbyshire. A third member would be announced later. In a statement made at the time, Norton's managing director, Gilbert Smith, gave the following 'official' reasons for the change of policy. He stated that streamlining, from the private owner's point of view, was 'undesirable as it added greatly to the first cost of the machine, was costly to maintain, made the power unit inaccessible and, by far the most important consideration, could in certain circumstances be dangerous'. Smith went on to say that only with some misgivings had Norton used a limited amount of streamlining the previous year and they had hoped that the FIM would have introduced a regulation to prevent the 'envelope' type of fairing being used in the future. The Norton boss also offered as a reason for the change in policy 'that further progress with the development of special works machines will lead to the demise of private owner racing, and the company had decided to revert to its original policy of racing a type of machine that can be sold to private owners'.

The bikes that Surtees and Hartle would use would only deviate from standard by introducing features that could be incorporated in the following season's production models, after they had been developed during a

During the early 1950s, the 250cc class in British short circuit racing comprised either home-built specials or sleeved down larger singles. One of the latter in the shape of a two-fifty Manx is seen here, circa mid-fifties.

JOHN SURTEES

John Surtees' first motorcycle race came about as a 14-year-old when his father Jack recruited his services as a sidecar passenger. The pairing actually won the event but were subsequently disqualified because of John's age.

His first solo victory came at 17, at the tree-lined Aberdare Park circuit in South Wales. He was riding a 499cc Vincent Grey Flash single which the young Surtees had built whilst serving his apprenticeship at the company's Stevenage factory.

Except for a 1953 TT practice accident whilst riding an EMC 125, John would probably have joined the Norton team that year. As it was Norton retired from the Grand Prix at the end of 1954 so he missed this piece of the action. However, riding a works development Manx he won the 500cc British Championship title in 1955, before being signed by the Italian MV Agusta factory to race its four-cylinder models during the 1956 season. In doing this, John was following in the footsteps of Geoff Duke (although Duke had gone from Norton to Gilera). His first competitive outing on one of the Italian 'fire engines' came at London's Cyrstal Palace circuit in early April. He then proceeded to win the first three rounds of the 500cc World

Championship, and even though he suffered a fall at the next round in Germany at the Solitude circuit, fracturing his arm, he had already amassed enough points to carry off the title. Although he could only finish third behind the Gilera pairing of Libero Liberati and Bob McIntyre in the 1957 500cc title race, he had the honour of giving MV its first ever victory with the smaller four-cylinder machine at the Belgian Grand Prix in 1956.

Then came the golden trio of double 350 and 500cc title years, when Surtees won just about everything in 1958, 1959 and 1960. Having nothing else to prove in the two-wheel world, Surtees moved to four wheels, first as a driver with Lola, then Ferrari (with whom he won the Formula 1 world title in 1964), Honda, and finally in 1969, BRM.

Then he founded his own team which lasted until 1978 and for which he drove until his retirement in 1972. Today he spends much of his time riding motorcycles in historic events.

season's racing. It was felt, Smith argued, 'that the present regulations tend to develop a motorcycle which is of no practical use to the normal tourist, certain international championship events being run on courses which call for a track machine rather than a road racer...Therefore, the Norton factory would no longer support the World Championship events, other than the Isle of Man Tourist Trophy races, which are run over what is regarded as an ideal road racing circuit, but will compete only in other events which will provide opportunities for development of the standard products.' Of course what all this meant in reality was that the factory could no longer compete at the very highest level and realised that only in the TT and certain lesser events could its singles still retain a chance of success. This move, of course, sidelined the proposed 1955 projects, which not only included a new single with the cylinder horizontal, in Guzzi fashion, but also the dohc four-cylinder design. It also meant the end of the road for factory race manager and development engineer Joe Craig, even though the Ulsterman remained on the Norton payroll for that year.

Surtees in action at Scarborough on his 350 in September 1955. He won the race and set a new class record at 64.95mph.

BOB McINTYRE

Robert Macgregor (Bob) McIntyre was born on the 28th November 1928 in Scotstown, a suburb of Glasgow. His father had worked as a riveter, building ships on the Clyde. Bob's first job was in a large garage near his home and his first motorcycle a 16H Norton of 1931 vintage. After completing his national service the young McIntyre returned home and purchased an Ariel Red Hunter - and it was upon this machine that he began his competitive career at a scramble event at Auchterarder near Perth.

After competing in dirt bike events for some months and getting hooked on bikes, Bob found a job with Glasgow dealers Valenti Brothers. His job was servicing and repairing touring bikes - the firm having little connection with the sport at that time.

After watching his first road race at Kirkcaldy, Bob borrowed a friend's 350 BSA Gold Star and entered his first race at Ballado. Riding pillion to the airfield circuit on the bike, they then removed the silencer and lights. His rivals were mounted on pukka racing bikes - including KTT Velocettes and Manxes, but the track was covered in loose gravel and McIntyre's scrambling experience came to the fore. The result was three wins in four races - and the only reason Bob didn't win that one was because he fell off.

At that time, 1950/51, there was very little trade support for racing in Scotland, however in 1952 Bob was asked to ride for Troon dealers Cooper Brothers in the Clubman's TT on another Gold Star. As Bob

was later to recall 'that race made me'. He finished runner up behind winner Eric Houseley and set the fastest lap (a new class record) at 80.09mph.

That September he returned to the Island, this time to ride an AJS 7R in the Junior Manx Grand Prix - Bob not only won, but riding the same bike finished runner up in the Senior!

From then on he mixed it with the big boys and after a spell working for AMC in Plumstead, south west London, began a highly successful spell with Bellshill, Glasgow tuner Joe Potts. (See chapter 12). Besides a famous two-fifty Manx, Bob also rode both 350cc and 500cc Manx models for the Potts stable, as did his close friend, Alastair King. By the end of 1956 the McIntyre reputation had become international, the result was that when Geoff Duke was injured at the beginning of 1957, Bob was signed to race the factory four-cylinder Gileras. He proved his worth by garnering a famous double TT victory in the Jubilee races that year. He also broke the one-hour speed record (on a 350 Gilera) at Monza later that year after Gilera had quit Grand Prix racing.

Later Bob rode works bikes for the likes of Bianchi and Honda, but it was on the British short circuits that he continued to make his mark. And it was one fateful day at Oulton Park in August 1962, when riding his Joe Potts-tuned 499cc Norton, that he crashed heavily receiving serious injuries from which he was to die nine days later.

The Motor Cycle dated 23rd August 1962 carried the following tribute, 'Though we mourned we can be proud that the sport that he graced and those who were privileged to enjoy his friendship are richer for his impact'. It continued 'A life of adventure was as compulsive to Bob as flying is to a bird. Challenge and conquest were food and drink to his spirit'.

On his record lap of 106.86mph during the 500cc race at the 1961 North West 200, on a Joe Potts 499cc Manx with five-speed gearbox and Gilera front brake.

The first motorcycle road race meeting of the season, at least in Britain, was held at Brands Hatch on Good Friday, 8th April, and large crowds watched Surtees dominate the proceedings with a pair of Nortons and a newly acquired German NSU Sportmax. This success was followed the next day at Snetterton, with three more victories. That month also saw veteran Jack Brett named as the third member of the Norton team.

Sunday, 1st May witnessed the 19th international race meeting on Belgium's 5¼-mile Circuit de Mettet. Although both races were eventually won by Fergus Anderson on a pair of the latest fully streamlined Guzzis, it was continental newcomer John Surtees who was acknowledged as the outstanding performer on his naked production-based Manx singles, with two superb second places. Meanwhile, fellow teamsters Hartle and Brett came home third and fourth respectively in both races. Surtees also set the fastest lap of the meeting in the 500cc event in 3 minutes 9 seconds, a speed of 100.54mph.

A tired, but jubilant E.F (Frank) Cope just after winning the handicap race on his sleeved-down 250 Manx, in the 1959 South African Port Elizabeth 200. He was then almost 65 years old.

Then to the TT, where, even if the official Norton policy was no streamlining, riders such as Bob McIntyre and Roy Ingram used 'dustbin'-type full frontal enclosure as used on the Italian works bikes. Even though they could not make use of streamlining, the 'development' Manx models to be used by the Norton trio benefitted from several departures from standard 1955 Manx specification, including 1954 factory cams, larger valves, improved port shapes, weir-type float chambers, rotating-magnet magnetos and new-pattern front forks with external springs.

In the Junior TT Guzzi took their expected victory, with Bill Lomas riding the winning machine, but not without a fight. First came Surtees, and from lap 2, McIntyre on his Joe Potts-entered streamlined Manx. Lomas finally got ahead on lap 5, but even so the Scot hung on to finish a brilliant second, with Guzzi-mounted Cecil Sandford third, Surtees fourth and Hartle sixth. Australian privateer Maurice Quincey rode a superb race to finish fifth after lying fourth at the end of lap 1, in front of many fancied runners, including Guzzi stars Bill Lomas and Ken Kavanagh. Interestingly, McIntyre put his success down to 'the bits of tin which enclosed the motorcycle'. This comprehensive streamlining had been made by McIntyre himself in sponsor Joe Potts's Glasgow workshop. The fairing was supported on a framework of square-section tubing (the same as on his Senior mount) and attachment of the fairing to the frame was by means of quick-action Dzus aircraft fasteners. A flexible hose took cooling air to the front brake. To prevent the footrests grounding on corners, McIntyre had raised the front of the machine an inch by means of a distance-piece above each fork spring, and the rear of the bike was raised by the same amount by the addition of a new sub-frame. The range of movement of the rear wheel spindle had been increased to 3½ inches by modification of the rear shocks.

Jim Redman's first TT appearance came in the 1958 Junior event. In those days he was a privateer in the true sense of the word.

As expected it was Geoff Duke and Gilera who won the 1955 Senior TT, with Reg Armstrong on another Arcore four second, Guzzi-mounted Ken Kavanagh third and Jack Brett, the first combination of British bike and rider, a well-earned fourth. For much of the race the Yorkshire veteran had held a brilliant third! Both Hartle and Surtees were forced to push in with silent engines, Hartle to 13th place and Surtees to 27th. Brett's average speed for the seven laps was 94.52mph, compared with Duke's 97.93mph, and the Norton trio took the manufacturers' Team Award. McIntyre rounded off a near-perfect week by finishing fifth, to add to his second in the Junior.

Tony Godfrey (7) leading another Manx mounted rider, British Championships, Thruxton, August 1958.

There were also a couple of sleeved-down 250 Manx models in the Lightweight TT. One was ridden by 60-year-old Frank Cope, but the courageous old-timer was forced to retire on the last lap. The other model came home seventh of only eight finishers.

If he had been disappointed with his TT results, the young Surtees certainly did not harbour these feelings for long. He was soon back with a string of successes on British short circuits. But not only this, for at the end of June he travelled to the Nürburgring to take part in the first German Grand Prix to be held on this ultra-demanding circuit since 1931. Constructed in 1927, the Nürburgring was the pride of German road racing. Its 14.165-mile lap was a series of undulations and a confusing sequence of bends, many blind, demanding the greatest concentration and skill. John Surtees displayed both with abundance in securing an absolutely superb third place on his Norton in the 350cc event. With only Lomas (Guzzi) and Hobl (DKW) in front of him, he soundly beat such stars as Sandford and Kavanagh (Guzzis), Hoffman and Wünsche (DKW) and the four-cylinder MV Agusta of Bandirola. The next British bike was way down in ninth place. In the 500cc race, aboard a factory BMW Rennsport twin, he was stopped in his wheel tracks when a float chamber fell off the German flat-twin mid-way through the event.

The Norton team then concentrated on British events, with Surtees notably successful at circuits such as Scarborough, Crystal Palace, Aberdare and many others. On the continent, Australian Keith Campbell had ridden a brilliant race in the 350cc Belgian Grand Prix to bring his production Manx single home third. Just as Surtees had done in Germany, the Aussie beat several works machines, including Guzzi and DKW. This was Campbell's first rostrum position in a Grand Prix and in achieving it he displayed some of the skills that were to make him a World Champion within two years.

Mike Hailwood and the Norton on which he finished 12th in the 1958 Junior TT, his first ever race in the Isle of Man.

Perhaps the greatest performance in 1955 for the Norton marque was when, at the end of July, John Hartle, John Surtees and Jack Brett scored a convincing one-two-three victory in the 350cc class of the non-Championship Swedish Grand Prix at Hedemora. Besides the Norton entries there was also works opposition from AJS, DKW and Jawa, so it was no hollow victory. Even though Geoff Duke's Gilera four took the 500cc event at an average speed of 102.46mph, Surtees finished second, at 100.20mph, with Brett third and Hartle fourth. It was a great day in particular for Joe Craig, almost at the end of his career as Norton team boss. Almost as good was the Ulster Grand Prix in August. Here Hartle and McIntyre were second and fourth respectively in the 500cc race, whilst Hartle made it a double with another second in the 350cc event, with Surtees third and McIntyre fifth. Bill Lomas took his Guzzi to victory in both races.

Then it was back to the British short circuits and a breathtaking duel in mid-September between Duke's four-cylinder Gilera and Surtees' Norton single at Scarborough's Olivers' Mount circuit, during the fifth annual two-day international meeting to be staged at the popular North Yorkshire seaside course. However, it was at the BMCRC (British Motor Cycle Racing Club) international Hutchinson 100 meeting on 1st October, that the young Norton teamster finally realised his greatest ambition by beating World Champion Duke and his Gilera. Leading from start to finish in the 20-lap 500cc Championship race on the 2-mile 1,618-yard Silverstone circuit, he thundered home 6.8 seconds ahead of the Italian 'Fire Engine' to share a new lap record with Duke of 96.28mph. Surtees finished his lap of honour to the tumultuous applause of thousands of spectators, officials and riders, who flocked to the grid to acclaim the 'victory of the year' as *Motor Cycling* called it. Surtees also won the 350cc race to round off a fabulous performance.

Geoff Duke with the 40M three-fifty special on his way to a superb 14th in 1959 Junior TT. His race average speed was 93.56mph.

Alan Trow receives the Slazenger Trophy from Mrs Gwendoline Slazenger at Brands Hatch on 23rd September, 1956.

Swiss sidecar ace Florian Camathias also rode solo, including this five-hundred Manx at Thruxton, August 1958.

The following day the largest crowd ever seen at the Brands Hatch circuit saw Surtees once again beat Duke to the flag. But this time Norton privateer Alan Trow also finished ahead of the Gilera World Champion. By now, the press were naming Surtees as 'Wonder Boy' and 'Future Champion'. With all this success it was perhaps inevitable that Surtees would be snapped up by one of the Italian teams - and in this case, late in October, the news broke that the gifted South Londoner had signed for the MV Agusta concern.

In March 1956 it was announced that the Norton team would comprise Hartle, Brett and newcomer Alan Trow, who had put up a number of excellent performances on his own Manx models, including a fourth place in the 1955 Senior Manx Grand Prix. Meetings 'officially' contested would be: Oulton Park, 2nd April; Silverstone, 14th April; Floreffe, 6th May; Aintree, 19th May; Junior and Senior TTs, 4th and 6th June; Swedish Grand Prix, 14th and 15th July; Thruxton, 6th August; Ulster Grand Prix, 9th and 11th August; Scarborough, 14th and 15th September, and the Hutchinson 100 on 22nd September.

The existing policy of mounting Norton factory riders on 'pre-production prototype' machines was to be continued. Perhaps the leading rider of Norton singles without factory support, as the 1956 season started, was Bob McIntyre, who had been one of the sensations of the previous year's TT races. For the new season he had not only had 349 and 499cc models, both of which were standard 1956 Manx models tuned by Joe Potts, but

also a very interesting 246cc model. The engine of this exceptionally workmanlike product started life as a 349cc Manx unit. The cylinder barrel was shortened and sleeved to a bore dimension of 70mm. In order to reduce the stroke to 64mm the original flywheel assembly was replaced by a one-piece crankshaft carrying an outside flywheel. The special light-alloy con-rod was split across the big-end eye, which was equipped with a shell-type bearing. Machined from a solid billet of high-duty steel and subsequently heat treated, the crankshaft had standard-sized main bearing journals, 1-inch diameter on the timing side and 1 1/8-inch on the drive side. The ball and roller timing side main bearings were non-standard. Diameter of the big-end bearing was 1 3/4 inches. To ensure adequate lubrication for the plain big-end bearing, oil pressure had been upped to 60lb/sq.in; this had necessitated the use of a synthetic rubber oil seal where the big-end feed jet entered the crankshaft at the off-side end. The cylinder head was machined from a 350 Manx Norton casting and the inlet valve was slightly reduced in size. The choke diameter of the Amal GP carburettor was 1 1/8 inches and the cams were specials manufactured in Joe Potts's machine shop. Of conventional duplex-loop pattern, the frame was constructed in 1 1/8-inch diameter Reynolds 531 tubing; the Earles-type front fork was made from 16 gauge Accles and Pollock tubing. The Manx twin leading shoe front brake featured a floating shoe plate and a torque linkage designed to isolate fork action from braking torque.

The 246cc Norton with which Bob McIntyre had so much success in 1956. The sleeved Manx engine revved to 8,000 and was capable of a genuine 100mph.

Fron Purslow on his 499cc 30M Manx at Thruxton, 1958.

The new quarter-litre McIntyre Manx was soon in winning action, with victories at Brough and Oulton Park early in the season. Capable of a genuine 100mph, the 'baby' Manx could exceed 8,000rpm.

At a very wet Silverstone in mid-April, Hartle and Bob Keeler (drafted into the squad) scored an easy one-two in the 350cc final; but in the 500cc final the 'official' Norton men did not make the first three, in a race won by Surtees on the MV and with privateer McIntyre in second place. Jack Brett had not been allowed to compete after being late for practice. In May Bert Hopwood rejoined Norton, to be responsible for all matters pertaining to design and production. The timing of his appointment is interesting, coming a mere five months after Joe Craig had retired. Sunday 6th May saw the Norton team riders competing over the 8.44-mile Floreffe circuit in Belgium. Sadly the meeting was marred by the fatal accident to former World Champion Fergus Anderson. The best placing obtained by a Norton rider was Jack Brett's third place in the 500cc event behind Surtees (MV) and Lomas (Guzzi). That month Norton machinery gained the first three places in the Senior class of the important Irish North West 200: Bob Anderson, Geoff Tanner and D.C. Chapman.

Few races in history have started so tamely and finished so dramatically as the 1956 Junior. In the final two laps two leaders were destined to retire, first Surtees (MV) and then Lomas (Guzzi). This left Ken Kavanagh, on

Geoff Tanner averaged 91.54mph to finish third in the 1958 Junior TT.

another Guzzi, to win by over 2mph from Ennett (AJS) and Norton-mounted Hartle. The remainder of the leader board was occupied by Sandford (DKW) and the Nortons of South African Eddie Grant and Alan Trow. But it had been the veteran Jack Brett who had put in the best Norton performance holding a gallant third for three laps. Even on lap 6, Brett was still holding fourth when gearbox trouble put him out at Quarry Bends. The Norton team leader came back in the Senior race when, after a truly outstanding ride, he finished third against full works entries from MV Agusta, Moto Guzzi and BMW. At the end it was a memorable day for Norton, as young Hartle finished second and Trow seventh, in a race won by Surtees and MV Agusta. Hartle averaged 95.69mph, Brett 94.69mph and Trow 91.36mph (Surtees's speed was 96.57mph). And Norton won the Manufacturers' Team Award. In the Lightweight TT, 61-year-old Frank Cope brought his sleeved down Norton home in ninth place.

Meanwhile, McIntyre had a miserable TT, retiring on lap 3 of the Junior and lap 2 of the Senior; with no entry in the Lightweight, his 1956 TT scoresheet was completely blank! This was a great pity because McIntyre's Potts-prepared Manx models had been fitted with pannier fuel tanks to enable him to complete the full race distance non-stop. By the important Aintree meeting in late July Bob McIntyre was back on song, taking the lion's share of the honours by winning both the 350cc and 500cc races on his Potts Norton. By now he had a travelling companion, Alastair King, who made it a successful day for the Scots by finishing third in the Senior and fourth in the Junior.

The Ulster Grand Prix some two weeks later saw Hartle score his first classic 500cc victory when he rode a superb race to outlast the opposition, which included such stars as Duke and Armstrong (both Gileras), Lomas (Guzzi), Zeller (BMW) and team-mate Jack Brett. Earlier, Hartle and Brett had finished third and fourth respectively in the 350cc race, behind the Guzzis of Lomas and Dale. Aboard a pair of Joe Potts Nortons, Jimmy Buchan scored an impressive double victory in the Junior and Senior Manx Grands Prix. Said McIntyre, when the bikes were returned, 'There's nothing to beat a Double Scotch.'

Mike Hailwood, father Stan and Graham Walker (far right) during an interview in early 1959.

At the International Hutchinson 100 at Silverstone on Saturday, 22nd September, spectators were treated to possibly the best race ever run on the Northamptonshire circuit. From start to finish of the 350cc Championship final titanic battles were waged between Hartle, McIntyre and Brett, all Norton mounted, until the 17th of the 20 laps. Brett showed that he had lost none of his old mastery and, with a terrific effort, put some 20 yards between himself and the two young riders, who continued to fight it out right up to the line, where the verdict went to the flying Scot by half a length. Hartle won the 500cc race from McIntyre and Brett, so reversing the order of the previous race. In the 250cc event, McIntyre brought his sleeved-down Manx home third behind race winner Sandford's Mondial and Chadwick's MV Agusta.

A 499cc 30M Manx engine is run up on the brake. During the late 1950s and early 1960s this was the engine for the top-line privateer.

At the Motor Trades luncheon held in Manchester on 15th October, Norton racing team manager Alan Wilson reaffirmed the existing policy of Norton Motors to be 'the same as you can buy'. Wilson went on to say that the 'Italians raced motorcycles that were nothing at all like the standard job, but they found it paid for the sake of prestige'. At the end of the year it was announced that both AMC and Norton would not be participating in international events during 1957 - not even with 'standard bikes'. However, the production of racing models such as the Manx and 7R would continue for sale to private owners.

Even without any factory support the 1957 season proved quite successful, including the classics. The highlight was Jack Brett's victory in the 500cc Belgian Grand Prix, which he won at over 113mph, although it must be stated that there were only five finishers. Even so, Brett also finished fourth in the Dutch TT in both the 350cc and 500cc races! Hartle also achieved some success with a fourth in the Ulster and a sixth at Monza, both in the 500cc category. Australian Keith Bryen also put up a number of excellent performances on the Continent and attracted the attention of the Moto Guzzi team. McIntyre had been signed up for the Gilera team, but still rode his Potts Nortons on the short circuits, with his usual aggressive style.

After the TT had come an exciting couple of days' racing at Scarborough. This had seen McIntyre, Surtees and Brett all duelling on single-cylinder Nortons. It was double TT winner McIntyre who controlled both races. Although the official line was 'no works support', an interesting mount appeared at the Scarborough International during September, ridden by none other than John Hartle. It had different engines for the Junior and Senior events. Prepared by Norton mechanic Arthur Edwards with an emphasis on weight saving, it scaled only 270lb in 350cc form and was fitted with a modified 1954 works five-speed gearbox. The most obvious departure from

standard Manx design was the absence of a normal oil tank, lubricant being carried behind the fuel in what was virtually a standard petrol tank divided into two separate parts. Other notable features were the fully floating rear brake, the torque arm of which was attached directly to the machine's frame to eliminate braking snatch and patter, and the front brake plate, which was equipped with a massive air scoop, with an equally large rearward-facing scoop to give an extractor effect. The seat had been reduced to Spartan proportions and no mudguards were used, a fact that proved a problem in the Junior final, which was wet! Hartle also found that the unaccustomed lightness made the machine rather difficult to control, though this was probably due to his unfamiliarity with it. Arthur Edwards's aim was ultimately to reduce the weight still further, to around 250lb.

During September 1957 Norton was awarded the Coppa Presidente dalla Republica by the FIM, for being the marque with the greatest number of finishers at the Italian Grand Prix that year. Managing director Gilbert Smith said, 'This award is very gratifying, for it vindicates our policy of concentrating on standard production racing machines which the public can buy, rather than on making a few special racing machines which are not available except to the top flight riders with works support.'

Some idea of the performance available from Manx models, albeit with special preparation, came from Australia, where Harry Hinton Junior broke the national flying half-mile two-way speed record at Coonabarabran, New South Wales, on Sunday, 29th September. Hinton's 348cc Manx averaged 126.76mph. Although not breaking the existing figure, on his 499cc model Hinton did two runs at 141 and 141.5mph. Former works rider Ken Kavanagh said recently: 'Harry Hinton Senior probably knew more about Manx engines than anyone outside the Norton factory.'

Rob Fitton (9) leading at Cadwell Park in 1959. Fitton rode Norton singles for many years and was one of the very last to race them at international level.

Superb action shot of Derek Minter on his way to winning the 350cc British Championship title on his Manx, at Thruxton in August 1958.

The following month saw former World Champion Geoff Duke back on Norton machinery at Oulton Park. This was a machine produced jointly by himself and the Reynolds and Woodhead Monroe concerns. Its engine and gearbox were standard production Manx components, but the frame featured a single down-tube and the front forks were of the leading link variety. Total weight saving was some 25lb. Duke appeared satisfied with the bike, commenting, 'the link fork seems to keep the front wheel on the ground and I can really use the front brake, but I'll have to alter the position of the seat, which is making me pull on the bars'. At the same Oulton Park meeting John Hartle's latest modification to the Edwards lightweight Manx special was that the megaphone now exited under his seat!

Despite John Surtees's contract to race four-cylinder MVs, he had none the less continued his association with the Bracebridge Street marque. For 1958, Surtees was building up a pair of new Nortons in an ambitious manner, aiming to increase the power output a little, lose some weight, improve the steering and enhance the stopping power. He also planned to keep his standard Manx jobs that had brought him so many wins during 1957. Regarding his plans with Count Agusta, Surtees said, 'My contract is due for renewal, though the subject (riding his private Nortons) still remains to be discussed.'

At the very tail-end of the British short-circuit racing season a new Norton star emerged, 25-year-old Derek Minter, who created a sensation not only by beating John Surtees at Brands Hatch on Sunday, 13th October, 1957, but also by setting some new lap and race records. His first success came in the 350 Experts race, where during a meteoric ride on his Lancefield-tuned machine he not only beat established stars such as Surtees, Brett and Trow but also equalled Surtees's 500cc lap record and set a new race record average speed. Then came the day's premier event, the Slazenger Trophy race. Although this was won by Surtees on his 500cc Norton, similarly mounted Minter set a new lap and track record at what *Motor Cycling* referred to as 'an astounding 75.15mph' for the twisting 1.24-mile Kent circuit. Derek Minter had arrived, and in style!

Former works star Geoff Duke campaigned this very special Reynolds-framed 350 Manx during the 1958 season. Its features included leading-link forks and a large diameter, oil-carrying down tube.

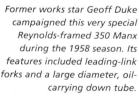

South African Paddy Driver, taking his 499cc Manx to victory in his heat of the Commonwealth Trophy, Thruxton, 1st August 1960. In the final his clutch came adrift, forcing his retirement when he was well placed.

With Moto Guzzi, Gilera and Mondial all announcing their retirement from Grand Prix events, and for that matter any road racing, many pundits began to question a full Norton return. This was heightened by news that the FIM would be banning the use of 'dustbin'-type streamlining. In the end all this speculation was to prove largely unfounded and Norton's 1958 involvement was limited to a few works development Manx models supplied to Manchester tuner and entrant Reg Dearden (see Chapter 12). The beginning of April 1958 saw Bert Hopwood appointed as managing director of both Norton Motors Ltd and the associated concern, R.T. Shelley and Co, Ltd.

Bob McIntyre, now fully recovered from an accident at the end of the 1957 season, was back in action on a very special 274lb dry weight, Joe Potts 499cc Manx at Brands Hatch on Good Friday, 4th April. Just prior to this, 1957, 350 World Champion Keith Campbell had visited the Bracebridge Street factory to purchase a couple of new Nortons - only to find the factory's complete output for 1958 was already sold. Undaunted, Campbell headed for the Continent and soon afterwards had secured a brace of Manx models on which to do battle. Maybe having Geoff Duke as a brother-in-law was of some assistance in this matter. As for Duke himself, he had signed up to ride a works BMW Rennsport twin. In the 350cc class he had purchased Derek Minter's 1957 Manx model and intended 'making extensive modification to it for the coming season'. This resulted in a most interesting special. The Reynolds frame bore some resemblance to the one that Duke used the previous season, but one big difference was the use of an oversize front down-tube, which also served as the oil tank. This was calculated to have two advantages, firstly that it brought a little more weight forward, considered desirable in view of the FIM limitations on frontal streamlining, and secondly, that without the conventional oil tank more room was available behind the engine for the carburettor and its 'breathing space'. The front forks (also manufactured by Reynolds) were of the leading link type used in 1957, somewhat modified, and the spring units, front and rear, were of Woodhead-Monroe manufacture. Braking was taken care of, at least initially, by an AJS 7R component at the front and Norton at the rear, both units featuring free-floating back plates.

A Silverstone shot of George Catlin with his three-fifty Manx in the spring of 1959.

John Hartle (28) and Derek Minter (31) duel on their Manx models in the 350cc race at Silverstone in May 1958. Minter won, with Hartle second.

Senior TT, June 1960. Canadian Dave Woodman (71) leads Jim Redman (18). Both ride Nortons. Woodman retired, whilst Redman finished 15th.

The engine was basically a 349cc Manx unit, but with a one-piece crankshaft, forged by Brown of Sheffield and machined by Laystall. The main bearing assembly differed in that the drive-side journal had a larger flange and the flywheel was outside the crankcase. A plain bearing big-end carried a con-rod of Hiduminium alloy and the forged piston operated in an aluminium cylinder featuring a chrome-plated bore, a system Duke had used for the past two years on his special Velocette, with which he had sponsored another rider over the preceding couple of seasons. Both the barrel and piston had been manufactured by Hepworth and Grandage and the engine dimensions were 80mm bore by 69.5mm stroke. Unlike the standard production Manx, the hairpin valve spring mechanism was completely enclosed. Another move to ensure that lubricant stayed where it should was seen in the use of an oil-bath completely enclosing the primary chain. Duke had the choice of a standard Manx four-speed gearbox or a special five-speed component. All-in-all a highly original and interesting variation on the Manx theme. Another ex-World Champion using a Manx model for 1958 was Umberto Masetti, who made his Norton debut at the Italian Championship race at Modena in mid-April.

At Silverstone on Saturday, 19th April, Geoff Duke thrilled a crowd of 40,000 by winning a hotly contested 350cc race on a conventional Dearden-tuned Manx. In the 500cc event Duke was way down the field before retiring on his BMW in a race won by Terry Shepherd from Bob McIntyre and Bob Anderson, all three Norton-mounted. In fact all of the first six men home in both the 350cc and 500cc races were on Manx machinery, proving, if proof was needed, that the venerable British singles were far from dead!

Derek Minter showed that his form at Brands Hatch the previous year had been no fluke by taking an impressive double victory at the important Castle Combe national race meeting held on Saturday, 26th April. A pointer to the future was an excellent third place behind Minter and Bob Anderson in the 350cc by a young man called Phil Read, who had earlier won the Non-Experts final. Yet another up-and-coming youngster showed promise for the future when the name S.M.B. (Mike) Hailwood suddenly began to show in the 350cc results - and later 500cc - on Manx models. His earliest win was at Brands Hatch in early May, when he beat, among others, that man Minter! As for the British Commonwealth Norton stars, there were several new names, including Tom Phillis, Jim Redman, Paddy Driver and John Hempleman, all destined to win works rides later in their careers.

At the Austrian Grand Prix on Thursday, 1st May, held over the 3.17-mile autobahn circuit near Salzburg, there was a thrilling climax after a race-long duel in the 15-lap, 350cc event between South African Driver and New Zealander Hempleman, with victory finally going to Hempleman. Keith Campbell proved he was still top line, even without works support, when he won the 350cc class at the international Rheinpokal-Rennen meeting at Hockenheim a week later. In Britain, Alastair King scored a highly impressive trio of wins on his Nortons at Aintree, defeating amongst others fellow Scot Bob McIntyre, Bob Brown and young Hailwood.

The American motorcycling press was devoting considerable space to a controversy then being aired in the Technical Committee and Competition Committee of the AMA, on the subject of the allegedly unfair ban on Manx Nortons for Class 'C' competition under AMA regulations. Top lawyers had presented a case on behalf of distributors of British machines in the States and some very forceful comments were made at the meetings of the Committees. The AMA remained unswayed by the lawyers' case and so the British double overhead cam single remained banned. Several years later (in 1962) it was readmitted, but by then its production reign was all but at an end.

Continental Circus Norton privateer quartet. Left to right: Rudi Thalhammer, Ladi Richter, Bertie Schneider and Eddie Lenz. The bike is a 1961 40M 350 Manx.

Rudi Thalhammer with his 350 Manx Norton in the 1962 Austrian Grand Prix.

At the end of 1957, Derek Minter was awarded this massive shield for best aggregate Brands Hatch performance throughout the year. Later his Norton exploits at the Kent circuit earned him the title 'King of Brands'.

Mid-May saw Jack Brett and Alastair King victorious in the Irish North West 200, in the 350cc and 500cc classes respectively. Brett, together with Alan Trow and Michael O'Rouke, had been recruited by the Slazenger company to race 350 and 500 Nortons tuned by Steve Lancefield.

Then came the TT. Here Surtees took an expected double on his works four-cylinder MVs. Behind him in the Junior race were Norton-mounted Dave Chadwick and Geoff Tanner. In fact the next non-Norton machine was an AJS 7R down in 14th position. Things were little different in the Senior, with Bob Anderson and Bob Brown leading home a whole pack of Nortons with only winner Surtees and Dickie Dale on a BMW (tenth) before the next non-Bracebridge Street product, a Matchless down in 22nd position!

Minter had an excellent day at the Dutch TT, with a third in the 500cc race and a fourth in the 350cc. Having his first ever classic race, 20 year-old South Rhodesian Gary Hocking finished a creditable sixth on his Norton in the Junior Dutch TT. Following a third place in the 350cc Dutch TT, Aussie Keith Campbell rode superbly in the Belgian Grand Prix the following weekend to finish third in the 350cc race and second - splitting the MVs of Surtees and Hartle - in the all-important 500cc event. In this, Campbell's average speed for the 131.42-mile race was 114.05mph. Sadly, the 1957 350cc World Champion was killed the week after the Belgian Grand Prix when, competing in the Cadours road races, near Toulouse, France, he crashed while comfortably leading the 500cc race, after earlier winning the 350cc event.

Next came a sensational German Grand Prix, where youngster Gary Hocking split the Surtees-Hartle MV domination during a blinding rainstorm and finally finished third. He had taken over the Slazenger Norton after veteran Jack Brett, who was to have ridden the bike, broke an arm in the 350cc race. Also at the German Grand Prix Geoff Duke did six laps on his newly completed Norton-engined lightweight 350, described earlier, and was reportedly 'delighted' with the results. It was also announced by BMW that Duke would be without his works BMW for the Swedish and Ulster Grands Prix. This was to lead to the following headline in *Motor Cycling* of 13th July, 1958: 'All British Victories in Swedish GP. Duke does the double!' Without the factory MVs, which had already clinched the 350cc and 500cc world titles, it was the first British double in a classic since the heyday of the works models.

The Ulster Grand Prix was held in miserable, wet, misty conditions, but even so, Surtees (MV) was unbeatable. Bob McIntyre put it across Surtees' MV team-mate Hartle in the 500cc race to add to his fifth in the 350cc event. In the smaller event Terry Shepherd rode a brilliant race on his Manx to finish third behind the MV duo.

On the British short circuits it was Mike Hailwood who was quickly coming to the fore, and soon headlines such as 'Hailwood Untouchable' abounded. Ernie Washer won the Senior Manx Grand Prix after Alan Shepherd

The 1961 Senior TT winner, Mike Hailwood, is seen at Signpost Corner. His Manx sports a Peel fairing and Italian Oldani front brake.

retired his Manx on the last lap, following victory earlier in the week in the Junior Manx Grand Prix on an AJS 7R. George Catlin snatched a last lap victory in the Senior final at Scarborough's international, and Mike Hailwood easily won the Junior. The special pair of Nortons that John Surtees had prepared for the final British short-circuit events of the 1958 season went unused by the now 350cc and 500cc World Champion, because of MV's insistence that he only ride their machines, so they were sold to Alan Trow.

Derek Minter was the first (and only) man to inflict a defeat on John Surtees during 1958. This happened at the end-of-season Brands Hatch meeting in mid-October. The Norton rider twice beat the double World Champion to restake his claim as 'Master of Brands'. The 'Mint' finished the year by taking second place in both the 350cc and 500cc classes of the ACU (British) Road Racing Championships. Mike Hailwood took the 350cc title, and Tony Godfrey the 500cc award. Nineteen year-old Hailwood was in only his second season and had also taken the 125cc and 250cc titles! Geoff Duke finished third in the 350cc World Championship and fourth in the 500cc (with some rides on a BMW).

Mike Hailwood (499cc Manx) during the 500cc Italian Grand Prix at Monza, 11th September 1960.

A youthful Mike Hailwood piloting a three-fifty Manx at the Aintree circuit near Liverpool, summer 1958.

MIKE HAILWOOD

SMB (Stanley Micheal Bailey) Hailwood was born on the 2nd April 1940, the son of a self-made millionaire motorcycle dealer; his father Stan having competed on both two, three and four wheels, before going on to build up the largest grouping of dealerships seen up to that time in Great Britain.

Mike Hailwood began his racing career aboard a 125cc MV Agusta under the watchful eye of his father and Bill Webster, a close friend of factory boss Count Domenico Agusta. This was at Oulton Park circuit near Chester, just after his 17th birthday. At the end of the 1957 season Stan packed his son off to South Africa, equipped with an ex-John Surtees two-fifty NSU Sportsmax and a three-fifty Manx.

It proved an excellent training ground and he came back with not only several wins, but experience enough to score an incredible trio of British Championships (125, 250 and 350cc - the latter riding a Manx Norton). Into 1959, and his first Grand Prix win was secured on a 125cc Ducati (his father had become the firm's British importer). He also won all four British

Championships - a feat he repeated the following year and one which no man before or since has ever equalled. For 1961

Mike had 125 and 250cc works Hondas, plus a 350cc AJS 7R and a 500cc Manx Norton. He gained his first world title, the 250cc, on the four-cylinder Honda, took the 125 and 250cc TTs and the 500cc on his Norton. On the latter machine he averaged over 100mph for the 6-lap, 226-mile race. Then he signed for MV Agusta and won the 500cc world title four years in a row (1962-1965). Mike rejoined Honda in 1966 and won both the 250 and 350cc classes on the new six-cylinder models, equalling this feat the following year before switching his attention to four wheels.

For more than a decade he largely stayed away from bikes (except for a couple of outings on BSA and Yamaha machines), before making an historic comeback TT victory on a Ducati v-twin in 1978. The following year, 1979, he rode a Suzuki to a final TT victory. But he soon retired once more - being a partner in the Hailwood & Gould bike business (with fellow world champion Rod Gould) in Birmingham.

Tragically he was to die in a road accident whilst driving his Rover car home after collecting a fish and chip supper in the Spring of 1981.

Mike Hailwood with the Bill Lacey-tuned 499cc Manx, Mallory Park Race of the Year, September 1961. Note four-cylinder MV front brake.

Factory development engineer Doug Hele experimented with this desmodromic version of the Manx from 1958 to 1960.

Geoff Duke with the special Reynold-framed lightweight 348cc Manx; Junior TT 1959.

In January 1959 it was announced that Norton intended to continue their quiet but effective programme of race development through a sponsor for another year. They were again tying up with Reg Dearden, and said they expected to have some rather special machinery for his riders to use. And that was where Terry Shepherd came in. Shepherd, who had already agreed terms with the Dearden equipe to ride Manx Nortons in 1959, was to be sponsored by Reg Dearden, along with Rhodesian wonder-boy Gary Hocking, who had spent the winter in the Dearden workshops at Chorlton-cum-Hardy. Early February saw Hocking over in the Isle of Man familiarising himself with the TT course on a road-going Dominator. In addition to his commitments to Shepherd and Hocking, Dearden said he would be providing Ewen Haldane with a pair of Nortons. However, now that 1957 Manx Grand Prix winner Alan Holmes had decided to retire from racing, sponsor Dearden intended to dispose of much of his race machinery.

Geoff Duke was set to team up with his Australian friend Bob Brown for the new season. Both would ride 350 Nortons and Brown would also run a half-litre Bracebridge Street model, but the former World Champion had decided to give up 500cc racing and hoped to ride instead in the quarter-litre category. In mid-February came the first public news that Doug Hele was working on a Manx engine (499cc) with desmodromic valve gear. If raced this would not be entered directly by the works, but through Reg Dearden. Development had begun the previous year.

The 1959 season got under way at Oulton Park at the end of March. This big national event sponsored by the *Daily Express* newspaper saw Alastair King beat down the opposition to carry off the main awards for the day. In the 350cc race he won from Derek Minter with just two seconds in hand, and he then repeated the performance in the Senior event when, at the end of a gruelling 52½ miles he, Minter and Bob Anderson crossed the line of the Cheshire circuit with a mere 1.2 seconds separating them.

After studying the Easter Oulton meeting, Geoff Duke thought the results 'very informative', as one or two 1959 Manx machines made their debut, and he found the racing 'highly competitive'. Duke also gained the impression that 'once again the greatest effort regarding development has gone into the 500cc unit'. He questioned 'why the poor "350" never seems to receive the full treatment from development "boffins"...this will always remain a mystery to me'.

Regarding his own 350 Manx special, the latest modification was the fitment of a newly designed Peel dolphin fairing. The aims of this were to reduce frontal area and improve handlebar clearance. Another benefit, the work of Cyril Cannell of Peel Engineering, Isle of Man, was full protection for the hands from the elements.

Duke also revealed that while being tested a few weeks earlier, his special 350 Norton engine had suffered a rapid fall-off in power on the first run up towards maximum rpm. Investigation revealed signs of a partial piston seizure, although clearances cold were thought to be adequate for a chrome-plated alloy barrel. However, as unsuitable material might have been the real cause, and time was short, it was decided to modify one of the old long-stroke 500 barrels (79.6mm) to suit. At the Silverstone Saturday meeting in late April, Bob McIntyre set a new 500cc lap record at 98.26mph for the event when finishing second to Bob Anderson, whilst it was Anderson who finished runner-up to Surtees's MV four in the 350cc.

Terry Shepherd 1958 Ulster Grand Prix.

In the 1959 World Championship series it was John Surtees and MV who completely dominated the season, winning every single classic in both the 350cc and 500cc classes. Behind him it was Gary Hocking who impressed most, with three seconds and a third. Geoff Duke put in a number of consistent performances, including a trio of third places in the final three 500cc Grands Prix, surprising in view of his earlier comments. Perhaps the Isle of Man TT belonged to Alastair King, with a third in the Junior and second in the Senior. Other riders of Manx Nortons who impressed were McIntyre, Brown, Shepherd, Hempleman, Driver, Phillis, Redman and the veteran Ken Kavanagh with an excellent fourth place at Hockenheim.

Terry Shepherd (left) consults with mechanics Eric Jones and Arthur Edwards during preparation of his 499cc 30M Manx for the Swedish Grand Prix, July 1958.

Phil Read taking his five-hundred Norton to victory in the 1960 Senior Manx Grand Prix. He also set the fastest lap at 97.09mph, a new record.

Reg Dearden took 14 machines over to the TT (excluding the 'works' bikes!). He also had on the stocks at that time a new oil-holding Featherbed frame. In this, engine oil was carried by the entire main frame, including the headstock. Chain lubricant was carried separately in the two horizontal seat stays, the ends of which were joined by a plastic tube incorporating a breather hole. The works development bikes also appeared in practice consisting of the 499cc desmo and a short-stroke 350. With the desmodromic model the opening cams operated the valves through hollow tappets, but the closing cams, driven by the intermediate pinions in a five-gear train, actuated forked rockers, which bore on the underside of collars held on the stems by split collets.

1959 was also the year of the FIM-inspired Formula One, which almost everyone else was against, including the majority of the leading riders. Soon after staging Formula One 350cc and 500cc races at the TT, the FIM abandoned its new baby. For the record, the races were supposed to be for standard production road racing machinery, such as the AJS 7R, Matchless's newly introduced G50 and, of course, the Manx Norton. May 1959 saw an experimental five-speed gear cluster appear on John Holder's 350 Manx. This was the work of sponsor Harold Daniell, the former Norton star.

In Europe, away from the Grand Prix trail, British Commonwealth riders usually reigned supreme during 1959. Typical was the 350cc race at the Sachsenring in East Germany during late August, where Norton riders filled the first four places. First across the line was New Zealander John Hempleman, who took 54 minutes 17.5 seconds for the 15-lap race (81 miles) and made the fastest lap at 91.77mph. Aussie Bob Brown was second, with Rhodesians Gary Hocking and Jim Redman third and fourth respectively.

Racing in South Africa, Paddy Driver (350 Manx) leads Dennis West (500 Manx), with Mike Hailwood (AJS – 18) and W. Van Leeuwen (500 Norton – 40), followed by national champion Mike Moore on his 496cc Matchless G50. Circa winter 1960.

Manx models were once again victorious in the September Manx Grand Prix races, with Peter Middleton the Junior winner and Eddie Crooks dominating the Senior. 'Duke's Day' said *The Motor Cycle's* headline in that journal's 17th September issue. This was a reference to the maestro's field-day at Locarno, Switzerland, where the former World Champion won the 500, 350 and 250 races and set record average speeds in the first two (65.34 and 65.55mph respectively for the 51½ miles), in which he rode his special Nortons; it was one of his last meetings before announcing his retirement from racing. At home, 1959 was a year in which Mike Hailwood emerged as a leading contender for major honours. This was illustrated by the 19-year-old being a comfortable winner of all four ACU Road Racing Stars, the forerunner of the British Championships. The other men in contention were McIntyre, King, Bob Anderson and Minter. At the end of the season Gary Hocking left for his Bulawayo home, secure in the knowledge that his superb performance in continental Europe had earned him a two-year contract with Count Agusta to ride the MV fours in 1960. As *The Motor Cycle* said: 'Surely such a contract has seldom been earned so quickly before?' Bringing down the curtain on yet another racing season there was a tremendous finale at Brands Hatch in October, with Minter beating McIntyre and Hailwood to the line in the 350cc race. Hailwood won the 500cc race after Minter came off at Clearways on the second lap.

An interesting 349cc Manx-engined special, featuring a Norton duplex frame with the bottom runs of the tubes cut out, appeared in March 1960 from the Monty and Ward stable. The frame modification was originally aimed at accommodating an outside-flywheel, 90mm-bore, 499cc engine, but work on that engine had to be shelved. So a smaller, more standard Manx unit of 1958 vintage was installed. This engine was converted to coil ignition and to the latest splined camshaft drive, but without the massive light-alloy housing for the drive. The original upper and lower bevel housings had been adapted to take the needle-roller bearing for the splined shafts, and so the old steel shaft tube was retained; an external oil drain from the upper bevel housing had to be arranged. A weight-saving device was integral with construction of the seat pan and oil tank in aluminium sheeting.

Another of the top British short circuit riders to choose a Manx was Banbury's Dan Shorey, seen here cresting the famous 'Mountain' at the Lincolnshire Cadwell Park circuit.

Hailwood in winning form on his five-hundred Norton at Castle Combe, Wiltshire, 15th July 1961.

Dan Shorey at Mallory Park's Race of the Year in 1961.

Race winner Dick Creith on Joe Ryan's 'Fireplace' 499cc Manx, Ulster Grand Prix, 1965.

Jim Redman and Peter Ferbrache proved it was still possible for a Manx Norton to beat an MV four on a tight circuit when both riders well and truly thrashed the Italian Remo Venturi at Barcelona, in the non-championship Spanish Grand Prix in early April. A week later Bob McIntyre pushed the cream of British short-circuit stars aside at Silverstone when he once again won the Hutchinson 100 on his 500 Potts-tuned Norton. Derek Minter won the 500cc class of the North West 200 after McIntyre retired, but the rival AMC race machinery was now much more competitive and second and third places were occupied by Matchless G50s; in the 350cc race AJS 7Rs were first and second. During May Phil Read scored an impressive double to win the 350cc and 500cc ACU Clubmans Trophy at Oulton Park. Read followed this up with an overwhelming victory in the Senior Manx Grand Prix later that year (in the Junior Manx Grand Prix he retired on lap 1 when a valve dropped in).

Former Norton three-wheeler star and World Champion Eric Oliver, not only entered a Manx-engined outfit, but also a 350 Manx solo for the 1960 Isle of Man TT. But the most newsworthy Norton entry in the TT was an experimental Junior model, referred to as the 'Lowboy', which was practised but not raced by the 1959 Manx Grand Prix winner Eddie Crooks. The chief focus of interest was the modified Featherbed frame, new front fork and unusual fuel and oil tank mountings. The main frame was a standard Manx type, but the rear end was considerably changed in order to accommodate the 3¼ gallon fuel tank. Of light alloy, this sat not only above the cambox, but also in the space between the main frame rear loops and extended back into the triangle formed by the subframe. Its base sat on a rubber pad above the gearbox mounting plates and a cutaway on the offside provided sufficient clearance round the carburettor bellmouth. A pump, driven from the inlet cam, lifted fuel to a small header tank. The oil tank was also a fresh piece of the panel beater's craft and was located down behind the gearbox and

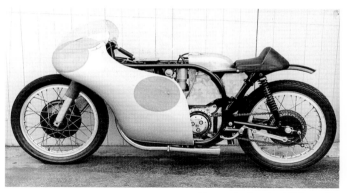

The works 'Lowboy' 350 used in TT practice by Eddie Crooks in 1960. It was not taken further.

ahead of the swinging arm pivot. In order to provide the necessary space, the swinging arm pivot mounting plates were welded to the rear faces of the frame tubes.

The exhaust pipe led between the front down tubes and directly under the engine. The megaphone was 'flattened' top and bottom and terminated under the oil tank some five inches forward of the rear tyre. There were other differences. The front fork was supported only by a single clip at the base of the steering column. A large one-piece lug formed the bottom clip, which did the job of two. The short, stubby handlebars were clipped to the stanchions, emerging through apertures in the lug, and were also located laterally by a light-alloy cross-brace. At its lower end the steering column operated in a 3 x 1¼ inch journal bearing. At the upper end the bearing was a conventional Manx component. The fork springs were of considerably greater diameter than usual and, of course, shorter and covered by rubber gaiters. The whole machine was considerably lower and had a wheelbase of just over an inch longer than standard and had, in fact, been designed to take a horizontal Guzzi-style engine that was rumoured to be under development at the factory. For its 1960 TT practice run, a standard 349cc Manx power unit was fitted, the whole purpose being to test the roadholding and general handling under race conditions. The machine was built over a six-month period preceding the TT, but as it did not appear again one can safely assume its handling and roadholding were not up to the standard required.

Norton, under Doug Hele's guidance, also had a desmo model on the Island. This was a 350cc model with a bore and stroke of 86 x 60mm. The very much over-square dimensions were explained by the fact that it was being used to test valves at high revs for the larger desmo engine. It also featured an outside flywheel with a two-piece crankshaft running on roller main bearings.

After a practice crash with his sidecar outfit, the former World Champion Eric Oliver was a non-starter in the Junior TT. But another old-timer, Jack Brett, was having his first outing since his German Grand Prix crash in 1958. The 1960 Senior TT was another milestone for the Manx Norton, when Derek Minter became the first man in history to lap the famous Mountain course at over 100mph on a single-cylinder machine. Until his fourth place in the Junior TT a couple of days before, Minter had been adjudged primarily a short-circuit star. With his 1960 TT performances he proved conclusively that he was truly world class. In the Senior, after lying third, Minter was forced out on lap 3 with a split oil tank. Mike Hailwood also lapped at over 100mph (but after Minter) on his way to third place, behind the works MVs of Surtees and Hartle in the Senior event. Meanwhile, veteran Jack Brett brought his Nortons home 17th in the Junior and 23rd in the Senior.

Derek Minter (11) leads Mike Hailwood at Oulton Park, August 1961. Both Norton mounted, Minter won, with Hailwood third. In the process Minter set a new outright lap record for the Cheshire circuit and became British Champion.

Next on the classic calendar came the Dutch TT at Assen. Here Mike Hailwood surprised everyone by holding second place in the 500cc race on his Lacey-tuned Manx, before being slowed by oil blowing from a cracked crankcase on to the rear tyre. He eventually finished fifth. On the home circuits Hailwood carried on where he had left off at the end of 1959, often winning all four solo classes! Also very much in contention were Bob McIntyre, Phil Read, Tony Godfrey and Derek Minter. At the Ulster Grand Prix in August John Hartle, now a privateer once again following his release from MV Agusta, put on a sterling performance with his pair of Manx models. Not only did he finish second behind Surtees's MV in the 350cc race, but he also beat Surtees in the 500cc event! Phil Read comfortably won the Senior Manx Grand Prix. The same rider also upped the lap record to 97.09mph, whilst Ellis Boyce took his Beart Norton to a record-breaking Junior victory.

At the big end-of-season British short-circuit meetings, Norton riders who impressed were Hartle, with a victory in the 500cc race at Scarborough and a 350/500cc double at the Aintree 'Century' meeting, and McIntyre, who cleaned up the larger classes at Mallory Park, although Mike Hailwood took the 'Race of the Year' event and its £1,000 purse. The season was brought to a close in mid-October with hotly contested meetings at Oulton Park and Brands Hatch. At the former the top Norton competitor was John Hartle with a win in the 350cc and a second in the 500cc races. Whilst at Brands, run in appallingly wet conditions, spoils were shared fairly evenly by Mike Hailwood, John Hartle, Phil Read and Alan Shepherd (on AJS 7R and Matchless G50 machinery). With that the curtain came down on yet another year's racing. It was Hailwood who had once again taken all four solo ACU stars, making it eight out of a possible eight in 1959 and 1960!

A pair of Nortons ridden by Rudi Thalhammer (53) and Bertie Schneider (54) having their own tussle during the 350cc class of the 1962 Austrian Grand Prix. Schneider later became a works Suzuki rider, and later still an FIM race official. Look at those cobblestones.

Tony Godfrey (Manx) after winning the 500cc race at the FIM sanctioned United States Grand Prix at Daytona, February 1961.

As winter came to Britain so it became summer 'down under' in Australia, where, at Fisherman's Bend in late October, Eric Hinton won the 350cc race by 8 seconds from Ken Rumble on another Manx. He retired his big Manx in the 500cc race after having led for several laps. Hinton had been expected to ride a home-brewed desmo 349cc Norton, but the job could not be completed in time. The design was the work of Eric's father Harry, and Harry's nephew David Stewart, an engineering graduate from Sydney University. The engine had normal bore and stroke measurements and compression ratio, but special bevel gears had been produced to stand up to the 9,600rpm the valve gear permitted. From a news point of view, 1960 will be remembered as the year Honda's four first appeared on the European scene and the year in which John Surtees finally called it a day on two wheels.

1961 got under way with the shock announcement in January that MV were to give up racing, but ultimately this proved incorrect. February saw Tony Godfrey on his Manx win the International Grand Prix of the United States over a 3.1-mile course at Daytona Speedway, Florida. Earlier, travelling companion Mike Hailwood had retired when his Norton developed magneto trouble. The British racing year started at Easter. Several leading Manx riders now used Italian Dell'Orto carbs and John Hartle was entered on a brace of new Manxes by Thames Ditton dealers Comerfords. He made an excellent start by winning the 500cc BMCRC Championship race at Silverstone in early April, with the 350cc event going to Derek Minter.

The 4.81-mile Nürburgring South Circuit in Germany was the scene of the fatal accident in which one of the most likeable riders of the era, Dickie Dale, was killed only five days after celebrating his 34th birthday. He was leading the 500cc race on his Norton, having put up a fastest lap, despite appalling conditions, at 77.5mph, when the accident happened. Earlier Dale had won the 350cc event on his smaller Manx from a star-studded field.

Norfolk farmer Dick Aldous rode this 1962 499cc Manx for over a quarter of a century at his local Snetterton circuit. Dick is seen here with his wife in September 1985.

Norton mounted Bob McIntyre (2) leads Alan Shepherd (Matchless G50) at Oulton Park in April 1962. In August that year, McIntyre was to meet with a fatal accident on the same machine. The motocycle world mourned one of its most popular brothers.

A week later Bob McIntyre averaged 105.4mph on his 499cc Manx, to win the North West 200, acclaimed as 'Britain's fastest-ever road race' by *Motor Cycling*. The same magazine had an even more significant headline a month later, when, in their 22nd June issue, they proclaimed 'New Boy Phil Read Scores First Home-Grown TT Win Since 1952'. Read's sensational victory came after first Gary Hocking's MV was slowed by an oil leak and later Mike Hailwood, who had taken over the lead, had been put out after his AJS 7R engine went sick on the last lap. None the less, Read had ridden a well judged race and only winners go into the record books! The previous all-British (not Commonwealth) TT win was Geoff Duke with his factory Junior Norton back in 1952. This obviously ignores the hollow 'Formula One' races.

Two days later on Friday 16th June, 1961, 21-year-old Mike Hailwood made history by becoming the first TT rider to win three TTs in one week and the first ever to average over 100mph on a British single, when he won the Senior TT on his Bill Lacey-tuned 499cc Manx. Hailwood's total time for the 6-lap 226.4-mile race was 2 hours 15 minutes 2 seconds, an average speed of 100.60mph. Norton machinery took five of the first six places. Behind Hailwood came Bob McIntyre, Tom Phillis (Domiracer), Alastair King, Ron Langston (Matchless) and Tony Godfrey.

Roy Ingram rode in the Senior with a duplex 7-inch diameter twin leading shoe front brake. The lining area was 45 percent greater than the standard 8-inch diameter single Manx brake. It was judged (correctly) that this dual front stopper would become standard ware on the 1962 production models. By then many of the leading riders were using other brakes, as exemplified by Hailwood's Senior TT-winning Manx, which sported an Italian Oldani component.

Another experimental factory Norton was a 349cc model raced by Derek Minter at selected short-circuit meetings, including Brands Hatch and Castle Combe, that summer. Besides a lower-than standard frame, it also had additional engine tune, including coil ignition.

Hailwood's win in the Senior TT was supplemented by a whole string of runner-up positions in the 500cc World Championship series, France, Holland, Belgium, East Germany and Northern Ireland, plus another win at Monza, Italy, and a second in Sweden, the last two results on four-cylinder works MVs, to finish the season as runner-up in the title race to Gary Hocking. In the 350cc hunt Phil Read came fourth, adding a fifth in Holland and a fourth in Ulster to his Isle of Man victory. Nortons also finished third (Perris), fourth (McIntyre) and fifth (King) in the 500cc series. Only Read, however, finished in the top five in the 350cc title chase.

On the British scene, the name of John Cooper was rapidly establishing a reputation at northern circuits such as Scarborough and Cadwell Park, with a string of wins and places on a pair of rapid Manx models. Meanwhile, at Brands Hatch, Derek Minter had regained his 'King' title for the popular Kent track. Hocking and MV won the 'Race of the Year' at Mallory Park, while Hailwood, back on a Norton, won the final Aintree meeting. The Manx Grand Prix saw the Senior won by Ned Minihan on a Beart tuned Manx; the Junior was won by an AJS 7R.

As 1962 dawned, the Japanese teams, headed by Honda, had signed up many of the leading Norton

Tom Phillips, seen here on his 350 Manx at Thruxton on August Bank Holiday Monday 1963, became a star overnight, after many race-winning performances on Norton and Greeves machinery.

privateers, including Redman, Phillis, McIntyre and Minter (the last named to ride for the British importer Hondis Ltd). However, both Minter and McIntyre, plus MV's Mike Hailwood, still continued to appear at many non-championship events on Norton singles. These, together with riders who included Read, Cooper and Shorey, meant that competition for places among Manx riders was as fierce as ever. One week it would be Hailwood, then Minter, then Read, and so on. It had been Read who had impressed many (the Italians in particular) with an inspired ride at Modena in late March, when he had battled with Remo Venturi (works MV) and Silvio Grassetti (works Bianchi), and *Motor Cycling* commented that it was 'nothing short of fantastic'.

Ellis Boyce showed his Isle of Man skills by finishing second in the Senior TT after several more-fancied runners struck trouble, and Nortons also filled third to eighth places inclusive, with the first of the Matchless G50s coming in ninth. In the Junior things were not so rosy. The leading Norton rider was Roy Ingram in fourth. Only eight of the first 20 home were on Bracebridge Street singles.

Berkshire rider Tom Phillips rose to fame as the British 250cc champion on a Greeves Silverstone in 1963. But much of his racing was on Nortons.

Vivid action at Union Mills during the 1962 Junior (350cc) Isle of Man TT from Tony Godfrey, who was lying sixth on his Manx, but was forced out by engine trouble on lap 4.

Royal Air Force Corporal Chris Conn, seen here at Mallory Park in 1963, could well have become a world class star if he had not been a career serviceman.

Norton, mounted Rob Fitton leads Matchless man Selwyn Griffiths at Cadwell Park on 14th September, 1963.

This picture was largely repeated on the Continent, where there were only three other top six finishers in the 350cc Grand Prix series with Norton singles, and the highest placed of these was Swedish rider Sven Gunnarsson, who took fourth place at Tampere, Finland.

It was still very much Nortons that ruled supreme once the MV fours had gone in the big class, except for the odd time when a Matchless or factory Jawa twin would finish near the front. All this goes to prove that Geoff Duke had probably got things about right with his comment a few years earlier, that most of Norton's development work on the Manx was devoted to the 500.

1962 saw the deaths of several leading competitors, including Tom Phillis, Gary Hocking (a racing car crash) and, perhaps most sadly of all, the much-loved Bob McIntyre, who crashed his Potts-Norton while challenging Phil Read for second spot at Oulton Park in early August. September saw London-Irish Joe Dunphy win the Senior Manx - the third Manx Grand Prix victory for a Francis Beart-tuned model in two years. But with terrible weather, speeds were well down on Phil Read's 1960 record. Once again the Junior went to an AJS. Interestingly this was also a Beart-tuned model and *The Motor Cycle's* David Dixon tried both Manx Grand Prix winners in a test session at Brands Hatch shortly after their return from the Island. Dixon found the Senior Manx easier to ride than the 7R. Particularly impressive was 'the smoother, more effortless power unit'.

At the end of December Jack Ahearn, who had just returned from a racing season in Europe, won both the Junior and Senior races in the Australian TT, held over a 3½-mile circuit at Banbury in West Australia on Boxing Day. In the Junior event the Norton rider rode superbly to beat Kel Carruthers on a works Honda four by over half a minute. Coming out of semi-retirement, Eric Hinton made a spectacular return to the Australian racing scene less than a week later, when, on New Year's Day 1963, he won three events at the Victorian Grand Prix, held on a brand new circuit in Winston Park, Benella, 120 miles north of Melbourne.

The new year in Britain started with the story that Geoff Duke had taken both Minter and Hartle out to Italy to test four-cylinder Gileras! This did not stop Farnborough tuner Ray Petty working on Minter's Nortons, which he was scheduled to race in British events, even if he obtained a works Gilera ride. A feature of the 1963 Petty-tuned 350cc bike was the high-level exhaust system that had proved so successful on the 500cc machine during 1962. This idea, which allowed the machine to be cranked hard over on right-handers without fear of the megaphone grounding, was soon to become a popular modification for many other Norton racing singles. Meanwhile, Minter's old tuner, Steve Lancefield, had arranged with Phil Read that he would prepare Read's brace of Nortons.

A massive crowd flocked to Silverstone on Saturday, 6th April to see the return to racing of the Scuderia Duke Gilera fours ridden by Minter and Hartle. After spending five years under dust covers at the Arcore factory the results were not quite as impressive as expected. Neither rider got within one mile an hour of their own Norton-mounted best, and Hartle was pushed hard all the way by Read's Manx single. It was Read also who was the lone challenger to the Gileras at Brands Hatch and Oulton Park over the Easter holiday a week later. Also at Snetterton on Easter Sunday Sven-Olov Gunnarsson became the first ever Swedish rider to win a major British race when, with his Torston Arguard-tuned Manx, he took the 500cc Molyslip Trophy after fighting off a determined challenge from Dave Degens (Matchless) and Dave Downer on the Dunstall Domiracer. The same day, many thousands of miles across the world, RAF serviceman Chris Conn became the hero when he won the 180-mile Malaysian Grand Prix on his Dudley-Ward-tuned 499cc Manx and defeated a formidable Yamaha factory team headed by Fumio Ito.

After an accident involving Minter and Downer (see Chapter 11), in which Minter was badly injured and Downer was killed, Phil Read was recruited into the Gilera team by Geoff Duke. When not on duty with the Gilera squad, John Hartle still continued to ride his own Nortons. Highlights were a win in the 350cc Austrian Grand Prix and a double over a short triangular circuit at Bourg-en-Bresse, France.

Belfast rider Ralph Bryans was awarded the Walter Rusk Memorial Trophy for the most consistent and outstanding performances in Irish road racing during 1963. Many of his victories were aboard Nortons.

Phil Read with his 30M Manx, Oulton Park 1962.

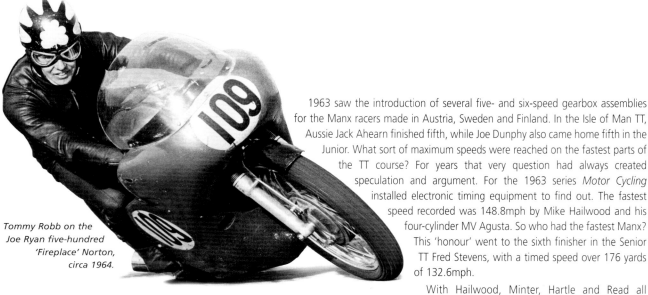

Tommy Robb on the
Joe Ryan five-hundred
'Fireplace' Norton,
circa 1964.

1963 saw the introduction of several five- and six-speed gearbox assemblies for the Manx racers made in Austria, Sweden and Finland. In the Isle of Man TT, Aussie Jack Ahearn finished fifth, while Joe Dunphy also came home fifth in the Junior. What sort of maximum speeds were reached on the fastest parts of the TT course? For years that very question had always created speculation and argument. For the 1963 series *Motor Cycling* installed electronic timing equipment to find out. The fastest speed recorded was 148.8mph by Mike Hailwood and his four-cylinder MV Agusta. So who had the fastest Manx? This 'honour' went to the sixth finisher in the Senior TT Fred Stevens, with a timed speed over 176 yards of 132.6mph.

With Hailwood, Minter, Hartle and Read all preoccupied with four-cylinder models, the British short circuits saw a few new victors, including John Cooper, Rob Fitton and Tom Phillips. The British Championships were now decided over one race meeting - at Oulton Park in August. Minter was back in winning action on the four-cylinder Gilera after a ten week lay-off, while Phil Read took the 350 title on his Lancefield-tuned Norton.

Generally there was little for Norton riders to shout about in the World Championship series in 1963. But in the Ulster Grand Prix the star of the meeting, at least as far as the Irish spectators were concerned, was undoubtedly 21-year-old Ralph Bryans, who showed scintillating form on his Joe Ryan Nortons in both the 350cc and 500cc races. After holding third for most of the race he was forced to retire near the end on his smaller Manx, whilst in the 500cc event he came home a creditable fifth. The only non-four-cylinder model in front was Alan Shepherd's very rapid G50 Matchless.

A new Senior Manx Grand Prix lap record of 98.18mph was set up by Norton rider Dave Williams in September; in fact Manx models swept the board in the race, with nine of the top ten places in the Senior going to Norton models. John Cooper was the star Norton rider at Scarborough's September international meeting, with a win and a second, while the same rider came sixth in the 'Race of the Year' at Mallory Park and was the first Norton rider home. Phil Read cleaned up at the majority of the British meetings during late September and October, to round off a highly successful season. Strangely, though, he had seemed far happier (and more successful) on his Lancefield-tuned Norton singles than the works Gilera fours.

Dave Williams 499cc Norton,
winning the 500cc class of the Isle
of Man Southern 100 in July 1964.
In September the same rider
returned to the Island to win the
Junior Manx Grand Prix. On both
visits he rode Norton singles.

Perhaps the most interesting Norton innovation that year was Ray Petty's 'back-to-front' cylinder head on a 349cc Manx engine, which appeared just as the season came to a close. This was first tested by Derek Minter at Brands Hatch in early November. The experiment was an attempt to extract yet more power from the now rapidly ageing single. It appeared a simple modification, but in reality it called for extensive work and many alterations.

'Moon Eyes' John Cooper was one of the top Norton short-circuit stars of the 1960s. Left: He is seen here at Scarborough on 4th July 1964.

George Leigh, another Manx specialist, began to offer various components made from titanium, including con-rods, gudgeon pins, inlet valves, gearbox bolts, wheel spindles and frame bolts. The advantage of titanium was that while it was just as strong as high-tensile steel, it was only half the weight. The disadvantage was that it was considerably more expensive. Rider Fred Stevens had been testing the titanium components throughout the 1963 racing season.

Another idea, from Ray Petty, was a 'big' Manx for use in the unlimited class at Brands Hatch in 1964. The idea was to enlarge the capacity to 636cc, as had already been done by certain sidecar boys, including Bill Boddice. In solo form this project was not developed further.

Derek Minter pictured in April 1965.

1964 saw Minter and Hartle back 'full time' on Nortons (Petty- and Lancefield-tuned respectively) and Cooper was also Norton-mounted. Read, however, was riding Tom Kirby entered AMC raceware as the season kicked off in late March at Mallory Park before a crowd of over 20,000 damp and half-frozen spectators. Hartle won the 350cc, Minter the 500cc. Other short-circuit stars that year with Manxes included Joe Dunphy, Conn, Shorey and Dennis Ainsworth.

There was now a new single-cylinder challenger to the British singles in the 350cc category, in the shape of the Italian Aermacchi. Early on in the season at Snetterton and Silverstone, Tom Phillips and the Swiss Othmar Drixel showed that these push-rod models were already a match for the best AJS 7Rs and Manx Nortons. One of the advantages of the Aermacchi was its light weight - it tipped the scales at only 225lb, some 90lb less than a Manx. I was fortunate enough to ride both in the 1960s and in my view this was the Italian bike's biggest advantage.

Len Ireland (83) and Ian McGregor (92), both riding Nortons, during the 350cc North West 200. McGregor won the race. Ulsterman Dick Creith, nicknamed 'Blue Streak', won the 500cc event on his Norton in front of some 50,000 spectators.

Soon Hartle put himself out of the running with an accident on his smaller Norton at Imola, Italy, on Sunday 19th April. He broke both arms and was warned that if he raced in future he would risk fracturing his arms in any further crash. Also on the continent local rider Heiner Butz took his Manx to victory in the international Eifelrennen meeting on the short 5-mile southern loop of Germany's famous Nürburgring. With 350 Aermacchis doing well, it was not long before there was talk of using an over-bored version for Senior events. And so the writing was beginning to appear on the wall for the venerable British big thumpers.

With Phil Read going to Tom Kirby and John Hartle injured, Steve Lancefield turned his tuning attentions to Rex Butcher, who repaid him by finishing fourth on his first outing at Brands Hatch on the Lancefield 350. Except for Minter, fourth in the 350 and second in the 500, Norton had a poor TT with the top privateer placings going to AJS and Matchless. Aermacchi had a terrible time, with only two bikes finishing in the whole TT series. At the important post-TT races at Mallory Park, John Cooper scored a double to stage something of a comeback after a disappointing Isle of Man visit.

By now Minter was supplementing his Norton rides with outings in the 250cc class on a works entered Cotton Telstar two-stroke. It was through this connection that he came to use the Mitchenhall 'Nose Cone' fairing. With this, the front number plate was mounted behind a pointed streamlined clear Perspex nose cowl. This was the subject of much attention from various race officials, with the result that it was eventually banned by the ACU (Auto Cycle Union).

After a series of excellent results in the classics, Phil Read won the 1964 500cc Ulster Grand Prix, followed by Jack Ahearn repeating this success in the 500cc Finnish Grand Prix at Imatra. With works MVs, Hondas and Yamahas at many of the important British short-circuit meetings, Norton victories were few and far between at international events staged towards the end of the 1964 season. However, Minter and Cooper had the satisfaction of taking their Nortons to victory in the final Brands Hatch meeting in October. It was at this meeting that Minter finally raced Ray Petty's back-to-front 350 Norton, almost a year after its first track test. Petty professed himself 'delighted' with Minter's third place, despite a bad start. In Germany Walter Scheimann (500)

Future Yamaha world champion Rod Gould winning on his three-fifty Norton at Rissington in 1965. Note high-level exhaust and Italian Oldani front stopper; plus of course the Peel fairing.

and Heiner Butz (350) had both taken their Manxes to the National Championship. Many Nortons in Europe (including Scheimann's) now sported a massive Friedl Munch front brake of such a diameter that it almost filled the entire wheel! Early 1965 saw Kel Carruthers put in a unique day's riding on Sunday, 3rd March, when he won five Australian TT titles at the 4-mile Longford circuit in Tasmania. In the 125, 250 and 350 classes Carruthers rode Hondas, but for the all-important 500cc and unlimited races, he switched to a Manx Norton.

The British season started with a renewed duel between the leading Manx runners, with 'First round to Moon Eyes', as *Motor Cycling* summed up Cooper's double in the 350cc and 500cc races. A week later, over Saturday and Sunday, 20th/21st March, the first United States Grand Prix to count towards World Championship points was staged. Mike Hailwood finished over two laps ahead of runner-up Buddy Parriott's Manx, as the MV star scored an almost casual 500cc victory on his four. At the last minute Count Domenico Agusta, unpredictable boss of the MV factory, cancelled plans to send a 500 four to Britain for Hailwood to ride in the Easter meetings at Brands Hatch and Snetterton. So Hailwood 'borrowed' an AJS 7R and a Syd Mularney 500 Manx. At Brands Hatch on Good Friday the best he could do was a poor 11th on the 7R. In the 500cc event he did so badly that he did not qualify as a starter for the 'King of Brands' race. As events were to prove, Hailwood

Joe Dunphy on his Francis Beart Manx at Ginger Hall during the 1965 Junior TT.

Norton mounted John Cooper (17) leads Matchless man Dave Croxford at Snetterton national road races, 20th March 1966. They round the infamous Russell's Bend – the first year it was used.

was down, but far from out. Two days later he came back brilliantly to win the Snetterton international 500cc 'Race of Aces' from a galaxy of British short-circuit aces on the Mularney Manx. The same weekend Derek Minter became the first official 'King of Brands' after winning the unlimited race, adding it to the 350cc and 500cc events he had taken earlier in the day on his Ray Petty-tuned Nortons. *Motor Cycling* said: 'He completely outclassed the opposition to win all three of the big races.' With fastest lap of the day at exactly 88mph, it was a jubilant Minter who received his crown, a replica of Henry VIII's, from the pop star Lulu.

Northern rider Billie Nelson (later a sidecar passenger with Helmut Fath), with his five-hundred Manx at Cadwell Park, circa mid 1960s.

The first European classic of the season was the West German Grand Prix, run for the first time ever on the shorter southern loop of the Nürburgring. In the 350cc race the first man home on a Norton single was Aussie Jack Ahearn, back in seventh place. In the bigger race Walter Scheimann finished a creditable third after a race-long duel with Jack Findlay (McIntyre Matchless) and Ahearn on his larger Manx. A week later Nortons finished in the top three places in the 500cc Austrian Grand Prix (a non championship meeting), with Dan Shorey taking a well-earned victory from Billie Nelson and Chris Conn. Irish Norton riders dominated the 1965 North-West 200 in late May, with Ian McGregor taking the 350 and Dick Creith the 500. Both were riding Manx models tuned by Ulsterman Joe Ryan, famous for his 'Fireplace' Nortons, scruffy but very quick.

For the TT John Cooper used the 'Camel', a Reg Dearden Manx with a 7-gallon glass-fibre tank-cum-seat. However, it was not short-circuit star Cooper who was the surprise of the 1965 TT but former Manx Grand Prix winner Joe Dunphy, who finished second in the Senior on his Beart-prepared bike. Dunphy also finished ninth in the Junior TT, at an average speed faster than his Senior time because of the atrocious weather conditions during the big race. Norton riders dominated the 500cc class of the international FIM-sanctioned Canadian Grand Prix at Mosport Park in July, with Roger Beaumont from St Hubert, Quebec, coming out on top in the 35-lap race.

An interesting technical development seen in 1965 was a pair of hydraulically operated disc brakes on the front of Tom Phillips' 500 Manx. These had been developed by Rhodesian Colin Lyster in co-operation with the Lockheed company, and were to set a trend which was to become the accepted norm a few short years later on both road and track.

Joe Dunphy, 30M Manx 1965 TT.

After being faced with a couple of expensive engine blow-ups, one in the 500cc Ulster Grand Prix, John Cooper went on record with his 'Big bills for John' problems during September 1965. In both cases his Manx engines were extensively damaged. Cooper commented: 'The last time that I wrecked a Manx engine it cost me £217 to repair it. Since then spares have gone up and are harder to get. Some people think that you can make a lot of money racing - they don't realise the expense.' Cooper was in a better mood a couple of weeks later at Cadwell Park, when he won £500 on his big Norton after beating Phil Read's 254cc works Yamaha twin into second place in the day's main race. Welshman Malcolm Uphill made it a Manx Grand Prix double by winning both the Junior and Senior races, but only his Senior victory was with a Norton. And, as if to remind John Cooper that racing could pay after all, the Derby rider clinched £1,050 prize money when he won the 'Race of the Year' at Mallory Park, beating Mike Hailwood (MV) and Phil Read (Yamaha). Cooper had prayed for rain - and he got it. He beat a star-studded field riding his Norton, which was specially prepared for the meeting by Ray Petty.

John Cooper looks back at Dan Shorey as the pair accelerate away from the Mere hairpin, Scarborough International, September 1965.

A line of British singles stream
down the hill towards Mansfield
Corner, at Cadwell Park in 1966 –
the majority including 71 (Billie
Nelson) are mounted on
Manx Nortons.

Norton riders Dan Shorey (16),
John Cooper (23) and Ian Burne
(19) scrap with Paddy Driver
(Kirby AJS) in the 1965 Dutch TT.

The problem of Manx spares was highlighted during November 1965 when it was revealed that although the parts position for AMC racers had eased a little, there was now a desperate shortage of certain vital Manx components, such as big-end bearings. *Motor Cycling* said the 'outlook is grim'. Other news was none too exciting for the future of the Manx as a viable racer at the top level. Colin Seeley revealed plans to build new engines and even complete bikes based on the AJS 7R and Matchless G50, 'but no Nortons'. There was also talk of a new larger-capacity Bultaco suitable for the 350cc class. If any confirmation was needed, the 25th December, 1965, issue of *Motor Cycling* ran the headline 'Manx story is nearing the end', in relation to a reply by tuner Ray Petty to a reader's letter asking whether a Manx or AMC racer would be best for him. Petty was no doubt influenced by the fact that his top rider, Derek Minter, was in the process of 'defecting' to race Colin Seeley AMC-based racers in 1966. But it was not all bad news for the Manx. South African Ian Burne, riding a 500cc model prepared by Allen Dudley-Ward, beat Honda team-leader Jim Redman to win the main event at the New Year's Day meeting at East London, Cape Province. January 1966 saw the Minter rumours confirmed, when he signed to ride for Colin Seeley. The following month a Manx Norton was purchased by Honda from Reg Dearden and air freighted to Japan. The basis of this saga centred around Mike Hailwood, who had signed to race Hondas in 1966. It is known that Hailwood was none too happy with Honda handling and their new signing had suggested that the Japanese company take a look at a Norton frame.

*Ray Petty preparing the
interesting reversed-head 350
Norton.*

Even though he was without the services of Derek Minter, Ray Petty still pressed on with the development of his beloved Manx engines. His project over the winter of 1965-66 had been an ultrashort-stroke, outside-flywheel 350. With a bore and stroke of 78 x 73mm (compared with the 76 x 76.7mm of the standard Manx), the engine was based on the 1954 works engine, but none of the original pistons were available. However, specialists Hepworth and Grandage co-operated by making two special pistons to Petty's specification. John Cooper was Petty's top runner for 1966 and he, together with riders such as Dan Shorey, Joe Dunphy, Ray Pickrell and Rex Butcher, provided the main opposition to little Bill Ivy. Unfortunately, new star Ivy was racing Tom Kirby-entered AJS/Matchless Metisse machinery, rather than Nortons!

'Moon Eyes' John Cooper established his name on Nortons (seen here) before switching to the likes of Seeley, BSA and Yamaha.

June 1966 saw the TT postponed because of a seamen's strike, Cooper scored a string of impressive victories on his Petty-tuned Nortons, and South African Ray Flack created a mini-sensation when he turned up for a Brands Hatch practice day with a 350 Manx-powered 'kneeler'. Based on the famous 'Flying Hammock/Silver Fish' works Nortons of 1953, Flack's bike was of his own design and built by Wallaby Frames of Acton, North West London. Unfortunately, its main claim to fame was the number of problems it created with race officials and scrutineers, rather than its performance out on the track.

In early July, Derek Minter was out once again on a 350 Norton when he won at Castle Combe after splitting with Colin Seeley. Interviewed following his win, Minter said: 'It felt good to be back on a Norton. There's something about them.' A couple of weeks later he 'rejoined' Ray Petty.

The AMC Group collapsed in August 1966 and a receiver was appointed. Later the Norton name was saved through its takeover, together with other sections of the fallen AMC empire, by Manganese-Bronze Holdings Ltd, who then formed Norton-Villiers Ltd from the ashes. Essentially this later era is outside the scope of this book, as by then AMC had already disposed of the Manx racing design and spares to Colin Seeley, as related elsewhere.

When the Isle of Man TT was finally held in late August the hero, at least for many British fans, was Chris Conn, who took his pair of Norton singles to third places in both the Junior and Senior TTs. Conn, an RAF corporal, was later voted top privateer of 1966 and awarded the Filtrate Trophy.

In December came the news that John Hartle would be making a comeback during 1967 after three seasons out of the sport, although he chose Aermacchi rather than Norton for the 350cc class. February 1967 saw Francis Beart begin work building what he claimed at the time would probably be the very last Manx made. Then in March, at Daytona, Mike Duff turned out on a specially prepared Yamaha twin. This was in fact the prototype of what was to emerge as the TR2 (and in 250cc form the TD2). Despite giving away 150cc to the winning Triumph, and 400cc to the Harley-Davidson v-twins, Duff qualified in eighth place at 132mph, and, as *Motor Cycling*

Ray Pickrell hurls his 350 Manx into Devils Elbow, Mallory Park, on 30th April, 1967.

Action at the 1967 Ulster Grand Prix. Norton riders Dunphy (10), Cooper (48), Conn (36) and Gould (21) fighting it out.

commented, 'proved that these new race-kitted Yamahas with piston-controlled ports really go'. When the new Yamaha twins became available in 1969, they achieved what the likes of Bultaco and Aermacchi had never fully managed: to finally make totally obsolete the venerable British single.

Before that, however, Norton still continued to figure in the results, even at Grand Prix level. Highlights of the 1967 season were Rob Fitton's fourth at the season opener in Hockenheim, West Germany; Steve Spencer's third in the Senior TT; Dan Shorey's fourth at Sachsenring; John Cooper's third at Brno, Czechoslovakia, and Billie Nelson's third in the Finnish Grand Prix. On the British short circuits the 'new' Norton star was Rod Gould from Banbury, later to become a World Champion on a works 250 Yamaha in 1970, whilst in non-World Championship European races the leading Norton rider was Bob Fitton. The same year also saw the introduction of the British Quaife five-speed gearbox, first race tested in June that year by John Cooper. The Manx Grand Prix in September saw Jimmie Guthrie Junior win the Senior event, a great way of remembering an illustrious father; it was fitting that Guthrie Junior's race-winning bike was a Norton single.

The 22nd of October, 1967, was, as *Motor Cycling* described it, 'the end of an era'. This was in recognition of Derek Minter's official retirement from road racing. The 'Mint' bowed out with two fine wins in a career that had spanned some 14 seasons since his first race at Brands Hatch on a 500 BSA Gold Star; and for a decade he had been acclaimed 'King of Brands', at first unofficially and later with official recognition. In December Ray Petty finally completed the outside flywheel 350 Manx engine. It was fitted into a standard Manx chassis with the bottom frame tubes cut out to accept the flywheel.

A quartet of Manx models dice it out at Oulton Park in 1967: Dan Shorey (74), John Cooper (18), Rod Gould (35) and Rob Fitton (29).

Billie Nelson, this time leading Lewis Young (7 - Matchless) during the 500cc race of the 1966 Czech Grand Prix.

For 1968 John Cooper quit the Norton brigade to race Seeley and Yamaha machinery. Besides Dan Shorey, Ray Petty's other runner was Percy May, who promptly scored an impressive double with his 350 and 500 Nortons at Snetterton in early May. Besides Shorey and May, other riders who continued to fly the Norton flag in 1968 were Rob Fitton, Johnny Dodds, Kel Carruthers, Godfrey Nash and Rex Butcher. The finest results were a couple of seconds on the Grand Prix trail, by Dan Shorey (500cc West German Grand Prix) and Rob Fitton (500cc Ulster Grand Prix). Besides the MV Agusta of Agostini there were now other challengers in the shapes of CZ, Paton, Vostok, Linto and Seeley (Matchless). Only Billie Nelson and Dan Shorey scored places in the top six of the 350cc World Championship. Here the opposition was even stronger: MV, Benelli, Aermacchi, Bultaco, CZ, Honda, Seeley (AJS), Kawasaki, MZ, Jawa and Ducati. The Manx Grand Prix saw the Scot John Findlay win both the Junior and Senior on his Nortons. By the end of the year it had become obvious that the day of the British single was virtually over, and with the announcement that Yamaha would be offering their new TD2/TR2 production racers, this is exactly what happened. *The Motor Cycle* went as far as saying quite openly in their issue of 9th April, 1969: 'End of an era for the British singles.' This was after the Manx, together with the Matchless G50 and Seeley machines, were soundly beaten in the French Grand Prix at Le Mans. Strangely, though, *The Motor Cycle's* main story centred around the new Linto, rather than the Yamaha TR2.

The Manx was to have a final fling, at least at Grand Prix level. During 1969 people had not yet got around to over-boring the Yamaha, and the Linto was to prove unreliable. So a Norton was to finish second overall in the 500cc World Championship series, ridden by Godfrey Nash, the surprise of the season! In achieving this, privateer Nash finished fifth in Spain, fifth in France, third in Finland and scored a memorable victory in Yugoslavia. The latter was to be the last ever win in a World Championship event by a British motorcycle.

Towards the end of September 1969 came the first news that Colin Seeley might be selling the Manx side of his business. He stated at the time: 'The people I'm dealing with intend to buy the entire Norton side, and their aim is to build complete Manx Nortons as well as keep the flow of spares going.' Some six weeks later, in mid-November, the mystery was solved and the buyer revealed as ex-sidecar racer John Tickle, who had retired from racing four years previously to concentrate on manufacturing accessories. Following the announcement, all existing spares, jigs and manufacturing rights for the double-knocker Norton single passed to Tickle and the stock was transferred to his factory at Eynesbury, St Neots, Cambridgeshire. Tickle also announced that he would be sponsoring 1969 Yugoslav

The RAF's pride Chris Conn.

JOHN TICKLE

John Tickle acted as the link between todays classic movement and the demise of the Manx as a competitive racing motorcycle at the end of the 1960s.

Born on the 3rd June 1936, much of his youth was spent tackling various sporting activities; notably swimming in which he was British Schoolboy Junior back-stroke champion. His father was a professional golfer, but John decided on a road racing career, at first with solos, thereafter with his first wife Cathy as passenger in sidecar. The pair raced at international level throughout Europe. The Manx-powered Tickle outfit was a regular sight at the circuits until the pair hung up their leathers for the final time in 1965. In that last year, racing had taken a back seat to a fledgling engineering business – started part-time in a rented workshop in Finchley, north London.

In the late 1960s the Tickle enterprise – which specialised in making bolt-on goodies for the café racer fraternity, moved to a factory unit at St Neots, Cambridgeshire.

The business then took over the rights to manufacture Manx Norton bikes and spares, after Colin Seeley, who had bought the rights from AMC, decided to concentrate on the AJS/Matchless side.

Tickle built a small number of updated 499cc Manx models, coded the T5; riders

included Robin Duffty and Tony Plumridge. The last of these was built in 1963. However, the spares and accessory business flourished with not only Manx parts, but five- and six-speed gearboxes, two leading brake conversions, and such roadster goodies as rear sets, clip-ons and headlamp brackets.

Mid 1970s and the business moved a few miles north to Peterborough, but then the partnership with former wife Cathy was dissolved and the remains of the business sold to Unity Equipe in Rochdale, who ran it for many years before selling it on to Andy Molnar.

As for John Tickle, he remarried (to Ruth) and moved to Wales. John died in Swansea Hospital on 14th May 2000 after a long-term, heart related illness. And so past a man of many talents, who also played a vital role in the history of Britain's most famous racing series, the Manx Norton.

A brand new Tickle T5 Manx at the London Sporting and Racing Show, the Horticultural Halls, Westminster in January 1970.

Grand Prix winner Godfrey Nash, and that Nash would race the machine, the Tickle T5, which would also be offered for sale. This featured certain changes, including a new frame and high-level exhaust system.

Also in late 1969 a leading tuner, Syd Mularney, revealed that he was working on a four-valve head, which on the larger Manx, he estimated, upped the power by around five to six bhp. In December that year John Tickle gained the services of 1955 double Manx Grand Prix winner Geoff Tanner, who was joining the 'factory' to take charge of Manx engine and machine building. In practice very, very few complete engines, and even fewer Tickle T5 machines, were actually constructed. One was the machine owned by sponsor Stuart Willis and raced by my brother-in-law Tony Plumridge. I was fortunate enough to ride this machine, which is important, as it has allowed me at first hand to compare its performance with that of a standard 1959 model 30M I had raced a couple of

The Manx's last Grand Prix victory was gained by Englishman Godfrey Nash, in the 500cc Yugoslav Grand Prix, 14th September 1969.

times earlier. History records the Tickle T5 as unsuccessful. This is not because it was any less competitive than the Bracebridge Street original, but just that by the time it arrived (1970) it was totally outclassed by the new generation of racers.

This is best illustrated by recalling that official Tickle rider Godfrey Nash finished in the top six only once that year in a Grand Prix, the 500cc Finnish at Imatra, in stark contrast to his success 12 months earlier. Norton's hopes also suffered a severe blow when Rob Fitton was killed at the Nürburgring. Fitton, then 42 and in his 19th racing season, was acknowledged to own one of the fastest Nortons in the business.

Ray Petty, now with only Percy May (Dan Shorey had retired in mid-1969) tried everything he knew, including Italian Fontana brakes, and a larger, near 600cc engine, but to no avail, for the day of the Manx as a competitive racing motorcycle was over. Eventually even the mighty MV could not stand up to the two-stroke challenge.

PERCY MAY
THE LAST MANX CHAMPION

Born in India on 6th February 1941– where his father was serving in the British Army – Percy May was destined to be the final British road racing champion on a British bike in the Classic period. In fact the only British riders/British bikes combinations to have triumphed since have been the Norton Rotary pairings of Steve Spray, 1989 Formula 1/750cc Supercup, and in 1994 Ian Simpson in the Supercup TT Superbike Championship.

When he was 18 months old Percy came to England with his parents. His father was wounded in the war and the family settled in Crookham, near Farnborough, Hants.

His first interest in motorcycles came whilst serving an engineering apprenticeship. In his late teens he owned a couple of Velocettes, at first a Viper and later a Venom. A friend used to take part in the MCC High Speed Trials at Silverstone. Soon the Venom was put to use by Percy to begin his competitive career.

Next came a Manx 'Bitza' – an early Oldhams coupling-type engine in a later chassis.

His first meetings on the machine came with the Wirral 100 and Bemsee clubs at venues including Oulton Park, Snetterton, Mallory Park and Silverstone.

After three or four years of club racing – ending with 17 wins in 1965 – Percy joined the national scene for 1966. By then he had met Ray Petty who lived only half a mile away in Cove, Farnborough.

At first a 350cc Manx was used; this later being joined by a 1962 499cc model. Ray Petty helped the machinist/toolmaker with discounts on items such as chains and clutches, whilst extra support came via Dunlop (tyres), Castrol (oil), Champion (plugs) and Ferodo (brake linings).

By 1970, the year Percy married wife Mandy, the smaller Manx had become obsolete, thanks to the wider use of enlarged Yamaha two-stroke twins.

1971 was Percy's racing swansong, and he did it in style, by taking his larger Manx to the British 500cc championship title. After this feat he decided to hang up his leathers.

Percy and Mandy had two children, Lisa and Derek.

Percy May, 1971 British 500cc Champion (the last British Champion on a British bike – Rotary Norton excepted).

14 The Classic Scene

Roger Munsey on his way to victory in the Vintage Race of the Year at Oulton Park, August 1980.

David May heading for 4th place in the 1989 Manx Grand Prix.

Gordon Russell preparing his 499cc Manx for the Post TT, Mallory Park, June 2000.

By the early 1970s, as the John Tickle enterprise had found to its cost, the Manx Norton was obsolete, even at the most humble of British Club events. This situation was inevitable ever since Yamaha had finally found out how to make their twin-cylinder two-stroke not only fast but also reliable. With the advent of the 350 TR2 in 1969, the Japanese company had the bike that was not just superior to any other production racer in its class, but also much faster than any 500! What this meant was that overnight owners of Aermacchi, Bultaco, Greeves, Ducati, AJS, Matchless and Norton singles were left with machines worthless for the task for which they had been conceived, namely winning races. The result was that you either bought a Yamaha or accepted the fact that you had about as much chance of winning races as going to the moon.

One day in 1973, I received a telephone call at my Wisbech dealership from Dave Bailey, race secretary of the local Newmarket and District Motorcycle and Light Car Club, to give it its full title at the time. The purpose of the call was to sound out my reaction to his club running a class for single-cylinder machines. Right from Dave's first sentence on the subject I realised that this concept needed support, which my company gave, together with a number of other interested parties, to help get the idea off the ground. This was not just because I happened to be a Ducati specialist, but having only very recently retired from racing myself, for the very reason that my Ducati was now so hopelessly outclassed by the new Yamahas, I had felt it was of no use to continue in the sport I had participated in for many years. So it came about that one day in July 1973 the first race confined to owners of single-cylinder machines took place at the Snetterton circuit.

The success of this inaugural event exceeded everyone's most optimistic forecast, including Dave Bailey himself. Not only was the event grossly over-subscribed, but the array of different machinery showed just why spectators had become switched off at the prospect of having an entry full of screaming 'strokers' with the word

The patter of feet as the starters flag drops and riders push their machines into life at a CRMC meeting, at Cadwell Park during the mid 1980s.

'Yamaha' on every tank. This wide range of bikes, their equally diverse mixture of different sounds, coupled with a unique atmosphere both in the paddock and among spectators, ensured that the Newmarket Club made the Single-Cylinder event a permanent fixture at its meetings thereafter.

The success of the reborn singles with full starting grids meant other clubs copying the Newmarket idea, with the result that by 1978 races were being run at several venues throughout Britain. However, it was left to the various clubs themselves to make their own set of rules regarding exactly just what could take part, as for one thing the Japanese were now offering their own brand of single-cylinder street bikes, such as the Yamaha XT500. Also, most single-cylinder racers tended to favour the 500s. This meant an owner of, say, a 125 Bultaco or 250 Aermacchi did not stand much chance of success. The first person to voice the idea of taking the concept a stage further was the late Stephen Finch from Kenilworth, Warwickshire. Earlier, the same man had been behind the setting up of the Ducati Owners' Club. Stephen's idea was to form an organisation to run races solely for the 'classic' racers of the period prior to the appearance of the Yamaha TD2/TR2 series. Sadly, before he could see his dream come true Stephen Finch was to be involved in a fatal road accident whilst on holiday in the Isle of Man.

The key that was to open the door to present-day Classic Racing as we know it was an incident that took place during 1979. Whilst at a Brands Hatch Vintage Club meeting, racer and single-cylinder enthusiast Alan Cathcart had offered Dick Linton (owner of FCL, the Aermacchi specialists) a ride on his Matchless G50 in a parade. It should be noted that Vintage Club rules banned the use of the G50 from actual racing, but there were

Geoff Duke at the official opening of the National Motor Cycle Museum, Birmingham, in October 1984. What more appropriate machine than an ex-works Manx Norton.

The 350 Manx used by John Armstrong in Vintage Club events during the 1980s. Note the use of non-standard Amal Concentric carburettor and the belt primary drive.

Another famous former Norton rider to get back in the saddle was Dan Shorey, seen here at Donington Park in the mid 1980s.

no real rules regarding non-competitive events such as parades. However, even though a group of Dutch enthusiasts had been invited to take part in this parade with similar 1960s bikes, an official, Jack Watson, violently disagreed that Linton should be allowed on to the circuit with Cathcart's machine. So annoyed were Cathcart and Linton over this seemingly petty matter that they decided to form a club themselves that would cater for the likes of Alan's G50 and other similar bikes. All interested parties were contacted (including myself) and a meeting was organised so that the new club could become a reality.

Held at Redgate Lodge, Donington Park, in December 1979, the result was the formation of what today is known around the world as the Classic Racing Motorcycle Club (CRMC). Currently with an active membership of some 1,500, it is the largest organisation dedicated to the use of post-war racing motorcycles conceived prior to the introduction of the Yamaha TD/TR models anywhere in the world. Conceived means that four-stroke models manufactured well into the 1970s, such as the Ducati singles and Honda's CB350K4, are eligible. However, no two-strokes after 1968 are allowed to compete, so preventing history repeating itself. Its first race was held in 1980. Then in the mid 1990's the rules changed allowing separate races for more modern two-strokes such as Suzuki RG 500's.

In the last few years various other parties have come on to the scene to organise events for Classic-type machinery, notably the Cathcart-inspired IHRO (International Historic Racing Organisation), which has succeeded in helping make historic bike sport popular in countries where interest had often languished. Other organisers in Britain who run races catering for Manx Nortons include the New Era Motorcycle Racing Club, the North Gloucestershire Motor Cycle Club, the North West Centre of the ACU, the Scottish Vintage Racing Club, Scottish Classic Racing Club and the Irish Classic Racing Championship.

The Isle of Man, for so long the centre of road racing, has seen many of yesterday's stars take part in a parade during TT week and in the Classic Manx Grand Prix, the latter first staged in 1983, during early September. Not only this, but the Classic movement has spread its wings, with events also being staged throughout mainland Europe, North America, Australia, New Zealand and even Japan. Another facet of the Classic racing scene has been a number of special meetings, notably Surtees Day at Brands Hatch, Hailwood Day at Donington Park and, more recently, the Ray Petty memorial meeting at Brands Hatch. The latter was staged during July 1988 in memory of the much-respected Manx tuner, who had died the previous year. The main race (limited solely to Manx models) was won by Chas Mortimer.

Prices... well in the late 1960s one could pick up a fully serviceable Manx for as little as £150. Now the same bike could, if all advertisements are to be believed, cost you in excess of £20,000! Even allowing for inflation, that sort of investment could hardly have matured elsewhere, even by the sharpest City of London stockbroker. In line with the huge increase in bike prices has come an ever greater shortage of spare parts. Even so, 1988 saw one person at least prove that it was still possible to build a new Manx from spares, for less than £10,000 (£9,513.45 to be exact). The bike, a 499cc model owned by racer Martin Ogree, is not a full Manx replica; it has, for example, coil valve springs, a Robinson 4LS front stopper and belt drive amongst a host of other 'non-standard' components.

Building a replica of a classic racer is a contentious business. Some people demand that everything should be original (which is obviously not possible in the 21st Century), and in any case certain modifications, such as belt drives and 18-inch tyres, assist in terms of reliability and cornering speeds. In fact, this highlights the split in the classic racing movement between those who demand originality at any cost (often feeling that replicas diminish their investment and that the use of and manufacture of replica components amounts to a form of immorality), and those who still see a Manx Norton as only a means of racing and do not view it as a piece of real estate that will be worth even more the following year. The needs

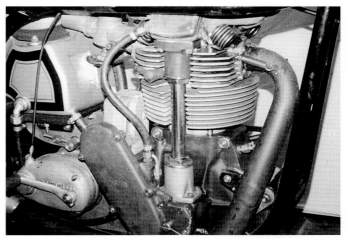

This 1952 long-stroke Manx engine was supplied new to Guildford-based tuner Francis Beart. It was later (still 1950's) modified by former Brooklands engineer Robin Jackson, with various special Jackson-made components including twin-spark head, cylinder, con-rod and flywheels. Now mounted in a post 1954 frame and fitted with a five-speed Quaife gearbox, current owner Dan Nash has just had the engine rebuilt by Norton specialist Stewart Rogers.

of preserving a bike in original (as built in 1960) condition and seriously racing the same item four decades after it was built will not work in harmony. A genuine 40-year-old racer will be tired, potentially dangerously so, and if it is used as it was originally intended, it will need rebuilding with certain vital parts, which are likely to differ from the original components.

Even in their heyday most classic racing machines were often modified for a whole variety of reasons, higher performance, rider's stature, even rebuilt with different parts following an accident or engine blow-up - so what is standard anyway! Standard can only mean as it left the factory's gates. Unfortunately, use changes originality, right from the moment the first modification or non-original replacement part was fitted. As time goes by it is inevitable that every Manx will become a little less 'as it left the factory'. Unless, of course, it is locked away and never used. One thing is certain, however: the day has long gone when one would find one of the legendary Bracebridge Street singles hidden away in a garden shed and owned by someone who did not realise its present (overinflated?) value. If considering buying, I strongly recommend that you vet your prospective purchase extemely carefully. Unfortunately, some Manx Nortons being offered are in a poor state of repair. The trouble is that they are now fetching such high prices that get rich quick merchants are building them up out of any old rubbish they can lay their hands on, (this does not of course include newly constructed replicas). You have been warned. Even so, the only conclusion that can be drawn is that in a free market economy, buyers and sellers have provided the clearest possible signs that the Manx Norton was a truly great racing motorcycle, hence its high price today.

Why? Well, besides the ability over many years to reign supreme on the world's race circuits there are three other reasons – sight, sound and smell. Three human reactions that give the Manx such a high rating. Strange but true, for many enthusiasts there is nothing in motorcycling to match a Manx Norton in these three areas, which combined to create a very special aura. Think about it. It is the only valid reason why a British single could have remained so popular for so long, even after its working life was long since over.

There is, of course, another reason – nostalgia. The Oxford Dictionary describes it in the following terms: 'Sentimental memory of or longing for things of the past.' And probably the Manx Norton portrays this phenomenon best in the world of motorcycles.

A popular modifcation for Vintage/Classic events is the Quaife five-speed gearbox.

DAVID & TINA MAY

David and Tina May,
Goodwood 1998.

The New Era Racing Club's secretary, Brenda Scivyer, phoned me up one day in the Spring of 2000 and said someone had entered the club's Supermono races at Castle Combe 'on an old Norton, and was it suitable?' My reply was that it (a Manx as it turned out), was not only eligible, but, in my opinion, more than suitable.

It turned out to be classic racer David May. After photographing his machine way back in the mid-1980s I decided to give him a call. It then transpired that David had married Tina – the late Ray Petty's daughter back in September 1991. And this led Tina to write the following words for this latest edition of The Manx Norton.

My father, Ray Petty, was passionate about bikes all his life. I can remember as a child how hard he worked, he usually took one day off a week to go fishing and would otherwise be in his workshop until at least 11pm. My younger brother Joe, my mum and myself would go on the annual holiday to Hayling Island (near Portsmouth). Dad would pop down and see us in the evening and then go home that same night. But because he worked in buildings at the bottom of the garden we would see him a lot. He was a smashing dad, with such patience and being older than the average parent (21 years senior to my mother), so very wise. During his career as a Manx engine tuner his customers included John Cooper, Derek Minter, Dan Shorey and Percy May (who is no relation to my husband, David). My mother recalls trips to the Isle of Man with the hotel where they stayed, The Douglas Bay (now demolished), also housing teams such as Benelli, Yamaha and Jawa. She remembers vividly being given a pillion ride around the circuit by Bill Ivy, 'he scared the life out of me', she said, 'he kept taking his hands off the bars'.

My mother was always supportive of dad and helped a lot with the day-to-day running of the business. I think she was very tolerant, especially as we always seemed to have a Manx Norton in the corner of the living room and magnetos in the airing cupboard!

I decided when I was 16 to get a moped, but dad was not impressed by my choice of a Suzuki two-stroke. He had offered to make me a motorcycle, but I wanted something modern – I wish now I had taken him up on his offer. I remember the Suzuki broke down and I told him it needed fixing. But because it was a two-stroke he wouldn't touch it, instead phoned a friend to do it. I decided to take my motorcycle test. I was encouraged by my future husband David and the late Leslie Boustead who was a larger-than-life character and editor of Open Megga the journal of the CRMCC (Classic Racing Motor Cycle Club).

Jane Petty and Bill Ivy.

I really wanted to find out what it was like to ride a Norton. David and I took the bike to a local farm road for me to have a go at bump starting. We should have had a video – picture an 8-stone female and a very pale owner of a Manx! But the good news is that I did get to start and ride the bike. My ambition someday is to parade a Manx.

David proposed marriage to me in the workshop whilst peering through the frame of a five-hundred Manx and then made me a titanium engagement ring on his lathe – romance is not dead! We were married on 14th September 1991 – and put a model of a Manx Norton on the cake – with a chequered flag as the tablecloth.

We now have two children, Sophia Grace May (aged 7) and James Raymond John May (aged 4). James is already showing an interest in bikes and often walks around the house with David's gloves and helmut on. When he's on his little trike he leans into corners and makes the wheels slide! It's genetic – James' Great Grandfather, Grandfather and father all had an unhealthy interest in speed and now James, a fourth generation speed freak with Petty blood.

David May lined up with the good and the great, Goodwood 1998.

FRED WALMSLEY

Fred Walmsley and Barry Sheene
at Philip Island.

Steve Tomes, Cadwell Park,
Easter 1999.

Fred Walmsley, Andy Molnar and
Manx engine, 2000.

Fred Walmsley and Steve Tomes,
winner of the Classic Race
of the Year, Snetterton,
September 1999.

Fred Walmsley was born in Bacup, Lancashire on the 16th November 1946. His father Clifford was not only a speedway rider for the Bell Vue team, but also rode the Wall of Death at fairs and carnivals. Fred's first motorcycle experience came at the age of sixteen, via a three-fifty AJS single. An engineer by trade, Fred was involved in club racing during the 1960s, at first with BSA Gold Stars and later the real 'love of his life', the Manx. He was married in 1970 and success in his business (as a Kentucky Fried Chicken franchise) allowed him to get back into racing via the classic scene in the early 1980s. This was to see Fred purchase an ex Jack Brett Slazenger Manx in 1981. This bike was kept until 1987. Also in the 1980s he helped Geoff Fowler and Nial Mackenzie, the latter on LC and TZ Yamahas.

Then came friendship with Mick Taberer and George Beale. This included building a replica G50 Seeley upon which Phil Nichols won the 1988 Senior Classic Manx Grand Prix. But this was only the start, later riders such as Bill Swallow, Hugh Anderson and Bob Heath rode for the Walmsley equipe, with Seeley machines.

Finally, 1997 saw Fred return to the Manx. As, thanks to the local engineer Andy Molnar, special parts were available to make the five-hundred Manx into a race winning proposition once more; with short-stroke engines using not only 86mm, but 90 and even 95mm bores.

Manx airline pilot Richard Coates, Welshman Jason Griffiths and Steve Tomes all rode Walmsley Manxes. Then in 1999 former F1 World Champion Damon Hill rode one of the Nortons at Goodwood. The following year ex 500cc world champion Barry Sheene had several outings on a Walmsley Manx, including the 2000 British Grand Prix at Donington Park, causing much public interest. To cap a brilliant year which included the Sheene appearances and Steve Tomes many victories, Glen English won the 2000 Senior Classic Manx in September.

THE MOLNAR CONNECTION

In 1978 John Tickle succumbed to economic pressures, partly due to falling demand for the products of his accessory business and partly due to domestic problems. He sold the Manx business to Unity Equipe of Rochdale. Several van loads of stock, mostly still the product of Bracebridge Street, together with all the existing jigs, patterns, supplier lists and most importantly the full drawing set and manufacturing rights for the Manx made their way north.

Unity was purely a retail operation and so mainly confined their activity to selling the existing stock, only having the simpler, high turnover items re-made. The jigs were all put into storage.

Close-up of Molnar Manx supplied to a Japanese customer in 1999.

In 1994 the sidecar connection to the Manx resurfaced when successful husband and wife Classic racers Andy & Kim Molnar bought the by now near dormant Manx business from Unity. Andy, an engineer by profession, had spent 10 years at British Aerospace before setting up Stainless Engineering Company with partner Kim, a buyer and production controller from the textile industry. They had already gained a worldwide reputation for their stainless hardware, replica drum brakes and G50 engines before embarking on the Manx venture. Stepping into their modern, well lit Preston factory packed with computer controlled machines provided a striking contrast to the bowels of the old Bracebridge Street works.

Fred Walmsley, Glen English and Andy Molnar, 2000.

It was the Molnar's plan right from the start to make all the Manx parts exactly to the original Norton drawings, so that every gear, screw, nut and shaft fitted straight into original engines. In October 1995 the inevitable happened, and 100% parts availability was translated into the first new Molnar Manx engine, an 86mm bore 499cc motor to 1961 specification, which made a fairy tale debut at Silverstone, ridden by Doug Jones to a win in it's first ever race. The standard spec engines continued to perform well and sold steadily, but it became clear that if the domination by the Seeley G50 in classic racing was to be overturned, then serious development work was required. In the 1996 Classic Senior Manx Grand Prix the first Manx home was in 15th position. Working together with trusted engine builder Gerry Kershaw, who had built engines for John Tickle, every single component in the engine was reviewed for weight and performance. At the same time the bore was increased, first to 90mm, then 95mm and the stroke shortened, allowing peak revs to increase to 9,000rpm and peak power to over 60bhp. This development work has achieved the desired result. In the 2000 Classic Senior Manx Grand Prix the first six finishers were all Manx mounted, the Manx is now re-established as the premier Classic race bike.

Glen English (riding the Molnar five-hundred Manx) pictured at Mallory Park Post TT meeting, June 2000, before his 2000 Manx Grand Prix victory.

By the end of the 2000 race season over 50 Molnar Manx engines had been delivered to customers world wide, and had notched up in excess of 200 race wins on every type of circuit from Go Kart tracks, through the speed bowl at Daytona USA to the road circuits in the Isle of Man and Ireland. A significant number of these engines have been built into the new Featherbed rolling chassis, also made by the Molnars, thereby keeping this Classic motorcycle in production over 50 years after it's debut.

After a protracted and costly legal wrangle with Norton Motors International Inc, Kim and Andy Molnar have registered the name Manx as a UK Trade Mark in respect of motorcycles and parts and fittings for motorcycles. They have also successfully opposed Norton Motors application to register Manx as a European Community Trade Mark.

To succeed in both cases the Molnars had to prove that all the rights to the Manx were sold by AMC to Colin Seeley in 1967 on the closure of the race shop, passing to John Tickle, Unity and then Stainless Engineering and that therefore no rights ever belonged to Nortor Motors International Inc, or any of it's predecessor companies.

SUMMERFIELD ENGINEERING

Jerry Summerfield on a 350cc Petty Manx, Mallory Park, 1999.

Derek Minter, Summerfield Manx 30M Post TT meeting, Mallory Park, Sunday 11th June 2000.

It all began on a whim back in 1983 when the Summerfield brothers Roger, Mike and Jerry, bought a well used Manx following an advertisement in a classic magazine. The bike was alright as a show-piece, but when the brothers decided to use it in earnest, the big-end promptly seized. This led the Summerfields to the door of Ray Petty, down in Cove near Farnborough, who although an ill man was still deeply involved with the Manx after some 40 years – many of them with the legendary Francis Beart.

After Ray died in 1987, his wife Jane followed instructions left by her husband, that the Summerfields were the concern to carry on the manufacture of 'his parts'. The wide use of the Petty name by the Summerfield operation since that time is an acknowledgement of this fact.

Manx Nortons seemed to breed a special set of individuals, with most parties seemingly working together in some way. For example Summerfields have had a long relationship with Bernie Allen from Marlborough, Wiltshire (who builds complete replicas of the 1962 Manx, using Summerfield engines); whilst Huddersfield-based White Rose Racing manufacture Petty frame kits, which the Summerfields sell with their engines fitted.

Summerfield Engineering, based in Somercotes, Derbyshire, also manufacture the PGT gearbox (based on the Schafleitner box later used by Colin Seeley up to the mid-1970s, when the design was taken over by Ray Petty). In 1989, Mike Summerfield together with Bernie Allen visited the Norton factory in Shenstone to obtain official permission to use the name. When Doug Hele, the man responsible for the development of the original Manx design in its final years, saw what they were offering, he gave their joint efforts his blessing.

For the last decade the Summerfields have sold around 100 Manx engines and countless spares for existing owners world-wide, in both 350 and 500cc variations.

Although Mike does not race, Roger and Jerry have both won many races on their own products. Most recently, the Summerfield Manx business has enjoyed unparalleled success, both on and off the track. For example, during 1999, not only did Bill Swallow finish 2nd in the Singles TT, lapping at over 108mph (the fastest ever Manx lap), but in the Classic Senior Manx Grand Prix, Summerfield machines came home 1st, 2nd and 5th (Swallow, Nick Jeffries and Mick Robinson respectively). And to cap a superb season they won both the 350cc (Jerry Summerfield) and 500cc (Steve Ruth) races of the Old Bike Mart 1,000 Guineas National Championship series.

Finally it was perhaps fitting that the former King of Brands and Manx Norton star, Derek Minter, should be another rider to fly the Summerfield flag on the race circuits of Europe, during historic events. And what a great sight it was to see Derek out on the circuit once more on the type of machine which made his name during the 1950s and 1960s.

New Summerfield Manx supplied to Max Hirthammer, Germany 1999. Petty frame kit is by Huddersfield based White Rose Racing.

THE LANDSDOWNE CLASSIC SERIES

Lee Moore, winner of the Landsowne Classic Series in 2000, 500cc class, on his 1962 30M Manx.

Richard Thirkell, Landsdowne Series organiser, with his 1959, 499cc Manx. 'Landsdowne' was in appreciation of Pa Norton's middle name.

Named after James Landsdowne Norton, the series was inspired by the first Goodwood Revival meeting in 1998 and aims to re-create, as far as possible, the spirit and spectacle of racing from the immediate post-war period until the mid 1960s. Besides the Manx Norton, other eligible bikes include Matchless G50, AJS 7R and Matchless G45. The Lansdowne series is especially aimed at original machines (or faithful replicas), and 'caters for mainly club riders wishing to race these valuable machines in a sensible racing environment without the white heat of competition from other classes'; says series organiser, Richard Thirkell, a competitor himself.

Nurtured under the watchful eye of the New Era Racing Club and its president Jim Parker, the Lansdowne series places as much emphasis on the spectacle as racing itself. Riders are encouraged to wear black leathers and ride unfaired machines. A typical grid in 2000 comprised 25 to 30 machines. About 70 bikes were registered at that time. There is a handicap system which favours total originality and the older long-stroke machines. Special awards are given for sportsmanship and personal performance.

The main sponsor of the Lansdowne Classic Series is Brookes Auctioneers (the organisers of the famous Stafford Classic Motor Cycle show auction); with additional support from Summerfield Engineering and Andy Molnar, manufacturers of Manx Spares.

BERNIE ALLEN

1961 replica 499 Manx in standard spec.

Motor Cycle News, in their 28th February 1990 issue, carried the following headline: 'Legend lives again' and went on to say 'The Manx Norton lives! The most famous racing machine in history is back in production, but at a price – £26,450!' This story's background was thanks to former Manx racer Bernie Allen, of Great Bedwyn, near Marlborough, Wiltshire, who had used his contacts and expertise to co-ordinate the project. Bernie Allen's background was one of professional bike restorer who had begun his working life as an apprentice at a Rolls-Royce dealership. He was able to offer the prospect of replicas of the final 1962 499cc 30M Manx thanks to his own enthusiasm – and the supply of parts from around the world. The engine and transmission components were manufactured by Manx specialists, Summerfield Engineering of Somercotes, Derbyshire, who also supplied the aluminium fuel and oil tanks.

Former Reynold Tubes man Ken Sprayston, by now employed at BSA's Gloucestershire factory, supervised the building of the Featherbed frames, using a jig owned by Summerfield – which they recieved from the late Ray Petty. Bernie Allen's comment at the time was: 'I'm not going to build too many, maybe five a year. I reckon it's better to make a good job of a few than get headaches employing people you don't know and trying to make a lot'.

Later, in the August 1992 issue of *Classic Bike* magazine, journalist Mick Duckworth tested what he called the 'The Ultimate Café Racer'. This was reference to Bernie Allen's road-going Manx (the only one he built). And except for a five-speed PGT (Precision Gear Transmissions) gearbox and Newby belt primary drive, the Allen machine was a very good replica of the real thing. For street use (by then the Featherbed frame had been made by Goodman Engineering), the following equipment had been added: Smiths 150mph speedometer, centre stand, six-volt battery (a BTH mageneto was used for ignition), horn, stoplight and switch, rear number plate and adjustable clip-on handlebars. Although Mick Duckworth was deeply impressed, he also pointed out 'anyone spending £22,000 for a road Manx must consider some hard facts. This bike has no kickstarter. It cannot be used discreetly. The steering lock is restricted. Riding will leave your hands and toes resonating with the after-effects of vibration! And more!'

Mick ended by saying: 'Leaving his place, (Bernie Allen's), I swapped the Manx Norton for a comfortable, sensible 1,000cc motorcycle with push-button starting and ample luggage capacity. How bland and boring it felt after the Manx'. All the above no doubt explains why, since this bike was built, only pure racers have been built and sold, with no more Allen Café Racer Manxes.

Bernie Allen at work in his Wiltshire workshop, with a new Manx in preparation.

Bernie testing a new 1962 replica at Goodwood during the 1990s.

INDEX

Figures in italics refer to captions

TITLES BY MICK WALKER

Ducati Singles
Ducati Twins
Spanish Post-War Road & Racing Motorcycles
Moto Guzzi Twins
Moto Guzzi Singles
MV Agusta Production Machines
Greeves
Ducati Desmo – The Making of a Masterpiece
International Six Days Trial
Italian Motorcycles
Manx Norton
Ducati & Cagiva Buyers Guide
Mick Walker's Classic Italian Gallery – The Road Bikes
Mick Walker's Classic Italian Gallery – The Racing Bikes
BMW K-Series Motorcycles
Café Racers of the 60s
Superbike Specials of the 70s
Ducati Singles 2nd Edition
Ducati Twins 2nd Edition
German Motorcycles
Ducati Singles Restoration
Ducati Twins Restoration
BMW Twins Restoration
Moto Guzzi Twins Restoration
Aermacchi
Benelli
MZ
Morini
British Performance Two-Strokes
Ducati Buyers Guide
Moto Guzzi Buyers Guide
Ducati
Yamaha
Suzuki
Honda

Moto Guzzi
Kawasaki
Endurance Racing
Kawasaki Fours – The Complete Story
BMW Twins – The Complete Story
Moto Guzzi V-twins – The Complete Story
Laverda Twins & Triples – The Complete Story
Ducati 4-Valve V-Twins – The Complete Story
Ducati 2-Valve V-Twins – The Complete Story
MV Agusta Fours – The Complete Story
Aprilia – The Complete Story
Gilera – The Complete Story
Mick Walker's British Racing Motorcycles
Mick Walker's Italian Racing Motorcycles
Mick Walker's German Racing Motorcycles
Mick Walker's European Racing Motorcycles
Classic Motorcycles
Performance Motorcycles
Miller's Classic Motorcycle Price Guide 1995
Miller's Classic Motorcycle Price Guide 1996
Miller's Classic Motorcycle Price Guide 1997
Miller's Classic Motorcycle Price Guide 1998
Miller's Classic Motorcycle Price Guide 1999
Miller's Classic Motorcycle Price Guide 2000
Miller's Classic Motorcycle Price Guide 2001
Ducati 2000 (exhibition catalogue)
Ducati, Taglioni and his World Beating Motorcycles
The Manx Norton